A SENSE OF TRAVEL

A BOOK BY

RODERICK CRAIG LOW

New Generation Publishing

Also by Roderick Craig Low

Novels

Going Nowhere

Three Hundred Hours

Rewards and Dilemmas

England 2026 – After the Discord

Promises of Love and Good Behaviour

Technical

Writing User Documentation

CONTENTS

*The author poses with 'Crab' No. 42765 (since preserved)
at Fleetwood, 26th May, 1963*

ACKNOWLEDGEMENTS

Obliging crew at Tollcross terminus, Glasgow.
August, 1961

This book is dedicated to my wife, Chantal, my two children, Rebecca and David, and my grandson, Joshua:

Over the years, and to a greater or lesser extent, they have unwittingly been a party to my passions – spending hours traipsing over rusty rails, looking at seemingly-worthless artefacts I, for obscure reasons, admire. They have indulged me at birthdays and Christmases with vouchers happily exchanged for books that they could not, for all the world, want to dip into. And they have provided the tell-tale signs of glazed eyes and whispered asides when I have overstepped the mark in terms of too-precise or overly-long explanations, when they, rashly, posed a question they might assume deserved a five-word answer.

I must also thank my DNA:

A grandfather who was a driver, a father who was an enthusiast, another grandfather who was an engineer – all fed my life and directed the shape it took.

I must acknowledge the thousands of unsung heroes who made this passion possible:

The railwaymen, tram crews, road-transport workers, those who went down to the sea in ships, captains and labourers of industry, the miners and quarrymen, fishermen, and others. Yes, and the people I have met on the way who sat on stubbly embankments sharing my enthusiasms and who, in many cases, turned their hobby into a lifetime of work.

I must also thank Alan Warren, who has permitted publication of two pictures from his collection.

Lastly, I must thank Colin T. Gifford:

Although I never met him, he published a book in 1965 that altered my view of railways. Gifford elevated railway photography to a point where we saw the railway in the context of its surroundings – in all its moods, set into the landscape, a part of the geography, instead of being falsely centre-stage and an end in itself. His magnum opus, "Decline of Steam", influenced and encouraged me to write my own book that attempts something similar – setting my memories into the landscape of my life and times.

To them all, thank you. I trust my book reflects a part of what we all were.

Roderick Craig Low
North Wales 2018

CHAPTER ONE

PROLOGUE

My grandfather, Robert Low, 4th from the right, second row. He is seen here as part of a cleaning squad at St. Margaret's shed, Edinburgh. The locomotive is North British Railway No. 612, built in August 1892, and probably fairly new when the photograph was taken as my grandfather started work as a cleaner in December of that year, before becoming registered for firing in March of 1895. No. 612 served in France during the First World War and, upon its return, was named 'Ypres'. As LNER No. 5269, it was withdrawn in July, 1947.

I believe I must have been about three and a half years old.

Equally blessed and cursed with a long memory, I can trust myself to that. I'm sure my brother wasn't there, as he came along in July 1949. And my mother wouldn't have scaled the scrubby upland of tufted grass and time-worn sheep tracks if she had been pregnant – my father, extremely solicitous where my mother was concerned, would have forbidden it.

So this must have happened in 1948, and probably in

the summer time, as we usually went to Scotland for annual visits to relatives during the hoped-for warm, summer months that invariably required the presence of a gabardine raincoat.

Where my uncle parked his sleek, low-slung, wire wheeled, chromium-headlighted, pre-war, silver-grey Jaguar saloon, I don't remember. The attraction was the Forth Bridge, only one in those days, of course, but I doubt there was a special car park or any semblance of an information centre in the vicinity. He would have nosed the big car around the lanes above South Queensferry until the sprawling vista of the Forth lay below us like an animated painting, and then bottomed it convincingly at the entrance to a field as he was wont to do. I remember the sun on the water catching the crests of restless waves, gulls calling and wheeling in the air, the wind in the grass making it murmur and rustle, and the request to 'stand back' while the adults pulled and pushed the marooned car until all its wheels had regained terra firma.

'See the ferry boats below the bridge?' my father commanded, pointing and sighing in exasperation at my not-yet identified astigmatic attempts to satisfy his request. From that angle, upstream of the colossal bridge, the Queen's Ferry hung so low in the water as to resemble driftwood, the only giveaway being the glinting paintwork on the roofs of the SMT buses and charabancs that went to sea. I would acknowledge sight of the ferry, even if I hadn't, although the smoke from the tall, black stacks and the churning paddle wheels once it had left the quay probably helped.

Even a structure as fine as the Forth Bridge has finite appeal for a small boy, and I am sure the appearance of a thin plume of smoke and steam through the tracery of steelwork did much to reduce the risk of the inevitable 'juvenile-inattention equals parental-frustration' equation that so characterised my early years. Rolling towards us from the Fife shore, at that distance there was no sound to drown out the mewing of the restless gulls and the

4

moaning wind in a stand of trees close by. But as it reached the final cantilever, the roar of the train on the bridge became ever more distinctive.

In my mind's eye, the train was long, the engine was black, and the coaches were brown. If I am right, odds are that it was a V2, but it could have been a Pacific still in its wartime garb. The roar came closer and then faded gradually away, like the volume control on my parent's valve radio being turned down by me when a scary passage from "Dick Barton" was broadcast, as the train gained the more silent masonry pillars and steel girders approaching South Queensferry station. Before the train reached the West Lothian shore, it was obscured by the curve of the hill, only the sound of the locomotive revealing its approximate whereabouts as it accelerated on the last leg to Edinburgh.

Satisfying though it was, that image was not all for that day.

Perhaps it would have been better if it had ended there, the family group standing obediently, if impatiently, as the Jaguar was moved carefully onto a flat part of the road, and then a gentle run back into Edinburgh for tea and, in my case, an appropriate three and a half year olds' early bed. And, with that conclusion, the day might all have been forgotten.

But grown-ups do their best and, sometimes, their best is far too much.

Abandoning the car, we walked down the hill, or very probably I rode on my father's shoulders, to the small goods-yard at South Queensferry. In the days before the bridge, this had been the terminus of the line from Edinburgh, but the bridge approach, high above the little town, became the obvious location for what was to be called Dalmeny station as soon as the permanent link was opened. At the cost of an exhausting clamber up the hill, the would-be traveller could now travel north and south by train and take his or her pick of destinations, instead of being restricted to the few stops into Haymarket and the

Waverley, the flat-bottomed ferry until then being the only option for a trip to the Kingdom of Fife.

Into the yard we strolled, where a small goods engine stood after making up its train. I remember it as a Holmes 18-inch goods engine, a J36. An unrebuilt example is illustrated at the beginning of this chapter. It may well have been 'Maude', since it was awarded the special treatment of a home in Haymarket shed, more usually dedicated to the big express types, rather than the heroic, hopeless chaos of St. Margaret's on the eastern side of the city. 'Maude' worked the South Queensferry pick-up for years so, yes, it was probably 'Maude'.

In spite of his pedigree – *his* father a then recently-died railwayman and possessing a number of other deceased relatives called in past years to a similar vocation – my father was a reticent fellow who found it difficult to talk to anyone he didn't know. Besides, he couldn't abide a refusal. It would have been my uncle, always an outgoing, gregarious type, who would have sown a kindly seed and been the unwitting instigator of my undoing. He would have clambered over the fence, introduced himself to the driver and, in no time, I was lifted over and thrust into the cab of the little engine. I remember the heat on my face, the dirt on my hands as I steadied myself on the unaccustomed and uneven floor, the smells of warm oil, dusty coal, hot water and steam. The driver lifted me to the window to see my family loitering at a respectful distance behind the fence.

And then the driver pulled the whistle cord.

I knew, from experience, engines frequently whistled before they started, and I have no doubt now that the kindly driver would have puffed slowly along the siding and back again to the delight of everyone, and the especial delight of yours truly.

But I was three and a half, and it was perfectly obvious to me at that tender age that I had been given away. Furthermore, my family appeared to be delighted to see me go, waving me off enthusiastically. Perhaps, I thought, this is what happens to little boys; their greatest joy, for I was already a total devotee of the railway, becoming their most formidable betrayer.

It is hard to write this.

No-one likes to confess such a thing, the more so at the beginning of a book of reminiscence. But I screamed. Louder than the NB whistle, over the extraneous sounds of my steed – the fireman's shovel perhaps, or the conversation going on by this time metaphorically and actually over my head – and shrill enough to be heard behind the fence.

Within a moment, I was hastily returned to the embankment and awarded solace by my mother with, no doubt, withering incomprehension from my father. And the little engine slumbered on, an exchanged conversation between the driver and my family papering over the cracks caused by my wailing.

That was the last time for many years I stood on the footplate of a steam engine. And certainly an early moment of, almost immediately felt, profound embarrassment and deep shame. Within a short while, safely ensconced on my father's knee in the front passenger seat of the polished wood and cracked leather luxury of the Jaguar (in those days, no one had heard of seat belts, and a small child was thought safer and more under control in the front seat wrapped in the protective and powerful arms of his father than romping about free in the back, stamping on his aunt's, mother's and cousin's pretty 'going-out' shoes), I knew I had committed a blunder of epic proportions that I would never forget. Had I been more rational, more wise, I would have had a memory to treasure, instead of a lingering humiliation. It is very likely I would have steamed grandly up towards the throat of the goods-yard, probably been lifted to blow the whistle myself, seen the engine halted and the reversing level pushed across the quadrant for a gentle run back. And, even at that age, I would have been admitted, albeit briefly, to the closed, unique world of the professional railwayman, otherwise denied me by the death of my still-in-harness grandfather engine driver a few short years before my birth.

If only my uncle had come with me, it might have been so different.

But he didn't and it wasn't. I panicked, and it was all over.

Although my first intimate memory of a steam locomotive's cab was so inauspicious, the sense of the thing – the sight of the little engine and its traumatic, dread-inducing interior, the sounds – familiar enough from my father's insistence on us 'going up to see the engine', much to my mother's consternation, before setting out on any journey, or being made to pause on a footbridge as the train roared by underneath, the smells – never more acute than in that Holmes 0-6-0, the taste of the coal dust in the air and the rust and sweat on my fingers, and the touch – unfamiliar, massive, unyielding cold steel, like climbing into the very belly of a malevolent machine – these were all learned that day.

And now, writing fifty years after steam locomotion ceased to be commonplace in Britain, and seventy years after my profound disgrace, where the memory *does* fade, scant details confined to notebooks and faded pictures, it is via the senses alone one can accurately conjure up the past.

When I think of a Fowler 2-6-4 tank slowing for the station in the village of my childhood, its bunker facing London, its smokebox in long conversation with an LMS 9-compartment composite behind, were there three coaches or six, and was it, after all, a Fowler, or a more modern, less liked, Stanier or Fairburn? And how much of that satisfying perspective and glimpsed animation within, of passengers rising to their feet, of umbrellas and briefcases retrieved from the racks, of faces turned, pale and indistinct, to the window waiting for the stop, is really of more modern memory, a diesel multiple unit perhaps, or an electric; or somewhere else altogether?

Certainly, the guard, standing on the station platform in

brief dialogue with the rather ferocious porter, consulting his watch, noting the signal pulled off, swinging his flag in a graceful arc acknowledged by a brief pop on the engine's whistle, hopping expertly onto the running board and keeping a watchful eye on the bottom of the footbridge staircase in case a late and unwary passenger decided to risk all in a dash for the rapidly departing train, is of reliable provenance. The diesel multiple unit guards always seemed more cautious, and anyway they 'buzzed' the driver from a button over the inside of the door and didn't need the flag except in an emergency. And when the electrics came, the guards had been consigned to history. So that, at least, was a 'steam' memory.

But I no longer remember the engine's number – once the most important thing in my world – and although I remember the porter's name, I can no longer recall his face. But I can hear his step. He wore highly-polished black boots with steel protectors nailed underneath to the sole and heel, and he had a habit of putting his feet down, heel-and-toe. 'Ca-tunk, ca-tunk', his feet went, staccato and rhythmic, like an endlessly passing goods train of four-wheeled wagons. 'Ca-tunk, ca-tunk', 'ca-tunk, ca-tunk'. He walked past the house I lived in as a child on his way to work and, in summer, with the window open, I would hear him before I saw him and knew the aural source.

Not that one would run out and engage him in conversation as a long-lost friend! He had ample reason to be suspicious of small boys – one of our number had a personal obsession with the idea of blowing up the fish pond on the station which was our worthy's pride and joy. So, with a school cap on, I learned to be wary of him. But, the year I left school and replaced the uniform for my first '40/- Tailor' suit, that same porter who had growled at me only the span of a school holiday before, touched his cap respectfully as he briefly checked my weekly young-person season-ticket from Harpenden to Green Park on the Piccadilly line.

These are the memories I am left with. Clear and unequivocal, but unsubstantiated by anything tangible. In the past, those long years ago, it was the actual, the detail, the full experience, the taken-for-granted familiarity of it all; as if it would never change. Even the grainy photographs, the carefully collated number books, the squashed pennies, the stamps, postcards, newspaper cuttings and tickets no longer seem authentic, in spite of the fact I took them, wrote them, placed them on the lines and then searched in the ballast for them, stuck them into albums and books and, in many cases paid for my passage; their provenance, the why-and-wherefore, largely forgotten.

Now, one must fall back on the sense of it all or, rather, the five senses that conjure up a world gone forever.

These opening paragraphs, with one small exception, have dwelt long and lovingly on railway matters. And it is true, this book is mainly about what is left in my mind about them. But there was so much more to enjoy in those days. Lurching, rolling trams; silent surging trolleybuses; road transport in general that had a sense of adventure about it – not the inevitable dull reliability of things today. So they will come into the story to, as will a smattering of aeroplanes (to use their old name), ships, yes, and bicycles, for the latter conveyed us reliably to see so much.

Join me, if you will. Perhaps, in this world where everything is about instant gratification and immediate access, where memory is a largely overlooked treasure house, it may stir things in your mind. Your heart. Your soul.

The struggle for recall and anxiety about doubtful memory, in contrast to the ease and certainty of Internet research, can sometimes be amply rewarded. Because, and as an example, attached to reminiscence of a too-small-to-identify steam engine threading the valley to the north of Church Stretton, there was all that surrounded it. The scenery as intricate as a Constable; the up-the-hill scramble rewarded by lofty outlook; the questionable permanence of a stone thrown on a cairn; the reality of a solid, boarding-house breakfast resting uncomfortably on the stomach; the ominous sight of clouds massing over the Long Mynd, with the distinctive tones and texture of A. E Housman's "A Shropshire Lad" defining the mood; the manners, moods and attitudes of those who, like me, caught sight of the column of smoke curling over the silent carriages and, just as quickly, dismissed the image in favour of pleasures at closer proximity.

Perhaps the memory is of the creaky tram, standing silently at the Fairmilehead terminus awaiting our last stagger up from Hillend Park at the foot of the Pentlands. What framed that image? What put it into the context of burning, tired ankles having walked endlessly from the other 'car' terminus at Colinton, sandwiches consumed on a hillside, landmarks pointed out, sheep scattered by careless peregrinations, ankles turned over and nursed, blae' berries scavenged and eaten – carelessness resulting in consumption of a lone, withered, sheep dropping in error – warships grey and menacing lying in the far distance on the Forth?

Or the half-cab, Class 'T' single-decker bus easily springs to mind, turning carefully in the Harpenden station approach to begin its train-replacement service to Hemel Hempstead; the crazy Far Tottering and Oystercreek locomotive – steam outlined but internal combustion-engined – at the Battersea Funfair connected with the 1951 Festival of Britain; or the sudden roar that announced the arrival of 'Cats-eyes Cunningham', the test pilot, dipping a De Havilland jet fighter over his home in north Harpenden to let his wife calculate approximately when he would be home for tea.

Why do those things remain and what were their contexts?

I was never a professional railwayman. Instead, the memories recalled here sit in the landscape of my life – never centre-stage, always on the periphery, like the sets, props and costumes in a theatre production where the play is king. But, a stage-play performed without these would be a poor thing, and my life has been immeasurably enriched by my non-professional experiences.

In subsequent chapters (following one that explains my provenance, my claim to a small part in the railway story), each of the senses – hearing, sight, smell, taste and touch – will be trawled, to, hopefully, stir something of my past experiences. In so doing, I will endeavour to explore a perhaps overlooked aspect of transport scholarship.

I also hope to have a lot of fun.

CHAPTER TWO

ROOTS

Bespectacled and happy at the prospect of a train ride up the 'Nickey' line, Harpenden to Hemel Hempstead. 11ᵗʰ May, 1954.

Well, L. P. Hartley got it right. The past *was* another country and things *were* done differently there. And it wasn't so very long ago, either. A lifespan is enough to be somewhere else, to be so far away from 'now' for it to be foolish to even try to make comparisons. The oft-repeated line, 'it was better in my day' is an unconvincing distortion for old folks frightened by the modern world, for it was not better, or worse – only different.

I was born as the Second World War was drawing to a close. Adolf was confined but still alive, apparently lacking any regret for his emerging and terrible legacy. People were talking about life after combat – a new beginning – and married couples were getting amorous.

The baby boom was about to commence and my parents had been quicker off the mark than most. My father didn't serve in the forces due to a serious but opportune illness in 1939 – his contribution was a stint in the Home Guard and fire-watching from the vantage point of a branch line railway footbridge – and so I came along in February 1945, together with a number of future friends a few weeks older or younger than me.

I suppose you could say I was a favoured little boy. I was born in Harpenden, Hertfordshire – a London dormitory that retained its village atmosphere. Indeed, everyone living there called it, 'the village', even though it had a population that could easily match that of a respectable town. We existed in a rather smug bubble, pitched much higher in the social rankings than Luton, six miles away and a symphony of shabby industrial clutter, and felt we had nothing to be ashamed of by being close to the city of St. Albans. It had Roman remains, mediaeval streets, a posh public school, and a Marks & Spencer, but we had plenty to be proud of – an enormous area of common land that green-speared the village from the south, the world-renowned Rothamsted Laboratory, a working blacksmith in the High Street, a Sainsbury's – deep, cool and tiled, with tall stools, deliberately inaccessible to small children but specifically designed for the use of the elderly and younger women with various unspoken 'conditions', and staffed by kindly, disciplined people, the butcher being appropriately named Mr. Leaney – and, in Anscombes, our very own department store – hardly the sort of emporium associated with a genuine village.

Anscombes had an overhead cash railway that would end up being one of the last in Britain, and a penchant for charging for items, particularly women's wear, in guineas. I perhaps should explain that a guinea amounted to one pound and five pence in present currency. Since there were probably no actual guinea coins in circulation by that time, a degree of arithmetical prowess was needed to convert, say, three and a half guineas, into the actual sum due. Fortunately, the customer only had to hand over a sum in excess of the price which, together with a sales chit, would be put into the cash carriage and spun along over the heads of customers and staff, clattering over curves and rails to its destination in a cashier's office where the relevant mathematics could be performed, change calculated, and returned with the receipt in due course for the purchases to be released to the happy customer.

Shopping in Anscombes was a leisurely process providing plenty of time for small boys to seek out the source of the clicking and hissing overhead and watch the little contrivances as they went on their busy way. Separation from one's mother was a regular occurrence when the cashiers were busy. The most problematical aspect of the system was the part that went upstairs in a sort of caged elevator – the technology providing many opportunities for jamming and general breakdown. If my memory is correct, that part of the system was the first to be abandoned.

But those were the lean years just after the war, and even the residents of Harpenden, with mortgaged houses and steady jobs – usually of the white collared variety – were far from wealthy and, while there were, in some cases, funds to educate the children privately, bicycles tended to be second-hand, and the lack of money spared the blushes of bullied parents as there simply wasn't much in the toy shops or, for the more precocious or female compatriots, the children's outfitters. Nor were there the endless but rather passive diversions of today – tablets, screen-based gaming, computers, music delivered by a bewildering range of devices, mobile phones – and, apart from a couple of cinemas – one of which in these days of heightened anxiety about cleanliness would have had to issue a health warning for its bug-infested upholstery – little or no entertainment away from the gramophone with its fragile records in cardboard sleeves, or the Light Programme and Home Service of the BBC.

Some frightfully serious children listened to the Third Programme and whistled chunks of the 'Four Seasons' to drown out our renditions of Uncle Mac's Saturday morning choices – the 'Teddy-bear's Picnic' and 'How Much is that Doggie in the Window' (although old Mac was even a bit sniffy about that!) – but, on the whole, we saw radio as very much a relaxation from the school-centred chores of Nature-study, Geography, Arithmetic and, because as I say I was 'favoured', the impenetrability of Latin. We were brought up, unquestioningly, as Christians, in the 'gentle Jesus, meek and mild' school of pre-Sound of Music sentimentality, and not having much pocket money (an old penny per week for each year of one's life was traditional), we largely had to invent our own entertainment.

Deprived of worldly goods, but spurred on by the 'I-Spy' books that could be bought for modest sums for us from our local W. H. Smith's, we learned to be observant and to set great store by recording locations for stone mileposts, road signs with the torch of knowledge to indicate the presence of a school, oak trees, newts, and the sight of an Emperor penguin at Whipsnade Zoo. We also collected a myriad of useful and useless things – stamps, matchboxes, labels that adorned the little triangles of cheese we sometimes ate for our teas, images on the backs of cornflakes packets (the seduction of children into determining items on mother's shopping list presented to the village grocer – in our case, Harriden's – each week for eventual delivery in a tiny van, is not new) and, for those favoured with parents who smoked, cigarette cards showing footballers, boxers, famous buildings and vehicles.

And we collected numbers: the numbers of everything.

Bus numbers, aircraft numbers, car registration numbers and, of course, train numbers.

Most of the people I knew – birds of a feather, and all that – collected train numbers, but this harmless and slightly eccentric occupation has to be seen as the consequence of our time and situation and the fact that it came on the heels of a desire to collect practically everything we could. The richer boys started to buy the latest 'Dinky' offerings illustrated on the back page of the monthly 'Meccano Magazine' – a magazine encouraged by our parents who wanted to open our eyes, often vainly, to a variety of topics with an engineering bias – and these die-cast models were proudly displayed on chests of drawers in bedrooms. They became collections in their own right; mint examples, I note, now reaching astronomical prices in 'antique' auctions.

But most of us could not aspire to a monthly purchase for pride-filled exhibition in the school playground or on bedroom furniture. We had nothing but grubby notebooks and well-thumbed Ian Allen spotter's books to, with greater or lesser tidiness and accuracy – even honesty in many cases – cross off the engines, seen or not.

We were 'spotters', and we were proud of it.

But this is to jump the gun a little.

♦

I was fortunate to have had a grandfather who was an engine-driver – sadly deceased before I was born – and a father who, while being one of those white-collar commuters to the Big City who had turned his back on his parent's way of life, was something of a railway enthusiast himself. Not a spotter, but a man blessed with a long memory and some good stories to tell. Like so many others at the time, he was not particularly good at parenting but, I fancy, he saw sharing his passion with his elder son as a bridge into the bewildering world of the young.

Railways were our generational dictionary, our linguistic phrase book, and the common denominator of lives otherwise lived apart. The past and the (then) present – two countries where, indeed, things were done differently, places inextricably separated, the gulf linked by two steel rails.

My father may have despaired my inability to understand even the basic concepts of mathematics and my extraordinary capacity for wasting hours with little or nothing to show for their loss but, when it came to trains, we shared so much. Most of my compatriots came to an enthusiasm for railways in the form of a lucky accident – for instance the chance purchase by devoted parents of children's books that ranged across whatever was available at the time, including "Thomas the Tank Engine". I was both read to and told stories seamlessly by my father, so "The Wind in the Willows" and "Alice in Wonderland" were intermixed with his tales of hiding under sacking to avoid the attentions of the authorities at Edinburgh Waverley on my Grandfather's much-loved Holmes Class 'C' 0-6-0 (later J36), the soldiers on guard duty on the Forth Bridge during the First World War, or graceful 'Jersey Lilies' pounding past Pinner, my parents' first southern marital home .

As slumber gained ground and I closed my eyes, it didn't matter whether the words came from a book or my father's recollections. I would drift off by turns to a preposterous Mr. Toad, a frustrated Alice, or the rumble and roar of No. 678 heading for Fife on a dark and bitterly cold night, equally satisfied and not seeing any real distinction or feeling that there was something out-of-place regarding my genuine tales from long ago. To a young child, there is little differentiation between what is real and what is not, and my early years were punctuated by drifting happily between both camps, feeling equally at home in either.

Having a 'pedigree', an ancestor who was actually a railwayman and – most romantically of all – a footplate man, gave me a certain kudos in my circle of largely middle-class friends. I had a position in life that, real or imagined, helped me through.

Had I been born in my grandfather's city of Edinburgh and in the district he called home, just above the reeking, smoke filled, man-made, never-dormant, volcanic hollow that was St. Margaret's engine sheds, I would have been two-a-penny, 'the norm'. In fact, many of my compatriots would have had greater claim to fame, as their fathers, elder brothers and other relatives would still have been employed in my grandfather's former place of work and doing the same jobs he had done.

But my father got an education, moved to England and lived in an oversized village far away, where most of my friends had fathers who also worked with their brains in white-collar 'soft jobs', as my grandfather, apparently, called them. Some of them were managers and directors who worked mysteriously at the Stock Exchange, the Bank of England or, mentioned in hushed tones, 'in business'. My father moved on from an actuarial position with the Friend's Provident and Century Assurance Company to become a professional civil servant who hardly knew what he did himself, lost in the corridors of obscurity at the Home Office, and scratching his head over the idiocy of interrupting the job to lop twelve inches off the carpet beneath his feet because he was of a slightly lower grade than his predecessor.

My grandfather, now. He was different. He was a railwayman. He stood head and shoulders above anyone else in my imagination and, even to this day, I am most proud of him, and his picture still hangs in my office, grainily-posed in front old 678, 'pourie' in hand – the oilcan carried almost as a badge of office by drivers caught on camera – or stiff and posed with his family in a photographer's studio, a proud, tired, head of household.

So, my enthusiasm, specifically for trains, but generally for all things mechanical, was fostered by my father, but less-so by my mother. She saw the risks attached to too much time spent on a love-affair she didn't want to get in the way of her aspirations for me, which, undoubtedly, included dreams of university, a brilliant career, a detached house, a loving and attractive wife, two-point-four, achieving, adoring children, and the defensive wall of God-fearing, life assured, pensioned, like-minded, respectability. Whilst those were early days and all that might still happen, her son was spending a good deal too much time drifting down to sit beside the railway embankment and seemingly only enthused by the reporting of a passing 'Patriot', a 'namer', or the deep throated roar of a 'Garratt' getting to grips with an up coal train escaping the cloying idleness of the permissive block and mixing it with the local trains that, heading for London, had, from Harpenden, a choice of fast or slow lines that made it imperative that the coal trains and other freights 'got a move on'.

There was always an 'atmosphere' in my home where railways were concerned.

My father – never-endingly preoccupied with work and a house that saw a month without a plumbing, tiling or rising-damp disaster as a month wasted – shared brief moments, reading articles from the month's 'Railway Magazine', steering Sunday walks so that they intersected the various railway lines within strolling distance, or, very occasionally, winning my towering gratitude by spending a precious Saturday at the Science museum or 'around the termini', armed with notebook and, sometimes, bearing a new spotting book for the region we were concentrating on that day.

London was the ideal location for the aspiring spotter, as a few stops on the 'Circle' line, with its hand-operated, sliding-doored stock in my earliest days, enabled one to see all that was best on all four regions – a 'Sandringham' in Liverpool Street, an 'Arthur' or a 'Merchant Navy' at Waterloo (which required a walk across a Thames bridge which was also a thrill in its own way), a 'Duchess' cowering under the filthy roof of Euston, and finishing up with watching adenoidal, congested Great Western 'Castles' and 'Halls' or a myriad small pannier tanks hauling seemingly endless trains of empty stock over baulk-timbered rails that resembled those being pounded by the most unlikely, superb singles in picture books of the 'Broad Gauge'.

My mother, on the other hand, tried to make me into a 'normal child', a model student, frustrated by my severe astigmatic condition that, until it was identified, compromised my education, and a mild form of dyslexia, unheard of in those days and only identified long after I left home and my parents were dead.

I would never have been that academic she so earnestly cherished, that boy whose success would undoubtedly reflect so favourably on herself. In those days, and in that town, there was a good deal of pressure on parents to conform and to succeed on their own account and that of their offspring. Gradually, I slipped backwards, railways taking the blame for my intellectual shortcomings. One by one, my equals, with a few exceptions, left me rubbing the dust of their progress from my eyes, and my determination to pursue my lifelong interest was compromised by a sense of guilt at the place it held in my affections.

'Roderick could have been anything he chose, but for his obsessions with railways,' they seemed to think, my father quickly seeing the error of his early, encouraging ways and joining my mother's battle to broaden my interests and, to some extent, curtail my excesses. But, once the seed is sown, the child becomes devious and cunning, finding a thousand ways to wear down the resolve of his parents until compromises are found and an uneasy peace ensues.

This provided me with many contradictions and conflicts. Access to a tin-plate '0' gauge Hornby trainset, added to each Christmas with seductive and gleaming plum and spilt milk coaches, a standard tank, and a wagon or two – all four-wheeled – would be denied me, as a form of punishment, when poor school marks were achieved. My father, profoundly unskilled at 'do it yourself' and a great expert at using the "Birmingham Screwdriver" (or 'hammer', as it is more normally known), laboriously – and heroically, I thought – built shelving to enable a layout to be built and used without the risk of backache, only to prevent, at least for a while, the screwing of the track to

21

the aforesaid base units.

I suppose he hoped the model railway craze might be temporary and the shelving could come in useful for other purposes.

Whether it was kinetic energy or whatever discipline was being exercised, I do not know, science never being my strong point, but a Hornby 0-4-0 running at full tilt towards a tight curve on a track laid loosely on shiny-side-up hardboard has an unfortunate tendency to take the track with it, and after plunging to the floor in a respectable imitation of the Tay Bridge disaster, dragging its string of four-wheelers behind it more than once and causing lasting damage to locomotive, rolling stock and sundry plastic farm animals forever regurgitating pretend grass, the Birmingham screwdriver was reluctantly used to whack nails through convenient holes in the tinplate sleepers and into the hardboard.

I experienced a continual process of changed priorities, of reward and punishment, of encouragement and prevention, of indulgence and denial. At times it seemed as though I was the only person in the family with any real consistency. I felt I was the infant rock around which adult tides of disharmony swirled.

The adult mind – always mysterious to a child.

I even, irrationally, hate the thought of G. K. Chesterton's "Father Brown" to this day. My father's frustration and not a little anger, no doubt spurred on by my mother, at the prospect one Sunday of my early evening disappearance to witness a friend's outdoor Gauge '1' model railway, unusually made available to the model railway fraternity, manifested itself in my being confined to quarters to read about the myopic priest's powers of deduction and crime-solving. Indeed, 'Father Brown' was seen by my parents as such an excellent way for me to spend a Sunday evening that I never did get to see that garden layout, each Lord's Day ending in the same way well into the Autumn of that year.

Those things, the appropriate ancestor, train spotting,

the ABCs and the toy trains, are the background to all this – an obsession that, fortunately for everyone around me, virtually ceased with the obliteration of steam.

But, by then, it was too late. In 1968, when steam was largely over, I was already twenty-three and had propelled my compromised life into a form of employment that would pay for an upcoming marriage and the responsibilities of adulthood. Undoubtedly, an enthusiasm for preserved steam can be absorbing enough, and in that I am still very interested. Similarly, when the day-to-day has gone, there is always the history of it all, and that can be satisfied by a library of books and periodicals and the occasional stroll around railway remains. But it doesn't compare with the 'real thing' – the everyday magic of the classic steam railway.

I hope this book will explain why those old passions live on for me and, I know, many others.

♦

Harpenden, in those days, had three stations.

After Nationalisation, British Railways kindly distinguished between the former LMS and LNER stations by calling them 'Central' and 'East' respectively. Until that time, some context was necessary to ensure everyone in the conversation was singing from the same hymn sheet. 'Great Northern' and 'Midland' harped back to the heady days of the pre-grouping scene, but only the well-informed would achieve precision from those terms. The 'big' and the 'little' stations would be more understandable, and sometimes East would be called 'Batford', even though that community did not commence until after the River Lea had been crossed.

The third Harpenden station, Roundwood Halt, had closed in 1947, and sat, ironically, the most modern in its concrete-platformed simplicity, on the now goods-only branch to Hemel Hempstead and Boxmoor. To the spotter, even the 'East' provided a feast of thin gruel, a few passenger trains each way a day, plus some goods, while the Roundwood Halt offering was a couple of return good trains each day and, without sidings, no reason to stop, other than for a bit of a blow-up after climbing the 1 in 37 from Luton Road bridge.

But Central was a very business-like station with four platforms, a small goods yard, and a signal box at the south end, with another less than a mile away at the junction for Hemel Hempstead. In spite of my preference for matters LNER, it must be admitted that Central 'had it' in terms of interest in Harpenden.

The East was the gateway to LNER glories in Welwyn Garden City or, in the other direction, the mysteries of the end-on junction with the old London & North Western at Dunstable, where large and improbable 0-8-0 goods engines would, from time to time, appear on freights

On the other hand, Roundwood Halt enabled one to trespass happily on the railway; where wooden keys could be knocked into (and sometimes out) of the chairs; where pennies could be squashed without similar consequence for the trespasser; and where slow worms could be caught, rabbits watched, blackberries eaten in season and, in later years, girls could be kissed.

But maximum railway reward was, undoubtedly, earned at Central.

Harpenden Central had everything a boy needed, other than peace and quiet or something to eat. Forgetting the bars of chocolate sold by Bob – and Bob's dad – at W. H. Smith's, the station was no place to be hungry and, on the whole, the railwaymen couldn't abide small boys who had a persistent tendency to behave badly. If we had sat quietly between trains discussing the ways of the world, we might have been allowed to remain on the platforms – even without a requirement to buy a platform ticket, price one penny.

But that is not what small boys do in the lulls.

Oh, it might start with noisy comparisons of ABCs, incredulity at obvious dishonesty being stoutly defended,

24

and withering sarcasm at not crossing off all the 'Garratts' that must all, sooner or later, clatter up and down between Brent and Toton. Only laziness, surely, or a lack of commitment, would allow a locomotive to pass through unseen, unspotted, and uncrossed off! But after those conversational topics had been exhausted, pleading glances towards the signalbox hoping for a 'look in' obstinately unheeded, and in the absence of an indication of imminent action such as a clit-clattering of a signal coming off, idle hands made work for the Devil – an observation often directed towards us by the station staff.

There were barrows, both two and four wheeled, that could, at least by our bolder fraternity, be purloined for nefarious activities which generally meant being charged along the platform with any number of small shrieking children clinging on for dear life. There were full-to-bursting pigeon baskets that could be investigated, usually with a sharp stick or a discarded piece of straw, as the confined birds awaited their release time and the long flight home. One boy even created some never-bettered speed records, as the seals were broken and the straps unbuckled to set the birds off in hazardous, direction-finding loops as they gained height a full hour before their planned departure time. The fact that this was not done during a gap in train activity may have consigned a few birds to their winged Valhalla, as the station staff always paused to give them the best chance of avoiding a collision with an up-express. Or, in winter, gas lamps could be extinguished as soon as they had been lit by use of the long pole designed for this activity and discarded carelessly beside the porter's door, or simply by shinning up the lamp post and knocking the gas tap off.

Sometimes the flame would go out but the tap continued to gush gas into the cold night air. The more nervous and imaginative of us pictured our fathers lighting their pipes as they made their way from the train a couple of hours later and receiving a greater surprise than any headline in the 'Evening Standard' could ever provide.

But, on the whole, the gas moaned and hissed into the night air unheeded and quickly forgotten. On his next circuit of the station, Albert, or one of his compatriots, would, no doubt, spot the recalcitrant lamp, curse the suspected miscreants, and restore light to the gloomy platform.

Or, when a train did come through, the crew of the roaring 'Jubilee' might blow the whistle in alarm, fulfilling our desire to have that same reaction to the vigorous up-and-down pumping of our hands, even though small boys dangerously careening about on the edge of the platform was their trigger, and not our wish to be friendly.

On the whole, our presence at the station was not welcome unless we waited in the booking office, which was of no use to a spotter since nothing much could be seen other than a flash of coaches or a string of trucks as they passed the open doors. If we waited in the booking office, it was so as to meet someone off the train – nothing more. So we didn't go, preferring the embankment or the footbridge in Carlton Road. There we could discuss earnestly or lark about with only nosy neighbours looking for a reason to reprimand. Taking to the embankment or causing road vehicles to abruptly screech to a halt to avoid a collision with a seemingly out-of-control boy on a bicycle could bring threats of calling the police or, worse, the condemnation of God. But, on the whole, there was an uneasy truce between the residents of Carlton Road and the spotters. Indeed, many of the residents' children were *also* spotters – much envied by those of us who lived further afield.

It was usually they who saw the rarities, the Midland 2Fs, the rare Scottish and Carlisle 'Jubilees' and, of course, all the 'Garratts' as they articulated sinuously around the curve on the approach to Platform 4. It was they who could listen to the stumbling exhaust of the 'Compounds' that still pulled many of the breadwinner's trains, and who watched the Fowler 2-6-2 tank as it reversed the stock from the Moorgate into the loop siding behind the platform at the end of the day, before shuffling off to St. Albans' shed for the night, long after those of us who lived away from the railway line had been summoned home for tea. And it was they who were lulled to sleep by roaring expresses, eighty-wagon coal empties, and strings of suburbans running late into the night taking lovers home from London's theatre-land, clutching their cheap evening returns and the remaining nuts and brittles lying unloved in an otherwise empty box of Cadbury's chocolates, heads lolling together or now parted, his against the condensation-soaked glass, hers on his now makeup-stained shoulder. From where I lived, the trains were still audible, particularly in summer when windows were flung wide open, but they were muffled, masked and less easy to distinguish one from another.

The sound of trains in the distance which, of course, we all loved, long before we knew the words to Paul Simon's song.

Wherever one roamed in Harpenden, one was never far from a railway. Remarkably lacking in conventional railway features – no engine-shed, no big marshalling yard, and a junction that barely lived up to its name – one was constantly aware of its presence. Whether it was the 'Nickey', passing north and then west on its explosive passage to Redbourn, Hemel Hempstead and the shamefaced shabbiness of Boxmoor Gas Works in the shadow of the London & North Western; the strings of main line trains bisecting the village from north to south, tying the nation together; or the Great Northern over to the east of the village, paralleling the Midland to the north or striking off south-eastwards towards Welwyn Garden City and its film-star trains, nobody was more than a few hundred yards from a railway. This meant that every activity was accompanied by the background noise and smoke of passing trains.

During a walk to the village, the unaware or distracted would be startled by the sudden roar of a train passing over Station Road Bridge. A walk up the Common would be enlivened by the sight of an 8F passing over the high embankment, above the houses and the convent, hidden but briefly by the trees when in full summer leaf. A game of cricket or a round of golf would be similarly animated, as would the tennis doubles match played by the stiff-backed ladies who scolded each other when the ball was not hit to fall neatly at the feet of their companionable competitors.

Those ladies, with their skirts mid-calf, their white blouses and thin cardigans, their short socks and heavy wooden racquets held firmly in frames and clipped, for transportation, to the front forks of their bicycles, who never worked up a moment of perspiration, even in July, who argued about whose turn it was to make their colourless tea diluted with soured full fat milk in the wonky club-house, have gone with the steam engines and the roads only occasionally dotted with the motorcars of the fortunate few.

A visit to the dentist; he of the masochistic smile, the articulated torture equipment, and strange-smelling knock-out gas dispersed from what looked vaguely like a tea-strainer; he of the glass of pink liquid that mustn't be swallowed but must be spat, bloodied and mucoused, into the diminutive sink that defied all attempts to capture the contents of a pained and swollen mouth, was compensated not at all by the passage of a down 'Manchester' roaring through Harpenden Central. One marvelled at the number of expresses roaring through while still confined to the iron-framed, wood-scratched, horsehair-uncomfortable, chair. One, two, three would go through until, coming around and dizzy-sick, standing too quickly, clutching the chair arm, or relieved at the arrival of the amalgam – dangerous, even deadly, poison slowly setting in filled cavities, surplus material scouring the inside of children's cheeks to be fished out for the rest of the night – we would, always polite in Harpenden, thank him for his butchery, and attempt to descend the stairs without vomiting or stumbling to the bottom. We would sit in the waiting room until it was safe to leave, especially after an extraction, the gas fire sighing and encouraging a return to nauseous recollection of what had gone before. And, too frequently, further dental appointments made. Still the trains banged through the station whistling loudly, heralding a form of hysterical longed-for freedom, the heady lightness of being, of life post-trauma, of a surprising possibility of continued existence.

Harpenden East was a very different kettle of fish. For me, it was solely associated with school holidays. And as I hated school with a dawning realisation that it was acceptable to be critical of one's lot in life, to dislike things so intensely and without shame, a realised ingratitude for the gift of life itself, the East, away from the school journey after the age of eleven, and after the walk to school before eleven – other than one year wedded to a London Transport bus – was pure joy.

At first, it was my mother's infrequent visit to the Welwyn Stores, a form of Garden City New Socialism, now part of John Lewis, where everything could be bought. I suppose it resembled GUM in Moscow, a Tsarist emporium reinvented by the Soviet Union and taking pride of place in Red Square, although Welwyn Stores was a trifle smaller. But, restricted to Anscombes in Harpenden, Welwyn provided an image of orgasmic plenty where imagination was only held back by the usual restricted budget.

Down to the East Station we would go, walking along the little access path that led from the lower side of the railway overbridge to a flight of steps down to the east-bound, up, platform. The sun would be shining. It always was, because wet weather would simply postpone the visit and, in memory, to children the weather was either wet or sunny, with no dry or dull in-between. Tickets bought in the little booking hall, so very different from the larger Midland example at Central, we would return to the platform, legitimate passengers now, and I would walk to the north end to watch out for the train. Great Northern somersaults would tumble and the N7 would eventually appear. Careful observation enabled a child to see the coupling rods on both sides of the locomotive for a moment, up and down, up and down, almost like a toy, as it turned towards the up platform situated in the passing loop.

It always seemed to be an N7 on the local passenger trains, the big, more pugnacious N2s commonly dominating the freights. This strict demarcation was only in my mind, though, passing time contributing to imperfect memory. The train of plywood boxes containing new Vauxhall cars going to Tilbury for export, for instance, was normally N2-hauled, and it would sit smokily in the platform waiting for a Luton-bound local and the release of the single-line tablet. Customarily, tank engines on the trains at both Harpenden stations worked chimney first out of London or from the London direction. Tender engines almost always faced 'the right way', except the Nickey branch engine that no longer had the luxury of turntables at either end of the line.

On those afternoon visits to Welwyn Garden City, traffic was light and the other platform was unoccupied. So, the N7 came in, backwards, with its two-coach Gresley twin, or perhaps two or three Thompson suburbans, some blessed with a short corridor and access to a lavatory (never a toilet). The porter, he might have just sold the tickets to my mother, would, respectfully, help us to board, while the signalman talked to the engine crew as the tokens were exchanged. A quick whirl of the guard's flag, an answering squeak from the whistle, and we would set off, under that other Station Road bridge, to regain the single line. The N7s enjoyed very rapid acceleration and in no time we would be bowling along happily past the sewage farm and into open country, the double wheel-beats confirming the brevity of our train and, usually, Mr. Gresley's economy beneath our feet. The little engine would whistle long and repeatedly for the level crossing at Leasey Bridge, there being no signal to protect the crossing in the up direction, although, curiously, there was a distant for down trains which was interlocked with the gates such that the signal could not be pulled off unless the gates were closed against the road.

Shortly afterwards, the train hit the points into the goods yard at the bottom of the sharp gradient up into Wheathampstead station at considerable speed, skilful driving and the forces of gravity contributing to a neat stop in the station with very little braking required. Off again, and maybe to pass a goods at Ayot, where the station had burnt down in 1948 and closed the year later. Ayot station was something to be feared by a small child terrified of fire. I had been traumatised for ever from witnessing 'Great Expectations' at a very young age and shown, innocently enough, by my school's film club, trying, vainly in my case, to encourage an interest in Mr. Dicken's literature. Ayot represented everything that was unnerving, disturbing and sinister.

Off quickly, then, towards our goal via Brocks Wood, memories of Tizer and sandwiches, and a father who could combine his two leisure-time passions – trains and walking – rather well in this locale, and the White Bridge that linked two separate parts of the Garden City more satisfactorily than the previous level crossing. Around the curve, with its hoped-for glimpses of Gresley express engines, before a quick descent from the train and the doubtful delights of Welwyn Stores.

On the journey home, the sun lower in the sky, one could watch the train's shadow as it slanted its way across the green fields, every detail finely etched as it rose and fell with the undulating countryside. Sometimes the image was so clear as to pick up the coupling rods and the three bogies on the two coach set. Arrival in Harpenden initiated a short struggle with the unfamiliar, shielded, safety door-handle and then, the train having pulled out, the walk across the level crossing at the end of the platform and the tired stumble up to the summit of Station Road, and home.

In later years, I befriended the signalman at Harpenden

East, a chap from Ireland with a passion for railways and an easy conversational style that was quickly appreciated. He would bring bundles of pictures down to the box and, during the long pauses between trains, he would sit me down and explain the images of named, blue 'Compounds' on titled expresses, oddities such as 0-6-4 tanks without numbers, rail buses that really did look like buses on rails, and 2-6-0s that resembled those I saw occasionally on the Southern Region. In return for pushing the hugely heavy wheelbarrow laden with weeds taken out of the beautifully maintained beds behind the platforms and tipping it into the remains of the cattle dock, I became a regular visitor to the box and did some of the token exchanging. No-one ever seemed surprised at the sight of a young boy brandishing the loop and pouch. It was probably a scene repeated up and down the breadth and width of the country.

Small boys and trains – forever drawn to one another.

That line was the first in the area to succumb to the arrival of the diesel railcars. The local paper sent a reporter to take a ride and even they saw just how like buses they were. There had been no attempt to mimic a proper train. This one had a couple of doors on either side and ranks of fixed seats facing towards the driver's cabs at the end of the coaches. They lurched about and, even in their youth, were noisy and odoriferous. But they had large windows that merely exaggerated the fact that we did not really want to look beyond, other than that swing around the curve into Welwyn Garden City station. We were looking inwards, and soon there would be nothing worth seeing – in or out.

And, although the railway proudly announced a huge increase in passenger traffic in the first few weeks (as they did all over the country when modernisation arrived), it was novelty that swelled passenger numbers, not need. In no time, passenger numbers fell again and, for our little branch line, the end came on the 24th April, 1965. Goods remained only as long as it took to build a link in Luton to serve a truncated portion to Dunstable and this, together with goods traffic at the short extremities from Welwyn Garden City and Leighton Buzzard, lasted for a few years more.

In Harpenden today, you would have to be an industrial archaeologist to know that a railway ever existed at the East, although the route can be traced where housing and the slick of tarmac between speed-discouraging roundabouts are avoided.

Those of my generation who loved the traditional railway were almost permanently sad. We were morbidly in thrall of death, fully paid-up members of a cult focused on terminal disease, participants in a relentless wake. Each month's magazines announced another line closed, another class of steam engine rendered extinct, another piece of unwelcome modernisation.

Today, we would be in therapy.

In those days, we suffered quietly and mostly alone.

And if that wasn't bad enough, trams and trolleybuses disappeared too, and old underground trains, and steam ships, and the whole tapestry of our world of traditional industry with its inter-connected transport needs. Fishing shrank with the fish stocks, and the fleets of brave little drifters and trawlers with their braver crews, and lines of dripping, blue or white ice-charged vans snaking from the ports to the consumers in London and elsewhere behind express locomotives running at express train schedules, retreated too. Meat carcases, bound from markets all over the United Kingdom for Smithfield, transferred to the roads. Broccoli specials, headed by those night owls, the 47XX 2-8-0s, rarely seen on the main line in daylight, ceased their sleep disturbing clamour through Devon and Somerset and Berkshire, a long trail of occasional firehole-door-lighted smoke curling invisibly into the night sky. Milk churns, which stood in inconvenient groups fouling the entrances to dozens of country stations, no longer blocked our passage. Coal trains, of course, whose contents warmed hearths, facilitated industry, powered our locomotives, fed the coking plants, and fired power stations, not to mention the innumerable gas works of small towns (and the giant ones that occupied hundreds of acres in corners of cities, now replaced by bijou flats and artificial open spaces – park-benched and tagged with depressing graffiti), ceased to run. Industry replaced. By what? Just more dwellings, more dual carriageways, more pelican crossings beeping occasional permissions, more parades of retail premises destined to be boarded up or converted into betting establishments, charity shops, or cheap booze vendors.

And with the end of that interconnectivity, that interdependence, came the isolation we all now experience.

No one feels a part of anything complete, any more. No one sees the bigger picture.

I once worked in the computer department of a pharmaceutical company that made life-saving, pain relieving, drugs, and it was at my request that we had a tour of the laboratories where these medicines were made. Few of us had any idea of what was involved.

We all worked tirelessly at something of which we had not a clue.

But, until that time arrived – until now, if you like – there was so much to experience, so much to feel, so much to appreciate, so much to value. But we had no inkling of how quickly it would fade. Distracted by life's preoccupations, we would turn away, and it would be gone when we looked back – the hours and the moments quickly passing, their impending irrelevance to be followed, inevitably, by our own.

CHAPTER THREE

HEARING

The interloper side-lined at Bedford shed, probably 1958.
Alan Warren collection.

I can visit several preserved railways, not to mention the
Great Orme cable tram, within not much more than an
hour of my home. Two hours gets me to two working
tramways – one a feast of nostalgia and the other a
resurgent and modern system where, ironically, they had
to dig up the tracks of a network closed at the end of the
nineteen-forties to lay the new rails. A quick search on
YouTube can fill my ears with the sounds of railways
across the world in places I will never visit. I know exactly
what a 'Big Boy' sounds like, and a 'Shay', and a Czech
behemoth with a red star on its smokebox door, and a
Melbourne tram.

Do you want to know how the railways and tramways
of the forties and fifties sounded? Well, it's obvious, isn't
it? Visit a preservation site, or look on your computer, and
it will all become clear.

Well, yes and no.

While preserved railways do so much to foster nostalgia in the old, and imagination in the young, so much can only be recalled in fragments … little shards of remembrance that, together, never make up a reassembled mirror in old people's memories or give an accurate sound-experience to the not so old. Yes, I can listen to a steam engine barking away from a wayside station and, occasionally, the satisfying rhythm of wheels on rail joints, I can appreciate the whine of a tramcar as its gears take the strain of lifting tons of lovingly restored truck and body from a standing start. And I can hear a shouted instruction from the ground to an observant crew as a shunt is undertaken. It is all redolent of the past. But it is also something else – a new, but distorted, delight. A curiosity. A piece of Baroque music played on modern instruments; or being served in a curry restaurant where the accents of the third generation clash with my memories of shy waiters more used to the syllables and stresses of Urdu or Tamil; or a shambolic, noisy, unloved harbour warehouse hung with cranes and rotted doors on every floor, reborn chic, silent, polished, security-entranced, and domestically-desirable as never before.

♦

In my youth, the little Johnson 0-6-0 that figures so frequently in my memory would puff into our goods yard every morning to assemble its train for the branch-line. In the afternoon, after not one but two peregrinations to the grass-grown sidings at Hemel Hempstead or Boxmoor, dropping wagons at wayside stations and bringing out emptied and filled ones for the north and south, it would return to the Harpenden yard and shunt, often well into the rush hour.

Our goods yard was hardly a yard at all. Two dead-end sidings and a pair of loops – one straddled by a dark and forbidding goods shed, the other somewhere to park the Moorgate stock once the bowler hats had returned home.

There was access to the north and south slow lines, and a large paved area where the coal-lorries would stand at right-angles to the track for the fuel to be weighed and bagged before being delivered around the village. If the merchants couldn't do this within the time constraints imposed by the railway and mining industries anxious to see wagons on their way back to the collieries, it would all be dumped into merchants' pens or just onto the yard floor to be dealt with later. Delay meant incurring extra charges. The sounds of shovelling accompanies the memories of the 0-6-0.

Sometimes that seemed to be it – a curious scraping cacophony – from wagons into sacks, from the tender into the firebox, from the ground into yet more sacks. We got the impression that everything ran on coal and, in those days without mechanisation away from the large centres, it all needed to moved, one lump at a time, from one place to another – by hand.

Even at home, my father mimicked the professional actions in the yard, coal shovelled from the coal-house in the garden into a bucket, and then tipped with a roar into the ornamental brass-covered coal-box in the sitting room. We burned coke too. Strange, light, volcanic-looking stuff, from which the gas had been removed by being heated in a retort installed inside Harpenden's little gas works. It, too, had arrived in Harpenden in the form of coal, and had been taken to the works next to the railway line, but dozens of feet below, necessitating a lift of about half a mile in a huge two-wheeled cart pulled by a Shire horse.

The long-suffering animal had to negotiate the descent from the railway yard and then down Station Road before turning left and clip-clopping its level way along Southdown Road, under the skew bridge, and then into the 'Do Not Enter' confines of the odoriferous gas works. Wet and dry, cold and warm, snow- and ice-challenged, the poor beast, whose shoes kicked up sparks that crackled in the air as it took the weight of the cart on the gradients on dry days, or slithered dangerously in the slush, its ears cocked backwards to the warning cries of its minder who walked alongside the more challenging measures, a comforting hand on the brass-ornamented harness, heedless of the other traffic that would give the assemblage a respectful wide berth. Motorists, cyclists and pedestrians were more patient in those days, and it would be an insensitive and haughty shopper who attempted to cross at the Belisha beacon-marked crossing when the coal horse came through.

But what of the little Johnson standing quietly in the yard while we discuss the heating and cooking arrangements for the majority of Harpenden's residents? Having laboriously moved from the fast lines that inconveniently provided the only access to the Hemel Hempstead branch, everything from and for the branch train had to be sorted, together with the coal wagons and anything else that had completed its journey in Harpenden. That might mean a new piece of farm machinery, boxes of footwear from Northampton for the shoe shops, fruit and vegetables for Harriden's Stores, shiny new furniture and carpets for Anscombes' department store, or scientific instruments – crated and lovingly cushioned with straw – for Rothamsted Laboratory. Some traffic went away from the yard, too – that was the way of things in those days – but to the Johnson and its crew, they were all just wagons, some for the north and some for the south.

The shunter, a sloppily-attired cove who had, at an earlier moment, walked steadily along the lines of wagons checking labels for en-route wagons and attaching new labels (carefully written out in the warmth of the booking office) behind their little sprung clips, now repeated his peregrination, astutely memorising destinations – Leicester (frequently spelled 'Lester'), St. Albans, Bedford, Sheffield – the obvious and the not quite so easy to define, as individual collieries or companies might take the place of towns on the map. But, to him, they were to the north or to the south, and the pick-up freight would collect them dutifully as long as they were assembled correctly. There would, of course, be further wagons for the branch, to be taken on the next trip westwards (it was essential, of course, that they, too, were coupled together in the right sequence), so he had to assemble his wagons into three groups – north, south and west – and then into the correct sequence within each group. He might end up with a rake of twenty wagons that needed to be broken down a dozen times to arrive at his three main categories – for instance, the first for the north, second and third for the south, fourth, fifth and sixth for the north, seventh for the branch, eighth for the north, and so on. And he knew them all by heart.

The 0-6-0 would awaken from its slumbers and pull all twenty up towards the south end of the yard and then pause as our shunter friend walked slowly down to the far end, changed the points by hand, uncoupled the first, and waved in the direction of the driver. With a brief toot on the whistle, the engine would start up and give the train a hefty shove before stopping abruptly with a grinding application of the brakes. If there was nothing in the siding before the buffer stops, the shunter would walk alongside the free-running wagon or, if the shove had been a bit too spirited, break into a trot to keep up. Another parked wagon would render his walk unnecessary, the new arrival crashing noisily into its companion and thus coming to rest. But if the siding was otherwise empty, with nothing but the buffer-stop to avoid an accident, or they were using the goods shed loop, the hand-operated brake had to be dropped by removal of the pin that held it off the wheels and skilfully leant on at the appropriate time.

As soon as the wagon came to a halt, the more cautious of his breed would reapply the brake. Harpenden yard, however, was largely on the level, so they could sometimes be left to their own devices. Meanwhile, No. 43245 would have gone back up the head-shunt with the nineteen and, points changed again, the next batch would be uncoupled and pushed back, this process being repeated until the task was completed.

Steam engines are largely silent when stationary, so the thunderous shunting movements and whistling would be interspersed with periods of quiet, the wagon couplings taking centre-stage with their clinking, accompanied by the occasional crash of buffers. Up and down, a dizzy operetta of sound and movement. Sometimes in bed in the evening, I fell asleep to this music, continuing, sometimes, well into the night.

The modern railway doesn't shunt this way anymore – most trains are permanently assembled into rakes, with only crippled wagons being cut from a fixed format, and preserved lines that try to give the impression of old-style shunting do it for the sole purpose of entertainment – the wagons being very mixed in style and often too beautifully maintained. My memory is of coal wagons, steel and wooden, box vans with unsecured doors, and low-sided three-planked open trucks for largely-unprotected wagonload traffic – often in a deplorable condition. As I came on the railway scene at the time of both railway and mining nationalisation, the once proud private-owner coal trucks displaying ownership, addresses and sometimes sales slogans, gradually lost their identities as they were patched up with new and sometimes second-hand timber. It becoming more and more difficult to identify their provenance as the months and years went by.

But that rhythm and the anticipated crash as wagons came to a halt, or the sudden bark from the locomotive as it seemed, briefly, to be getting somewhere, was a false promise. The starting would be repeated after the next crash, and the next, and the next. We could tell it was just preparing for the next round of its wrestling match with the trucks. Freedom to play on the main line would have to wait, usually after sleep overtook me.

♦

Jointed track gave much of what we experienced in terms of our ears. While, thanks to the heroes of the preservation scene and the tolerance of those who run our main-line railways nowadays, I can still enjoy the sight and sound of an express train hauled by a steam engine, jointed track out on the main line is becoming a rarity, while steam hauled goods trains with four-wheeled wagons are very much a thing of the past.

That beautiful 'one-two, one-two', out-of-step, marching sound of wheel on joint, like a man with a gammy leg wearing nailed boots, dot and carry one, 'click-clack', 'click-clack', punctuated by the occasional insertion of a long-wheel-based four-wheeler, bogie wagon or six-wheeler, could set the hairs on the back of one's neck on edge, and we would wait for the elongated patter from the brake van sporting a slightly longer wheelbase. Dun-dun, dun-dun, dun ....pause ...dun. What a satisfying conclusion, rather like the triumphant crescendo at the end of a piece of music.

I suppose that was what it was ... music.

There was irony in the fact that, when pop music came along, it unconsciously adopted the four-beats-to-a-bar rhythm of the quickly-disappearing two cylinder steam engine and the four-wheeled truck.

One of the very best trains, aurally, was the return milk empties, usually pulled by a 'Crab' 2-6-0. Bulk milk wagons needed to run smoothly, and the best railway solution to that requirement sported a six-wheeled frame. Before young people turn their noses up at the idea of milk being carried in a railway wagon, consider that the tank was glass-lined, baffled to prevent surging, and thoroughly washed out at the end of every trip. Those wagons rode more smoothly than a Pullman or any road tanker. Most of them, when full, ended up at dairies conveniently situated beside the railway. There was one at Cricklewood that had an early abomination in the form of a blue diesel shunter that came to life only when the tankers arrived and needed to be discharged, one-at-a-time, in the dairy.

So, along would come the 'Crab' on the down-slow at Harpenden with the empties, steam shut off in anticipation of its move to the fast lines at the Junction, The six-wheeled rhythm was beautifully syncopated with two six-wheeled vans for the guard, presumably reflecting some sort of dividing of the train further north. Curious to us, neither van was at either extremity of the train. It was a very rare sight in those days to see a train terminated by a wagon sporting a tail lamp which had to be checked especially carefully by successive signalmen. It was one of their tasks to make sure a passing train was complete, and a brake van with its tail-lamp would easily convince them of the train's conclusion. But the milk train required particular observation as the final van might be six milk wagons nearer the locomotive.

While one would be correct to assume the noise of the locomotive in terms of the action at the chimney or the safety valve (and a certain looseness around the valve gear and coupling rods) headed the list of sounds associated with a passing passenger train, the rail joints were almost always the first sounds we heard. This is now, sadly, no more, as we live in a world of welded rails with very few imperfections resulting in any of the old 'clickety-clack' heard in the days of which I write. Almost any train in those days would announce its arrival by a fast drumming of the wheels. This was especially true of tank-engines on the front of London-bound locals which, in our case, might have meant a twenty-five mile slog from Bedford, with another twenty-five to go before reaching St. Pancras. As they invariably 'faced north', our Fowler, Stanier, Fairburn and, later, Riddles 2-6-4 tanks would treat us to a complex and satisfying percussion as they slowed for Harpenden station. The 'Jubilees', on the other hand, would scream past – the carrying wheels at the front acting like a herald, or the percussive, rhythmic drum in a bagpipe band – precursor to the roar of the coupled wheels and the follow-up of the tender and then the settling down of the coaches, sometimes slightly upset by the sound of a twelve-wheeled dining car.

The most complex wheel-beat was when the first of the

curious Metrovick Co-Bo diesels, always in pairs, appeared on a down 'Manchester' that passed through St. Albans as we waited indolently for our local train home from school. The diesels were often coupled with their six-wheeled bogies together, and the first coach was followed by one of those twelve-wheeled diners, so there was magic in the air as the beat went 2-3+3-2 for the locomotives, followed by 2, 2+3, 3+2, 2+2, and so on, four to the bar, to the end of the train. As those diesels were blisteringly dreadful and rarely ran as quickly as the steam engines they were introduced to replace, we had plenty of time to listen to their painful passage through St. Albans.

♦

While the clickety-clack of bogie coaches was almost universal on passenger trains, there were variations that the discerning among us would recognise and appreciate. We all knew the moment when, as the train accelerated, the regular four beats to the bar would gather together into a sort of gallop, and the sound would subtly change to a speedy 'tattle-tattle, tattle-tattle'. If I try to imagine it now, I would have to say it took place at about forty miles per hour, and so long as the bogies were of standard size, this would be true on almost every line. When I first started to take a serious interest in railways, pre-Nationalisation stock was dominant, and I have already mentioned the Gresley articulated coaches on the former LNER lines where the sound made by the wheels was, effectively, halved – one bogie performing the task of two on other lines. But the Great Western also had its idiosyncrasies, and I well remember a trip out to Reading when, with my head hung out of the window as we bowled along through Sonning Cutting on the up, I was aware of the sound made by extremely long Great Western bogies bolted to the ends of extremely long Great Western coaches. Instead of the rhythmic 'clickety-clack', we were hearing 'dum diddy dum', the sounds in proximity being made by the last axle

43

on one coach and the first on the next.

Wheel beats on London's tube lines were always a bit of a mystery. At the time of which I am writing, welded track was very much a thing of the future, and one would expect the familiar beat elsewhere to be impersonated by the tube stock. After all, the stock was borne on bogies passing over jointed track, just as on the main line. Whether it was the confined space in the tunnels, the length of the cars relative to track length, or that we experienced sound coming from the cars to front and back in partial duplication, I do not know, but five beats to the bar could be heard quite distinctly. There was also a certain rhythm to this with the 'five' being in a group of three, followed by a pair, as in 'du-du-du' pause 'du-du'. As the tunnels the trains ran through were only twelve feet in diameter, with much of that lost to the track and running gear, passengers were extremely close to both the rails and the tunnel walls, and it seems likely we were hearing a lot of noise from elsewhere on the train. But, recently, I travelled on new tube stock on the transformed London tube and, while the trains are new but essentially of the same basic design as those built in the nineteen-thirties in terms of their running gear, I could not hear that elusive fifth beat.

Before the advent of almost universal welded track on the main line, standard rails came in sixty-foot lengths. But the LNER, always a bit ahead of the game in my view, fitted up some parts of its racing stretches with ninety-foot track. My dad would point these out on our long hauls to and from Scotland, and we would listen to the long pauses between the wheel beats. The change of rhythm had the curious effect of making one rock one's head, as if listening to a piece of music. This would go on for perhaps a mile or two before there would be a riff and a clattering as the sound resumed its more normal tempo, and one's head would ignore the more normal rhythms.

♦

Watching trains in those days was a matter of delicious anticipation, and nothing heightened the excitement and sharpened the senses more than sitting within earshot of a signal box. I suppose this can be experienced today but, at best, it would resemble a branch line for its intermittent nature and infrequent animation. It is true there are still some mechanical boxes in the country but, I suspect, few people sit eagerly anticipating the arrival of a Type '66' diesel, although I appreciate everyone has their favourites. Also, the accompanying sounds of the swish of the semaphore wires through the sheaves, the satisfying clunk of the point-rodding, the melodic ring of the block bell or the tuneless whistling of the signalman in the box is probably, with a few exceptions, something of the past. Those fortunate enough to visit signal boxes enjoyed more intimate sounds, the crashing release of a single-line token, the soft click of the block instrument needle, and sometimes the sigh of the gas or oil lamp illuminating the desk upon which the block book, always open at the last page, would await detailed and usually neat entries as to locomotive number, train reporting number (taken from the notices or, in some cases, a number displayed on the front of the locomotive) and the all-important time of passing. There must have been thousands of those books, studiously completed every day with sucked pencil tied with string to prevent loss, and then sent off, often via the local station master, to 'Control' who would, we all assumed, cross-check and update.

Probably, however, after a decent interval, they were consigned to a hearth somewhere and quietly forgotten.

What a world of individual responsibility it was! A world where thousands of men and a growing army of women went about their tasks largely unsupervised but where the needs of the travelling public were almost embedded in their DNA. They knew what they had to do and, on the whole, it was done. They were the unsung heroes of the railways and, obviously, of us, their admirers. The railways were a leveller in our minds. We may have mostly been destined for white-collar jobs and enjoyed, if that is the word, superior educations to the army of railway servants, but they were 'it', the people who did a real job, the people who deserved our respect. We could only stop, stare, read, write down numbers, and dream. But they 'did', and were therefore, sorry to use the metaphor again, the actors up on the stage while we crunched our metaphorical (and often actual!) Maltesers in the stalls of our chosen theatre, watching, anonymous, indistinct and irrelevant in the darkness, while the play, which quickly became a tragedy, was performed before our eyes.

◆

For every memory, there are components that bleed from one sense to another. Seeing and hearing, for example, often go hand-in-hand.

When I was very small, my father would take me to London on the occasional Saturday – the excuse might be a birthday or the start of a school holiday. Often the desire for intellectual enrichment would be an essential part of the experience, so long treks around museums or visits to Greenwich, the Regent's Park Zoo, or the Tower of London would be preceded by the purchase of the appropriate I-Spy books and, even occasionally, an Observer's Book that impinged in some way on our topic of the day. These accoutrements would be checked before departure, as would the presence of pencils (sharpened), an India-rubber (cleaned and ready for non-smudgy use), and a small notebook.

There always seemed to be a piece of subterfuge going on. Yes, we would visit the zoo or whatever. Yes, the I-Spy book would be carefully annotated with espied penguins or cheetahs, the distinction between Indian and African elephants would be duly noted, or we would stand on the meridian at Greenwich, and look into Buckingham Palace to, as always, never see the King or, subsequently, the Queen. But there was always a sense of urgency about the worthy aspects of the day out.

Perhaps my father had to report back.

If the weather was good, and dad felt like a bit of exercise, we would walk from St. Pancras, along the Euston road and then dip down into Bloomsbury. This seemed to me to be the very best London had to offer. Straight streets, dignified terraces, intimate, iron-railinged squares and, in those days, an atmosphere of sophisticated, near-silent calm.

It reminded me of my 'second home', Edinburgh, and no city I ever visited in those days could match them.

My father clearly liked the area too, and he would adopt a rapidly-undertaken, zig-zag, disorientating route that would, eventually, lead us to the bottom of Southampton Row where a small convoy of trams coming in from the Angel gave the street scale and dignity. We would soon cross to the centre of the road and climb aboard what I now assume was an E/3 maximum-traction bogie car. They were always 'cars' in my memory, since few of the people we knew possessed the rubber-tyred version.

My only other proper experience of trams in those early days was that of the Edinburgh fleet – neat, traditional, interestingly-liveried, well-maintained four-wheelers that were, at that time, being added to by new vehicles. It was not a system in decline. So, catching sight of the London trams was a bit of a shock.

I knew they were being phased out and that the pre-war plan to replace them with trolleybuses had been abandoned due to the assumption that the rebuilding of London after extensive bomb damage would require a simpler, more flexible solution to the need for public transport. Even stringing trolleybus wires along roads where demolition and realignment were the order of the day could not be justified, while a motorbus could easily be diverted around obstacles and utilise new road layouts.

Knowing for over ten years that the trams were doomed

had taken its toll on maintenance of vehicles and track and, while miracles were performed on the permanent way, a shrinking requirement meant that the best cars could always be transferred into areas where they were still needed. To make things more difficult, and as was to take place with the London trolleybuses when they fell into disfavour ten years later, the best and most modern cars were sold off to other cities (notably Leeds), leaving Londoners to endure the most broken down, neglected wrecks until the end came in July 1952.

Our goal was a ride through the Kingsway Subway, of course, an acutely important feature since it was the only central physical link between the northern and southern halves of the vast London tram network. London's reluctance to allow railways and trams to cross the centre of the conurbation is a problem, notwithstanding the Elizabeth Line and Thameslink, that is still with us today. The ring of railway termini is still a hindrance to service development that many other cities in the world have endeavoured to overcome, while others, notably Paris, share London's challenges.

As the tram route 31, north of Westminster, was a rush-hour car only by the times of my visits, our car would have been a 33 or a 35. Up the stairs we would stumble and, if we were lucky, the curved bench above the driver's head would be unoccupied. Almost as soon as we had boarded, the car would set off with a grinding of the gears and, crossing High Holborn, it would immediately dip its nose onto the one-in-ten gradient down to the mouth of the tunnel. If we hadn't gained our desired seat before the car set off, we would be propelled ignominiously in a sort of free-fall that demonstrated both gravity and the, sadly, unshared benefits of having sea legs.

The first and abiding impression was of the noises the cars made. The bodywork, unlike those found in the Edinburgh fleet, was as loose as granny's old occasional folding table. There was a noticeable pause between the moment the driver, watched from the top of the stairs

48

when the trapdoor was left open, moved his controller, and the car surging forwards, the body reluctantly following the substantial bogies and under-gear with an audible groan and a great chattering of the window frames. These were added to by the driver constantly winding on the brake handle and, again, notching up.

Trams were not silent in those days. As the car plunged downwards towards the tunnel mouth, it accelerated very quickly, the whine of the gears rising and then being checked by braking and the rapid closing of the controller. Each change of velocity put a strain on the body that sighed, creaked and rattled in protest. Then the lights were switched on and we roared into the tunnel, the single headlight, still blackout-hooded years after the war ended, reflecting dully on the rails. The noises in the tunnel were deafening – the clatter of the wheels on the rails, the actions of the driver, and that cruelly under-maintained body reverberating off the vertical walls of the tunnel. In spite of the tight confines, the car swayed like a quickstep dancer, and we would look for the track bellying outwards for the first tram-tunnel station, Holborn. Due to the desire to have as few staircases as possible at the tunnel stations to reduce the footprint in the middle of Kingsway, the platforms were narrow islands placed between the tracks. This resulted in another challenge – the need to let passengers leave and join the car through the front entrance, normally reserved for the driver as it was, effectively, in the middle of the road – a dangerous place for passengers to be leaving in normal circumstances. On one occasion, we got off at one of the subterranean stations and then boarded another car simply for the experience.

On we went through the Aldwych stop and then ground around the corner into the sunlight to join the reserved track along the Victoria Embankment before crossing Westminster Bridge with its panorama of London, much of it bomb-damaged, and a vast amount of river traffic, mostly tugs and lighters skilfully negotiating the arches of the bridges at what seemed like considerable speed. Up there, on the bridge, the sounds the tram was making reduced as speed increased, with only the bodywork complaining as we swayed along.

On one occasion, we changed onto a 36 or 38 and rode out to Abbey Wood which included observation of overcoated members of staff uncoupling the plough pick-up in its little slot and resuming our journey using the more conventional trolley pole which added a new sound – that of the swishing trolley contact on the overhead wire. That was best heard from the other end of the top deck, but nothing was more memorable to me than the creaking of the body on a London tram in the Kingsway Subway.

♦

In the days when one could have closed one's eyes and identified a locomotive simply by its sound, we used to try to put together a form of locomotive phrase book using the alphabet to accurately describe and, with care, replicate the sound. The problem was, how do you put into phonetics the sound of a London & North Western 0-8-0 tender engine in a form that looks noticeably different from, say, a Great Central O4 2-8-0? It was pretty well impossible. So one had to rely on experience and an amount of contextual guesswork.

Some small engines made a sort of 'chaff, chaff, chaffing' sound, a softer beat than, say, a more powerful or more modern locomotive. Three-cylinder engines normally spoke more quietly at six beats to the bar. Four-cylinder engines mostly emulated their ubiquitous two-cylinder cousins in their four puffs to each revolution of their driving wheels, although the Southern's 'Lord Nelsons', perhaps to give the impression they were moving more quickly than they really were, puffed eight times for each revolution of their 6 feet - 7 inch drivers.

Most locomotives made the first 'puff' the strongest, which gave authors of children's books the opportunity to stress the courage of the steam locomotives in their stories.

In the 'Thomas the Tank Engine' books, the locomotives frequently talk in phrases of four syllables, imitating the most common locomotive 'voice'. 'I can make it, I can make it', says Edward on one occasion while struggling with a heavy train on a steep gradient, while, in a more serious set of circumstances, Percy complains, 'I want to stop, I want to stop' as he careers along, driverless and out of control. However, in the real world, some two cylinder engines had the emphasis on the second beat – 'puff, PUFF, puff, puff', and so on. This was particularly noticeable on London & North Western engines.

By the greatest of good fortune, one day in the early seventies, I was driving home to Guiseley, West Yorkshire, where I lived at the time, when I saw locomotive smoke rising over the retaining wall at Shipley. Wondering what it was, I scooted around to the station and parked the car. I couldn't believe the sight and sound of 'Flying Scotsman' and the Webb 'Precedent' 2-4-0 coupled together. They were being turned on the triangle before going back towards Leeds. The effect of this reversal put the ancient 36 ton (together with its 25 ton tender) 2-4-0 at the front, leading its 158 ton east-coast young rival. Whatever the thinking at Head Office was, I am not sure, but I assume the two crews had a bit of a plan that rather countered 'best practice'. When the two locos were signalled to leave, the 'Pacific' was doing no work at all and, together with its own tender, the little one-hundred year old LNWR 2-4-0, 'Hardwicke', had a trailing weight of very nearly 200 tons – the sort of train-weight it would have drawn in its heyday.

If I could have a recording of that sound again, I would pay good money for it. There, for all to hear, was the second-beat emphasis; there was the chaff, chaff of the ancients; there was everything aural that one could have requested and, for good measure, the smoke effects were pretty memorable too. As soon as it left the platform, it was nothing but a receding Gresley tender obliterating the view. But I stood there until the two locomotives disappeared, still accelerating and with the 'Precedent' roaring from the chimney.

I have heard bigger and stronger, but I have never heard better.

♦

Of course, where railways are concerned, locomotive sounds take the top spot. Double headers make interesting sounds and, on the line where I was brought up, the expresses were often double-headed. The contrast between chimney talk from a Midland 2P and an LMS Class 5 was extremely impressive. Both two-cylinder engines, they shared a 'four beats to the bar' rhythm, but one had six foot and the other six feet nine or even seven foot drivers, and this contrasting exhaust was extremely interesting to small boys perched on the fence in Carlton Road, Harpenden. Visually, too, it was amusing to see the elegant 4-4-0 high-stepping along at the front, its tender buffeted by the Class 5 behind, wheels racing around, almost like a child running with its parent.

♦

Paddy Wood always knew.

Paddy Wood, who worked for the railway but was, nevertheless, one of us, a hopeless train-spotter and model railway enthusiast, clearly used his inside knowledge to good advantage and never did anything other than share what he knew, to our lasting benefit.

He was our own Railway Oracle.

''Derbyshire Yeomanry' is coming up on Sunday', he would report, as he threw his huge and heavy bicycle against the wire fence. Carefully removing his trouser clips and pressing them over his crossbar with a satisfying double 'ping', he grinned before casting his gaze over the four familiar tracks. Down fast (what we called 'Line 1') fully pegged, meaning a clear run at least to Chiltern

Green; up fast ('Line 2') pegged; down slow ('Line 3'), nothing showing; up slow ('Line 4') pegged. That most distinctive smell of late summer – controlled-embankment-burning – in the nose, gentle, sweet and rancid, the work of a few days before; the cockerel in the garden on the opposite embankment demonstrating once again his profound ignorance of time; small late-afternoon birds making continually changing sheet-music on the telegraph wires; something unseen scuffling in the burnt grasses below us; a new 'RF' briefly rumbling past the end of Carlton Road as it took a momentarily level rest before tacking the second half of Station Road hill; Harpenden Central station looking deserted, save for a porter wandering aimlessly along the island platform wielding a long handled brush that never seemed to come into contact with the ground.

'Derbyshire Yeomanry' was *our* 'Patriot'. At that time a resident of 17A, Derby, she was still a rare visitor, spending most of her life on the Gloucester road, but there were, occasionally, specials that brought her to London. I suppose, with a name like that, it should have been a 'he' but most locomotives were called 'she', except where the name was obviously male.

Over at Welwyn Garden City, 'Oliver Bury' was always a 'he'.

Having checked up on where action on the four-tracks might be anticipated, Paddy would divulge more.

'About half-past four going back north,' he said. 'Maybe twenty-to-five. Depends on, you know, things...'

His voice would trail away. Paddy was quite shy and not a great conversationalist. Besides, a gaggle of small boys must have been of limited interest. As well as that, there were today's activities to observe and, while he was talking to us, the railway was behind him. He would turn back to the railway lines, fielding the odd question while pulling a large cotton handkerchief from his trouser pocket and blowing his nose noisily.

Perfect. Half-past four, you say? A reasonable time

after bible class, which convention determined couldn't be missed, although the thought of an unrebuilt 'Patriot' clashing with 'Crusaders' might have generated a serious conflict of interest. I'd be expected home by four-thirty, so here was a difficulty.

I always wanted to avoid domestic debate about my time-keeping, especially where trains were concerned. The problem was, they came much higher in my priority list than, say, tea, 'Children's Hour' and 'Sing Something Simple' on the BBC or, perhaps, bible class, but parents didn't always appreciate these matters.

I decided I'd risk it. I wouldn't tell.

Came Sunday, another beautiful late-summer day.

Choruses, prayers, notices, hymns, bible readings and then sloping off to our individual classes based upon age and, as we saw it, superiority. That over, we bade our farewells and, consulting my Timex wrist-watch (I had progressed from the much-hated and embarrassing Smith's pocket watch by that time), bicycles were retrieved from around the back of the Friends' Meeting House and a course set for the railway embankment.

Twenty-past four and a gaggle of train-spotters was already gathering.

After straight-facedly telling us she had already gone and relishing our disappointment, the lucky heathens amongst us, free of tiresome religious commitments, laughed and all looked in eager anticipation at the signals. Sure enough, a little too late for comfort, the down fast starter clanked into the 'off' position and, in the time it takes for signalmen to telegraph each other, the distant operated from the Junction box also rose. Clear run for the 'Patriot'. Soon we'd hear that Fowler roar and witness the plunging parallel boiler as it took full advantage of the downhill from the top of the Harpenden Common.

But …. Paddy's words of warning rang in our ears. 'About half-past four going back north. Maybe twenty-to-five. Depends on, you know, things...' Perhaps it had been delayed or the signal has been pulled off for something quite different? Instead of the eagerly-anticipated star, we might just get a dirty 2-6-4 tank and a three-coach set. Owing to our other Sunday obligations, to most of us the Sunday afternoon train timetable was unfamiliar.

Four-thirty came and went, but nothing else blocked the line. Hope springs eternal. Four-forty and still nothing. My mind was filling with an image of angry faces at home. It was about three minutes on the bike, nothing more. I'd go the long way around to avoid Station Road hill – just a little climb to start with and then nothing but bends to deal with on an otherwise level route. I started doing the maths. Say it came at four-forty-five, add three minutes, I'd still be in before ten-to. That allowed time for the usual whoops, shouts and smiling goodbyes before I cycled home.

Where was it?

At ten to five, I bottled it.

I suggested to everyone that it was probably not coming and, without Paddy's presence and greater authority – he was probably working that day – I did cause a small stir of agreement with my theory. The last thing I wanted was to have left and, two minutes later, the object of the exercise come roaring through without my presence. Too much pain and disappointment, for me. Too much glee and pleasure, for others.

But that is exactly what happened.

Off I went, reminding people of my theory of a 'no-show', and hoping I'd convinced them to go, too. Looking over my shoulder as I turned the corner, I realised they were ignoring me. I had reached sight of my home, well away from the railway, when I heard, unseen, the full-throated and deep roar of a Fowler 4-6-0 hammering across the steel girders of the bridge over Station Road.

To add insult to injury, I got a telling off for arriving home late without a satisfactory explanation!

♦

Thinking of wheel beats on rails, I was, in a sense, fortunate, to live a long way from most of my relatives. Distance meant that visits, usually annually but sometimes more frequent, resulted in long-distance train rides to Salisbury, Macclesfield and Edinburgh. In the days of which I am speaking, the visits to Edinburgh took eight hours and only gradually reduced to six and a half. Add to that, the run up to London – always in good time for the walk across to King's Cross – plus the taxi from the Waverley to either leafy, semi-detached and villa-blessed Davidson's Mains or stern, vertiginous Piershill, and we were in for a ten-hour trip. Minimum.

My father, always the experimenter and endlessly curious, varied the itinerary by occasional use of the Midland main line, with its Settle & Carlisle and the Waverley Routes, or the line from Euston by way of Carlisle and Carstairs, while variation on the East Coast main line could be achieved by using the 'Queen of Scots' via Leeds and Harrogate.

One Waverley Route adventure stretched out to well over twelve hours. I remember the A3 backing onto our train in Citadel after five o'clock in the afternoon, by which time the sandwiches for the train had long-since been consumed and it was too late to buy anything from buffet or restaurant. Of course, Salisbury via Waterloo, or Macclesfield via Euston and Stoke-on-Trent, were shorter, but I must not forget home to Bregenz in Austria (via Calais, Lille, Basle and Zurich), about twenty-four hours, or from home to Linz-am-Rhein in Germany (via Folkestone, Ostend, Brussels, Aachen and Koln) which must have taken about fifteen.

All these long journeys had one thing in common. Wheel-beats. Normally, every sixty feet in the UK, one rail was connected to the next by means of fishplates – one pair on each rail. As the fishplates filled the narrow piece of bull-headed rail at the waist, the plate prevented one rail from rising above its companion and, of course, kept the rails connected to each other. But as there is a need to allow for expansion in summer and contraction in winter, in normal conditions a narrow gap between the rails was provided. Flat-bottomed track, now the normal profile for rails, worked in a similar fashion, using plates to join and maintain associated rail height. So, the gap was necessary, and it was the sound of the wheel imperceptibly dropping in and out of the gap that conveyed the sound to our ears.

When I started to travel by rail, there was virtually no welded track – I think the first stretch was on the LNER somewhere on the east coast main line. So, the 'di-di-di-dah' was an integral part of the business of travelling by train. Musicologists will tell you it is a wonderful rhythm – completely satisfactory to the human ear and providing a percussional theme that dates from long before the advent of popular music. Take Ravel's 'Bolero', for example – that is just one instance that conveys an urgency, a dynamism, and a sense of positive optimism that is so appealing. Of course, composers play with this basic four-beat structure to their own ends, introducing syncopation, changing stresses, and employing other musical devices, but so, quite by accident, did railway engineers. Track-laying mile after mile of sixty foot lengths would eventually come to crossovers and points, and they did not necessarily occur exactly at sixty-foot intervals. The occurrence of a long curve also tended to throw things out – the inner rail, as it were, getting to a destination before the outer rail. Anyway, on British railways, it was normal to place rail joints on both rails opposite each other, unlike the United States of America where they were, and are, staggered, giving an almost continuous clatter, together with a slight left-and-right rocking motion. So the continually repeated four beats to the bar heard when travelling in bogie coaches would suddenly stumble, pause and stumble again, quite deliciously when encountering a complicated junction. When two double-tracks connected, a fine old din would ensue when your train crossed one line before merging with the next. This would eventually be followed by a return to the 'di-di-di-dah' of before. I say sixty-feet was the normal length, but there were still stretches of forty-five feet when I was a boy.

On those long journeys I referred to earlier, this sound was so much a part of the pleasure of travelling that I find it sad, if inevitable, that it has now become comparatively rare. And even though the track was well-maintained, the mere fact of the gap in the rails and its Meccano-like connection to its companion, meant that the passage of the train and its rapid movement from one rail to the next caused an up-and-down motion that gradually crushed the ballast near the joint. This was the weak spot in all jointed track. Sleepered and chaired rail, followed by a fishplate unsupported from below, followed by another rail also chaired and sleepered – well, you can imagine the stresses this caused. Professional lengthmen or platelayers spent their lives looking after a few miles of track and it was those track joints that occupied most of their time. We could often spy them from the train with their giant spanners for tightening the chair and fishplate bolts, and long-tined forks for scraping and repacking the ballast. All to keep the track in good order and, incidentally, to deliver that distinctive sound to our ears.

♦

I was pondering over something the other day.

I think I have always lived in earshot of a railway.

In some cases it might be a bit of an 'ask' for you to believe me, but you must bear in mind that railway enthusiasts are blessed with acute if selective hearing. From the background of noise and conversation, the railway enthusiast can sense a train like a thrush can hear a worm. It can be as slight as a distant whistle, unconfirmed by convenient repetition. It can be just a rush of air in the stillness of the night. Sometimes, the presence of a tunnel or bridge can alter the background noise so that it is merely the 'change' we are aware of – not the 'before' and 'after' but, momentarily, the 'in between' of it all.

Sometimes what we hear is the clatter of wheel on rail, but that has been continuously-welded out of the experience of many of us, and we may only hear wheels negotiating points and crossovers. Nowadays, it is more difficult, as the distinctive sound of a steam train is rarely heard and a diesel train resembles a truck or a bus. I have noticed recently, however, that, from a distance of about half-a-mile, I can hear the whine of the electric motor beneath a diesel-electric multiple unit here in North Wales, while the purr of the diesel engines is lost on the wind.

Whilst living near a railway would mean that the sound is constant, daytime noise is now so omnipresent that relative distance may make the railway appear silent. At night, with the bedroom window open and struggling with insomnia, the train makes its presence felt. So many of my 'from the home' memories, therefore, took place at night. Living in France for eleven years, we were just within earshot of one of those long, French single-lines that meandered across the country for miles and miles. Some nights I would lie awake and hear a long goods train, diesel hauled, as it clattered around the hills near Rocamadour. Then, suddenly, it all stopped, and the goods train went another way – much to my disappointment – or maybe it just ceased altogether.

The shrinking railway is not just a British phenomenon.

♦

In Harpenden, living midway between Central and East, the roaring expresses, the cavalcade of coal trains, empty and full, the cacophony of yard-shunting, and the 'local trains' as we called them (never suburban, at least in my memory) on the main line, and the occasional presence of branch line passenger trains and a long, slow goods at the East station, were my earliest and probably most charged memories.

By the time I left the family home in 1965, the best was over. The Welwyn Garden City branch, with its preponderance of 0-6-2 tanks and all the trappings of a delightful branch line, had transmogrified into multiple units and Type 1 diesel locomotives that failed to prevent closure, so it went altogether. The track had subsequently been lifted and windows in the station buildings and signal-box had been broken by the youth of Batford and, no doubt, Harpenden proper, the quaint little footpath that led from that same Station Road, switchbacking along the top of the embankment at the back of the station, was weedy and desolate, the heavy-quality gate lifted from its hinges, and the blue station signs removed from their frames.

The main line through Harpenden Central was still there, of course. It still is. But I had been born into a world of roaring 'Compounds' and 'Garratts', 3Fs and even 2Fs, 2P 4-4-0s, spoffling Fowler 2-6-2ts, and the many defiantly noisy products of Messrs. Stanier, Ivatt and Fairburn. These had gradually removed the interesting engines of before and were themselves partially replaced by 'Standard' types that went, it seemed overnight, in the face of 'Peaks', boxy Bo-Bos and diesel multiple units that, even when new, seemed oddly out of date.

Our most prestigious steam local trains, notably the 8:10 am from Harpenden and the train at about 6:18 pm from London (the times changed slightly over the years), contained nine coaches, three containing one-third brakes, 864 seats, and plenty of room for standees. These were replaced by eight coach diesels with four cabs, four brakes, and accommodation for about half the number of seated passengers. The diesels were slightly faster ... but not much ... and they were dreadfully noisy and poisonously smoky in the tunnels.

The 8:10 am from Harpenden, headed by an elegant Bedford 'Compound', ran non-stop to London St. Pancras, taking 29 minutes, hardly bettered today. Going home, it took a little longer. On another up train, with two stops (Radlett and St. Albans), the journey to London took forty-four minutes, but this was in April 1947 when my father started to work at the Home Office. It was in acceleration from station stops that steam suffered, which is why the non-stops could almost equal the performance of the diesels.

♦

The two old men stood talking over the garden gate. The much younger wife of one of them stood by, taking in the moment, eyes blinking in the warm later-summer sun. Occasionally, small cars and vans broke the silence, save for the conversation – the postman in his little red van, saluting the man behind the gate, no letter for him today, a tourist, clearly lost, condemned by the single carriageway to drive onward and upward to above the tree-line before any change of plan could be exercised.

A September sun shone down on the winding lane above Lake Padarn near Llanberis until, a distance away, the unmistakeable roar of one of the mountain railway engines floated across the lake as it began its hour-long struggle to the top of Snowdon. Over the viaduct it must be going, ploughing a smoky furrow through the wooded valley at the bottom, its precious cargo of tourists hanging out of the windows, savouring a unique experience in the British Isles.

'They were good days,' the man behind the gate muttered in his second language, for the benefit of the two walkers. English spoken with a Welsh accent so pure, so precise, so deliberate. So poetic. 'Over forty years I was in the quarries. Here, and later at Penrhyn. After this one closed, there was no proper alternative. Not if you wanted to work.'

Small talk ensued. The cottage was beautifully kept, long and low, one converted from two, a pretty, well-kept garden flowing down to the garden wall, grass newly cut. We complimented him. Not flattery. It was genuinely very fine. From his boundary wall, a convenient gap in the trees opened up a vista of the hillside beyond the lake. High on

61

the hill, the familiar signs of quarry workings bruised and blistered the otherwise unspoilt green sward.

'All the same slate vein,' he said, anticipating my question. 'Here at Dinorwig, Penrhyn at the back over the hill, that one on the hillside opposite - Glynrhonwy, Nantlle. Down to the Lleyn, it turned to granite at Trevor. All the same vein. Sometimes wide and sometimes not so wide, sometimes deep. Fortunes made and lost. But it was very hard work, you know.'

We agreed. It must have been. On a balmy late-summer day, the gentlest of breezes parting the leaves, the sounds of that noisiest of British narrow-gauge engines beginning to fade, it was hard to appreciate the industrial past.

But it must have been hard.

'They were good people, you know,' he insisted. 'With no money to educate their children – send them to college, like – they just stayed and walked in their father's footsteps. Followed them into the quarry. But they weren't stupid, you know.'

Why should they be? What a thing, even to contemplate! Those grey, unkempt men in their working clothes grinning or frowning at the camera in a thousand museum illustrations, posing self-consciously, it made you wonder again, in spite of volunteering unquestioning agreement. It made you think about what kind of men they were. Made you rethink what it meant to be a working man in those days of education-exclusion on the basis of income and 'place in life'. It was not just a matter of us and them: simply what was possible and what was not.

The rack engine suddenly bellowed again. Was it turning a corner or a simply a change of wind direction?

'The quarry was a place for intelligent men,' the man behind the gate confirmed. 'It took skill and it was dangerous. You had to have your wits about you. Have you seen the hospital?'

We said we had. And the morgue, with its two slabs. And the sinister drain-holes in the floor.

'Not a place for fools. Not many people think about

those things.'

A faint whiff of coal-smoke drifted up towards us from the lakeside train, silent in its easy passage along the foreshore. Driver Owen would be meticulously uncoupling the little 'Hunslet' and running around the train, while the guard checked tickets and joshed with the passengers. Second-generation immigrants from the Indian sub-continent are drawn to Lake Padarn and they always appreciate help with group photographs, smiling shyly and modestly at the camera, not unlike the quarrymen of two generations and more before. At the main station, Hefin would put his railwayman's cap on a child's head and they would stand in the cab. The doting parents would demand smiles and click away happily. Another image for posterity; sent to relatives thousands of miles away in an instant.

The old man behind the gate sensed the attention paid to the little steam locomotive. 'Of course, there were lots of little engines in the quarry. Some of them spent a lifetime up there on the galleries. Some of those are down at the lakeside now.'

A small pop on the whistle heralded the departure of the little, unseen train.

'You can't imagine what it was like,' the old man said. 'Three thousand men working at the Dinorwig slate quarry. Three thousand! I walked there every day from here for work.'

That made us think.

We had walked up from the car park, up flights of steps to the hospital, on along the few yards past the last of the buildings and then struggled up and down over treacherous rocks, tree roots, streams, the little lane where some hippies now live, under the bridge that took waste from the small Faenol quarry on the hillside, disused since 1912, and then up and up to the road down which we had just walked. What was it? Two miles? Two miles of hard walking on a sunny afternoon? Think of it in winter! Think of it as the daily morning and evening commute, in the dark, in the rain – or snow. Quarrymen, be they splitters, dressers, explosives men, engine drivers, shunters and waste tippers, hookers-on and -off at the inclines, where life could be dreadfully cheap and the hospital with its morgue beckoned.

A mental image of the Snowdon Mountain engine still biting its way up the rack came to mind. It had been doing that for over a hundred years, throughout the days of plenty at the quarry, days of plenty in the sense of predictable work for the men, but pitifully low pay.

But the camaraderie!

'They were good men. Mostly gone now. But the discussions and debates we had! The politics and religion, the singing, the 'being together' in the *cabans*, the courage, humour and heroics. You could rely on people, then. If you were injured, they'd get you home, however late. Now?' The man spread his arms, looked around and changed the subject. 'It gets lonely, you know. And the nights are so very long.'

'We'll look out for you when we walk again,' we said.

'I'm getting some logs cut for the winter,' he replied, oblivious to our concern. 'As soon as it is dark, the temperature up here drops. Need some logs. Cut them every year at his time.'

We set off down the hill in silence. A blackbird sang high in a tree, followed by squabbling sparrows dancing in the branches below. A chain saw buzzed unnoticed somewhere below us.

'It's about seeing it all in context, isn't it?' my wife uttered. 'I mean, all this work, all this labour. Your trains in the landscape – a part of something long gone.' She pointed at the scarred mountain opposite. 'Heroes. Forgotten men working thousands of tons of rock – ten tons of waste to one ton of usable slate, isn't that what you said? Paid piece work, not for mere attendance but for what they did. A hundred and twenty slates prepared to be paid for one hundred, to allow for breakages in the trains and ships. Where is the justice in that?'

I clutched my stick and nodded in agreement. 'But, think of our friend,' I said. 'What a noble man, proud of his memories, proud of what he did, proud of his life.'

At that moment, a fast-moving car caused us to scuttle to the relative safety of the side of the road. A bright red Audi with a well-heeled couple inside shot by, the driver adjusting his sat-nav while his wife flicked the screen of her iPhone, blind to the breathtaking scenery around them, and presumably ignorant of the man-made scars in the hills.

'Posh car,' my wife said.

'Certainly was,' I agreed. 'Wealthy people, I assume. But not as rich as our friend, back there. Not *really* rich.'

They could probably have bought and sold all of us before breakfast and not even noticed it.

But were they really well off?

♦

It must have been about eight in the evening. My usual time for getting back to St. Albans in the late eighties – eight o'clock or later. It was dark, too, as I traipsed between the last of the parked vehicles in the sprawling car park that was once St. Albans City railway goods yard. As I was an early morning arrival, my car was in the privileged serried rank facing the boundary fence. It had spent the day facing the up-slow, with its continuous file of electric multiple units and occasional freights.

It was one of those occasional freights that met my eyes … and ears. The train was slowing and there was a roaring sound from the brake pipes behind the locomotive. Clearly something was amiss as another sound assaulted my ears – a heavy, rhythmic banging. I realised what had happened and ran along the car park waving hysterically at the driver who had brought his train down to walking pace.

He opened his window.

'It's off the road!' I yelled, over the hiss of the brakes.

'What?' he replied as the train stopped. I know nothing

about air brakes but I assumed that the severed pipe had applied the brakes and that was what had alerted the driver.

'First wagon!' I gasped, running through the car park and demonstrating my overall lack of good health. 'The bogie's off, first axle, and it's hitting the chairs.' They probably weren't chairs at all on the flat-bottomed and welded track, but it wasn't a moment for precision.

The driver looked shocked. I suppose he was visualising what might have happened if the train had reached the station. The first bogie wagon – I seem to remember it was a container train – would have been just enough out of alignment to foul the platform which might have resulted in a serious derailment. It was lucky his brakes had failed so comprehensively just before the station. My contribution was nothing more than that of messenger.

The driver hopped down with a large torch and we both walked back to the offending wagon – him on the scrunching, dark ballast and me in the muddy car park. Sure enough, the first axle was hanging down with the wheel firmly outside the rail. It had banged up and down on every track fastening for no-one knew how long.

I left the professionals to their task and drove home, anticipating chaos the next day. I knew the up-slow would be closed for a minute inspection of the track and, with everything running on the two fast lines, the timetable would be shot to pieces.

And it was.

But, better that than what might have happened.

♦

Early nineteen-fifties, it'd been a long haul from King's Cross. The weather was hot and distinctly clammy and there was no opening window, save the little sliding ventilator that was not living up to either its name or purpose. Mercifully, as the afternoon wore on, the sun moved over towards the west, but it was still high in the sky and the morning had been torture.

There had been an incident with an overtoppled thermos-flask which was not entirely my fault but it was well known I could be very clumsy. It's as though issue-closure could be speedier if blame could be attributed, so I took it without argument – two (adults) to one child with one abstention (my brother who, on this occasion, was blameless) was hardly going to be a fair fight. The thermos' descent to the lino floor had been complicated and speedy, with two unfortunate consequences – no-one had any tea to drink for the rest of the journey from that moment onwards, and the ominous broken-glass rattle from within assured us all that no-one ever would again.

Most people would seek a remedy to such an eventuality – such as a quick walk along to the cafeteria car for replacement liquid refreshment – but my parents thought life-lessons could and should be learned from such incidents. So, we had dehydrated steadily for over one-hundred miles, a situation not helped by the necessary beverage-free consumption of cheese sandwiches in thick slices of white bread, with but a thin scraping of butter.

My mother sighed a lot.

The train was full and, as the compartment seated six people and the family occupied only four seats, two strangers had had to endure a shallow puddle of tidal tea sloshing left and right across the floor all the way from York where the incident took place. Despite frequent adult apologies, and some ineffective mopping with a tiny paper napkin, the couple, who were elderly and who had already made their presence felt by instructing my parents to keep us boys under control as 'father' (she called him 'father', but he was certainly not mine) 'had a war-wound that was still playing up'. To me, he looked too old to have suffered his misfortune in the Second World War, so I was impressed by the idea of an affliction lasting over thirty years. But, of course, another life lesson, they can.

Anyway, there was a lot of tutting from two mothers

and hard stares from the fathers and I felt pretty miserable, I can tell you. My brother kept a dignified silence and distanced himself from his errant elder sibling.

Fathers should really try to avoid telling their sons to, 'look this way' and 'look over there', and ask 'where's your pencil?' or 'did you get that station-pilot number written down?', while mothers simultaneously ask their offspring to 'pass the flask' and 'don't drop crumbs', or demand that their sons deliberately ignore their husband's, let's face it, far more interesting interjections while domestic activities concerned with consuming lunch are completed. It can all become too much.

And there can, as I have explained, be consequences.

We were sitting in Newcastle station while station duties were undertaken, and our engine was exchanged for another, when I was distracted by a rhythmic tapping sound emanating from down on the track.

'What's that?' I asked.

'Chap checking the wheels,' came the reply from dad, distracted from "Operation Come-down-on-Roderick". 'Want to see?'

Anything, I thought.

So, into the corridor we went and walked along to the transverse passage that gave access to the exterior doors on either side. Putting the window down, and gulping clean, fresh, Newcastle air, we were distracted by the laboured passage of a Q6 with its train of coal empties working westwards from the coal staithes on the coast. But, putting my head out after the goods engine had cleared the station and noise had abated to the slow and deliberate clicking of the wagon wheels over the rail-joints, there, again, was the sound of the wheel-tapper, who could now be seen with his long-handled, light hammer and brown-tanned bald head. He didn't so much grip the hammer but held it in such a way that a pendulum-action could be achieved. My memory says, three rings from each wheel, all accomplished from one place on the rim.

I was told to listen. It was a distinctive, sustained 'ting', a bit like our grandfather clock at home. Every wheel was tested carefully – an unhurried and vital occupation, but undertaken on one side of the train only.

Maybe the other side had been dealt with, unbeknown to me, at an earlier stop. I wondered about that for a long time, but didn't ask.

Testing done, whistles were blown from the platform and our 'Pacific' whistled in reply for the road. A square-looking green electric unit slid across our path from the high-level bridge and into one of the bays on the north side of the station. Another pop on the whistle from the engine as it got a green light and we were off on the last long – and dry – leg of our journey. One hundred and twenty-four and a half more miles without a drink.

I didn't step on the toes of our travelling companions on our return to our seats but was unable to keep up my good record as a consequence of a cunning scheme I prepared for myself a few miles later on. A solitary visit to the lavatory – one of the privileges of being about eight years old – was, in this case, more about consumption than drainage. A cupped hand under one of those LNER push-down taps can bring liquid-deprivation to an end, if you are prepared to ignore the exhortations never to drink train tap-water.

On my return, my parents were still fully preoccupied with apologising to 'father' for my stumbling over both of his once pristinely-polished shoes to notice the water dribbling down my chin and onto my shirt.

I think my brother noticed, but he didn't let on.

♦

Railwaymen in the years leading up to the end of steam were heroes. They were as close as they could be to being film stars, at least to the railway fraternity. But, not only to them. Newsreels at the cinema would sometimes include some exciting railway exploit, and craggy-faced railwaymen would be persuaded to say a few words to the camera at the conclusion of some high-speed run on the 'Cornish Riviera', or showed off their 'Coronation' to the press at Euston Station. Even the advent of the LMS diesels warranted an interview with the driver and the in-name-only 'fireman' for the cinema audience, but they looked shamefaced as though they were off to a funeral – smart and clean after hundreds of miles and, in our minds, less deserving of complements and admiration.

So, in the lengthy period between the supporting feature and the main film, we would be delighted when a railway item slipped easily in between the flashlight-popping newsreels of Princess Margaret, the Aga Khan or Betty Grable, who all seemed to live glamourous lives that were endlessly diverting and full of ceaseless pleasure, or Winston Churchill displaying his fun-filled 'V for Victory' sign which he used up until his departure from public life.

In the railway press, not a month would go by without a driver being photographed and his career described – usually upon his retirement. We were enthralled by these men who had joined the Great Western, the London, Brighton & South Coast, or the Great Northern, when the twentieth century was still in its infancy, and who now leaned, smiling, from their 'Castle', 'King Arthur' or 'A4', oily rag in hand, looking utterly at home in their place of work and who, inexplicably, were looking forward to a life of pigeon-fancying or tending the allotment.

How could they.

It's not like that now, of course. The job is highly pressured, extremely stressful and frequently lonely, it doesn't have the romance, and it rarely warrants a mention on the media, except when something goes wrong. The days of interviewing the engine-driver went out with the end of steam.

♦

Bill Hoole was one of those heroes. He was a Merseysider by birth, who never lost his accent. After the Great War, throughout which he served his country in uniform, he entered railway service on the Great Central Railway at Neasden shed in London. Marrying his landlord's daughter, just as my grandfather had in Edinburgh a couple of decades before, he rose through the ranks and, in LNER days, became a qualified driver in 1926. Redundancy quickly followed, but he applied for a post at King's Cross shed and worked there from 1927 until he retired in 1959.

He duly appeared on those hallowed 'retirement' pages in the "Railway Magazine". Rightly so, because his distinguished career had included the fastest post-war trip with steam – again an A4 – and, I thought, that would be it. Never forgotten but, presumably, out tending his allotment or breeding winners in some clichéd pigeon-loft.

But no.

He moved to the Ffestiniog Railway – single 'eff-ed' in those days – and I managed to photograph him on a Double-Fairlie at Tan-y-Bwlch in 1961 *(see illustration, Chapter Eight, 'Conclusion')*. He had a reputation, I heard, for driving them as quickly as possible, just as he had on the A4s from King's Cross shed.

Later, when I was a volunteer on the Ffestiniog, we were assigned to Boston Lodge and pottered up to Minffordd with a few wagons behind 'Prince'. The driver was Bill Hoole. After shovelling something or other in Minffordd yard – many volunteers have spent long days shovelling something or other in Minffordd yard – the chap who had accompanied him on the footplate to that point sloped off on an errand and Bill asked me to act as look-out on the return trip. It was all about making sure we still had the whole of the train behind us, but I was to be his quasi-fireman for the rest of the day.

I gladly agreed and, in the meantime, we talked.

Or, rather, he talked.

I listened. Fascinated.

Some people seem to reach retirement age without having anything to impart. Bill Hoole was not one of those. He was wise, clever, and a great conversationalist, with a wealth of stories.

He told me of his earliest days on the footplate, and how, one night, he was firing one of the former Great Central 'Atlantics' on the up line. It was a dark, wet night and, even in one of Mr. Robinson's capacious cabs, the two men were freezing cold. Somewhere near Aylesbury, they hit something. They heard and felt the slight bump, above all the noise and the driving rain, but they carried on, assuming no harm had been done to the engine. The schedule, after all, had to be maintained.

On arrival in Marylebone, they walked around the engine and noticed the lower side of one front buffer was bent backwards through ninety degrees. As enthusiasts and engineers know, buffers need to be immensely strong and are, consequently, made of a thick piece of steel.

And this one was bent into a right-angle.

On returning to Neasden shed, the incident was reported, as these things always were. Footplate men gain a precise knowledge of every yard of the route and, even allowing for the conditions, the location – near a foot crossing – was clearly identified. Bill said they wondered if they had hit an animal, but dismissed that theory on the basis that it must have been something a great deal heavier. How could such damage be inflicted by an animal?

The following day, when Bill and his mate returned to the sheds at Neasden, repairs had been effected and they thought no more about it.

Things happen.

On with the job.

In broad daylight, they backed down to Marylebone to pick up the return working, the 'Jersey Lily' nicely polished, well coaled and watered – a credit to the Neasden staff. In bright sunshine, they were going to enjoy a straightforward run down to Leicester – so different from the stormy hell of the night before. Coupled up and ready to go, Bill took a look back along the platform to wait for the guard's signal but saw, instead, an inspector approaching in a hurry.

'I'll be coming with you,' the inspector reported. 'I've a bit of news. It's about that damage you reported last night.'

Bill and his driver readied the engine, anticipating a criticism on some count or another.

'What was it, a blown tree or something?' enquired the driver.

'No,' came the reply. 'It was an eight year old girl.'

The driver and fireman were incredulous.

'A child?'

'Well, there were two of them. The girl and her mother. Both dead. That's why I am here. Not easy to keep working when something like that happens. Not that it was in any way your fault.'

Bill and his driver were in shock and glad of the company.

'I don't get it,' the driver said. 'The buffer was bent backwards!'

'The mother was proper smashed up – run over by the wheels, they think. It wasn't her. And the girl was perfect. Just looked as though she was sleeping.'

'How do you know it was the girl?' the driver asked weakly.

'I said the little girl was perfect,' replied the inspector. 'And she was, you know, except for one thing. The imprint of part of the buffer – just the right shape – was on the side of her head.'

Engineers know about drop-forging, where metal can be formed into complex shapes by being forced quickly into materials that are, in themselves, insubstantial – such as dropping it into sand moulds or even plastics. The metal takes the new shape even though the mould is destroyed. But this was an odd one. Apart from a mark, the 'mould' was unaffected, but the steel took up a completely new shape.

They drove north in silence, going over the sad

73

curiosity of it all.

And all those years later, in front of me, Bill shed a tear.

'I can still hear it,' he said. 'Oh, I suppose I can't really, not in a normal sense. But I *think* I can. I can remember that cold night with the driving rain and recall it all as if it were yesterday.'

With his reputation for speed, Bill threw 'Prince' back down to Boston Lodge with him facing the road ahead, hand behind him on the regulator, and me counting the slate wagons in a vain attempt to do what I was asked.

He was a lovely man. Full of generosity and humanity. He remembered the North British 'Atlantic' at Marylebone sporting a new LNER livery for inspection by the LNER directorate in the days following the Grouping. 'They were very fine,' he said, to my revelation of my grandfather's parallel existence, so far away – a common experience 'by proxy', a railwayman talking to the grandson of a railwayman and finding common ground.

There we were, two generations apart, experiences unshared, different histories, contrasting accents, almost foreigners to each other, and yet conjoined at the hip by a crazy affection for steam and what it meant to us. To him, it represented a lifetime of absorbing toil. To me, my initial two decades had been a strange, self-inflicted, living tragedy – the suppression of steam and the regretted passing of Bill Hoole's own world. And there was the link – one man's life, and another's arm's-length sanitised devotion, fetching up on that confined, historic footplate.

'Prince' propelled the works train into a siding and the other volunteers dropped out of the slate wagons and looked at me enviously. 'Lucky bugger,' someone said, and, yes, I suppose I was lucky. But my head was bursting with words and thoughts, with images and anecdotes, with so much more than mere childish one-upmanship. So much to try to remember, so much to share modestly, so much to change my point of view. So much to 'be', from that moment on.

Bill Hoole handed the engine over to someone for disposal and, with a brief wave, he set off home.

I felt a sadness. I can't explain it, fully. But I did. It was all over – for that little girl and her mother, for the men, for the trains and…. in the fullness of time, for me.

How transient it all is – life.

It is desperately short and even in those short years, everything changes. Just the senses remain and one of the most reliable is that of hearing.

CHAPTER FOUR

SIGHT

The probable subject of my Thornton Junction memory. Here,
the locomotive is stored at Dunfermline. Later restored to
service and withdrawn in 1954. Photograph, Alan Warren.

A picture is worth a thousand words, as the English idiom
has it, but what does visual memory hold? It can, of
course, be a means in itself; perhaps the strongest sense of
all. Furthermore, it can act as the skeleton key to the doors
of all the other senses. Even a photograph in a magazine,
hardly the stuff of memory, of a large steam express
locomotive on shed, can conjure up the acrid smell of coal
dust or hot oil and grease warmed by mechanical
movement, the taste of smoke in one's throat, the
unyielding, cold feel of the vertical hand-rail that provided
an aid to enter the hallowed portals of the locomotive cab,
and the sound of drain cocks opened to clear the cylinders
of malevolent, uncompressible water.

Also, when speaking of the sight of a locomotive or
railway installation, every year that has passed since those

bleak days of 1968 when workaday steam was banished from the main line has, paradoxically, brought us new things to see – restorations and even new-builds to 'fill in the gaps' caused by over-enthusiastic scrapping; reopenings and extensions of preserved railway lines; rebuilding of station buildings and other railway paraphernalia; recreated signalling systems; coaching stock that we can ride in today that has spent half a century or more providing sanctuary for a flock of chickens or an old couple living in Chatham; and the charming sight of window boxes and hanging baskets, strewn suitcases and milk churns, enamel advertising panels and staff dressed self-consciously in flamboyant versions of the more shabby uniforms of yesteryear.

We are still recreating the past, but also elaborating upon it and, in so doing, distorting what was familiar. What we see now is not what we saw then. One-time branch lines, hosting little more than two-coaches pulled by a small tank engine, are now served by six- and eight-coached trains pulled by pensioned-off express or heavy goods engines, often working tender-first, a visual rarity in the past. But what can you do when two or three hundred people descend upon your village station wanting a ride? It must also be appreciated that preservationists are very much in the leisure business and they must respect the fact that most of their custom comes from people who neither know nor care about authenticity. Nor should they. We just all hope they will continue to turn up, spend their money, and enjoy themselves. So, each year that passes adds to the wealth and variety of what we may enjoy but, at the same time, takes us one step further away from 'what was'. And visual memory can be fragile and mendacious – easily confounded by the strong images of today, even where memory is betrayed by recent misrepresentation.

What was it like, really like, to be able to see the *real* railway?

My father was born in 1907 and, through the good offices of his *own* father, he was familiar with the steam railway at its peak. He saw the North British Atlantics and their North Eastern counterparts. He rode the footplate clandestinely on the long haul from Edinburgh to Carlisle, and saw blunt North Western engines and a run-down Maryport & Carlisle 2-4-0 in appalling condition, but also admired Midland 4-4-0s backing down onto the passenger trains from Edinburgh to St. Pancras. He observed the blue 0-4-4 tanks of the Caledonian treading over Haymarket shed on their way to Leith and Barnton, and smiled at the sight of unimaginable numbers of small, well-kept shunters ('Pugs', they called them in Scotland) at just about every industrial site beside the line. And even *he* said he didn't see the railways at their best – when it was the train or nothing for passengers and goods alike; when single-drivers dominated the expresses; when cities like Edinburgh, before the onset of the tramcar, were threaded by suburban passenger lines that dived under, through and past the city streets, and where small tank engines in magnificent condition pulling close-coupled four wheelers provided the only practical form of urban transport, other than the horse bus.

He used to tell me *he* had witnessed the decline of the railway, so what have I seen? I, too, witnessed a contraction – where everything could have been lost; where there were serious plans to sweep the railways away; where buses were to use the route into Marylebone, London, in place of trains – but I have now seen a resurrection where one can witness 'customers' (horrid term) flocking back in ever-increasing numbers in spite of the general unpleasantness of present-day British rail travel.

Even at my age, and you have to be my age to remember very much at all of what I write, we saw the absolute nadir of the railways – closures, wrong decisions, political interference, incompetence, the tragedy that was the virtual death of a way of being.

And yet the things we saw were wonderful.

♦

One of my earliest memories was on Thornton Junction Station in Fife. We had been to Largo on what had been a beautiful early-summer's day. In those days, the coastal line was fully open and trains threaded around the beaches on their run to and from Dundee via St. Andrew's. As it was summer, and my aunt, who was still working at the time, was with us, it was probably a Sunday. We had come over from Edinburgh and changed at Thornton, much more of a Junction than a destination, been to the beach, eaten our sandwiches, probably dribbled ice-cream wafer down our clothes, and here we were going home. The day had been filled with the innocent joys of the new fifties decade. Women in still-fresh, full, petticoated skirts carrying large woven bags, as smart as they could be. Men, all with jackets and mostly wearing shirts with ties and a hat, having a break from their labours. And children, miniature versions of their parents, but with short socks and polished sandals, milling around waiting for the connection that would be a through semi-fast from Dundee or beyond.

I remember it as though it was yesterday; can feel the balmy early evening, see the blue sky, recall the broken stone and pebbly shambles of the platform beneath my feet, blink at the sun slowly sinking into the west, and hear the birds rejoicing as the heat retreated. A slight breeze picked up the corners of the women's dresses, not enough to embarrass but just sufficient to awaken a certain concerned caution. The children were eyeing each other up and down, wondering whether to make a move in terms of a smile or an intervention in an adjacent and hitherto unknown brother and sister's childish games. Newspapers, carefully folded earlier in the day, were now retrieved from men's jackets for a surreptitious glance at the racing form. Railway staff were loitering, striving to look purposeful, and yet lacking any measurable achievement.

My father and I left my mother, brother (in his pushchair) and aunt as they stood looking at their watches and staring eastwards whence the train would appear. I followed him as he walked along the platform and was soon aware of the object of his curiosity. Nothing more than a dirty and woebegone tank engine, somehow elegant in an Edwardian fashion, with its short smokebox set well back on the frames, bunker filled with coal, the driver walking around his engine checking bearings and topping up the oil in a dozen reservoirs, his fireman sweeping the floor of the footplate – the coal dust, a slow cloud dropping to the steps and cascading onto the trodden-down clinker and ballast. The familiar sight of a steam engine waiting in a siding between duties. Idle steam engines rarely provide an aural memory, unlike the diesels of today. Consequently, this old North British 4-4-2 tank said next to nothing as it rested.

As I lived in England, a mere twenty-five miles from London, this was a distinctly unusual sight for me. While there were still many classes of 4-4-2 tank still operating in Britain at the time – I suppose it must have been 1950 – they were unknown in Harpenden. But that was not what spurred my father. It was the livery that attracted his eye. The engine still wore the garb of the LNER.

When the railways were Nationalised, and the identity of locomotive stock was altered to remove duplicates, a huge effort was also made to obliterate evidence of previous owners. So much so, that old North Eastern electric locomotives were painstakingly renumbered, even though there was never any intention of using them again and they hadn't turned a wheel in donkey's years. But this old engine, the one we were looking at, had escaped the British Railways paint pot.

'There you are,' my father said. 'I don't think you will see that again.' And, pre-the preservation era, he was probably right. My last LNER engine, with its distinctive font and bold numbers painted on its side-tanks. Proudly, I was *unable* to cross it off in my number book which reflected the nationalised scene. But my father had obtained an early Ian Allan book during LNER days and, after we went home, I found the engine and crossed it off.

Now, the book seems to have been mislaid and I cannot be absolutely sure of which one it was – the C15 and C16 classes not being strangers in Fife (although I think it was No. 7462) – but I can still see it, noble, antiquated, competent, sitting in the fading sunshine before it was obscured by the arrival of our 'Shire'-hauled Edinburgh train and we were summoned to help with the practical tasks of getting the womenfolk and my brother into the Gresley corridor.

By the time we had settled ourselves, our train had moved off and the Reid tank engine receded from view. But the deed was done. That view was forever imprinted on my mind and the sights of thousands of other engines and a life of multifarious experiences has not in any way diminished that memory. The unforgettable sight of a nondescript little locomotive, invisible to the throng on the platform, the wind-ruffled, sunburned women, the tired and happy children, and a hatted and suited father smiling contentedly at a shared experience, a complicity, a moment he may have subsequently forgotten but which remains with me to this day.

♦

Nobby, one of the Canadian Pacific Thompsons – I don't remember which one, Snikpoh, and Drof were larking about on St. Albans Midland station with me in late 1958. I was Kciredor Wol at the time, after the then-current fashion of reversing names, mine being particularly excruciating as some felt, with my wire-glasses and myopic expression, I physically resembled the owl in 'Winnie the Pooh' and now, hilariously appropriate to some, had one of the literary character's names. We had three Thompson's in our class and their initials reflected the 'CPR' of the Canadian Pacific, hence their collective nickname, coupled to the obvious fact that reversal didn't really work with the name 'Thompson'. Nobby? Well, he was simply Nobby.

In between stopping to watch the passing trains, we had already pursued our long-term and ill-judged project to fathom out the code on the Jamaican porter's bicycle padlock. He trustingly left his personal transport on Platform 3 while diligently pursuing his portering vocation, little knowing of our criminal intentions. We had circled the waiting room to gaze at the impossibly beautiful girls from Loreto College as they gossiped and cantilevered schoolbags on raised knees in innocently-erotic, scholarly fraternity. We had watched the Post Office staff struggling with a fully-charged, four-wheeled barrow as they negotiated the boarded crossing that linked the platforms at the north end of the station. This was a somewhat risky activity at any time of year, there being no signals other than those that only-incidentally aided the postmen – home signals on the down lines at the extremities of the platforms, and up signals frequently out of sight at the London end – but made much more precarious in the dark, which it was that day, it being November, and about four-thirty in the afternoon.

We often willed the barrow to come to grief and nursed visions of uniformed postal workers scattering like characters in "Oh, Mr. Porter", while a 'Jubilee' reduced said barrow to matchwood. To an extent, we were rewarded in this vein a couple of years later, when the barrow remained intact but a consignment of children's plastic telephones in gaily-illustrated cardboard boxes cascaded onto the down-fast just as a Manchester passed through, the satisfying sound of crunched plastic and cardboard added to the roaring engine. In those days, before over-regulation, the train just marched onwards, leaving the station staff and postmen to clear up the mess between subsequent passing trains.

The up-slow home signal clattered into the 'off' position and a Class '5' strolled around the corner under the road bridge, its bufferbeam and smokebox door lamps winking in the cold night air, denoting a half-fitted freight.

Smoke, illuminated by the open fire-hole door, lifted high over the engine as the fireman got down to a spot of shovelling after a severe check. The chilly evening sharpened the white of the exhaust from the safety valves as the string of vans tightened against the tender coupling, the 'one-two' rhythm of the trucks' wheels satisfactorily quickening as the train passed. What we were especially looking for, the thing that caused our keen and specific interest, was not, however, the 'Stanier', with its hard-working crew, for this was winter and we were hoping for one thing and one thing above all else.

Snow.

In those days in the Home Counties, the first snow always seemed to come from the north and there, on that bitterly cold evening, it was. A smooth coat on the roofs of the vans, unmarked by the passage of the train or cinders bouncing in the tunnels. Did that mean the snow was near, south of Sharnbrook, perhaps? Or simply that conditions the train encountered left it unspoiled? No matter. Snow was on its way and, with it, the prospect of nonsense in the gardens and school playing fields and, because skiving was something highly valued to alleviate boredom, perhaps a late train in the morning or some cancelled games lessons.

Many of us were far from sporty.

As the train rounded the curve past the engine sheds, the brakevan, with its red lamps blinking their farewell to us, disappeared from view.

Only the arrival of our Fowler 2-6-4 tank made us forget, briefly, the prospect, the anticipation, the great expectations those frosted vans promised.

♦

Being blessed with a photographic memory where railways were concerned (but sadly absent from any conventionally useful discipline), there was always a tendency for me to 'know' what I was looking at – even if

I had personally never seen it before. Magazines, books and the local libraries (three of them – 'Public', Boot's and W. H. Smith's) fed the powers of recall, too.

Thus, walking to the platform-end at Lindau – just in Germany, but on the Austrian border and within sight of the extraordinarily beautiful Bodensee (Lake Constance), in the summer of 1962, the curious conical smokebox and vacant lot under the boiler of a huge locomotive, while something striking and certainly never seen before, was quickly identified as a Bavarian 'Pacific'. Although the locomotive had been heavily and surprisingly reconstructed well inside the era of diesel and electric traction, it still proudly displayed its 1907 Maffei-built, S3/6 heritage. Imagine! A 'Pacific' design as old as my father! That was simply impossible in the UK.

Those amazing Bavarian locomotives held off dieselisation on the expresses to Munich, Nuremburg, Stuttgart and Heidelberg for years and, even today, their legacy on the lines radiating from Lindau is that they were dieselised so late that electrification is still, as I write, on the 'to do' list of Deutsche Bahn. Fortunately, there are several of these amazing four-cylinder locomotives still in existence.

I remember I had to gently correct my father as we stood on Dinard station in Brittany during the summer of 1959 (a line now, sadly, closed), and looked carefully at our train's motive power while he announced the 2-8-2 was one of the American and Canadian-built locos that came over to France in huge numbers after the war. It simply didn't look right, being older and, somehow, more 'French', and the number wasn't right (141C123). This was no 141R.

Now, in my seventies, I sometimes find my memory deficient or just plain wrong.

The more you know, the more you don't know.

And the more you remember, the more you forget.

♦

Sometimes, even the obsessed crank gets a surprise, and it is then that the recollection is more firmly established. Many of those happy visual memories date back to earliest times for me, since each year that passed increased knowledge and, at the same time, reduced scope for new discovery. The baby tram, bright yellow and unbelievably short, standing in a shopping street in Koblenz, was a very happy discovery in 1960, as was the three coach interurban further down the Rhine that took us, lurching and grinding, to Bonn, then the capital of West Germany. There was always a tingle of excitement at the knowledge that what we saw as undiscovered and strange, was matter-of-fact for so many others.

The mere act of walking into the middle of the street in Glasgow, defying rubber-tyred traffic in our purposeful mission to board a slowing tram and realising we were joining a huddle of biddies who did this every day without thinking as they rode to the shops for their messages or went on hospital visits to see aging relatives, was interesting. What a thrill for us, but why didn't that surely-justified excitement register on the faces of plastic-coated, rain-mate hatted, message-bag wielding Fiona, and Moira, and Jessie, who spoke their special patois to each other through intermittently-toothless gums. They were expert in the process of boarding (downstairs, rarely up – up was mainly for working men who smoked incessantly), familiar, light-footed and deft in their own way. In contrast, we, the enthusiasts, the experts, the knowledgeable, who could tell, at a glance, the difference between a Coronation or a Cunarder, a Kilmarnock bogie or a Standard, and knew not to risk the street when, joy of joys, a dark, maroon works car ground its way towards us along Great Western Road, shuffling by with its load of granite setts and odoriferous melting tar, stumbled clumsily up the, to us, unfamiliar steps, decided and then changed our minds over which grasping hand to use, and tangled our limbs in the straps of our shabby haversacks.

How many of us, momentarily and embarrassingly-defeated by the strangeness of it all, subtly copied the retreating Maggie as she turned quickly into the saloon, having right-handed the pole in the doorway and left-handed the rail on the bulkhead next to the uncollected fares 'honesty-box', before dropping sensibly into a seat before the car started to move. We were often left half-way up the stairs, and not yet in sight of the leather-cushioned order of the top deck, when the car set off, grabbing anything to steady us, our eyes already smarting from the cloud of blue cigarette smoke, and our ears full of hacking coughs while we fought gravity and came to terms with the fact that we would never properly get our legs accustomed to the motion of a double-decked tramcar in full flight.

♦

One railway employee whose work could be keenly observed was the tube train guard.

He spent his working life cloistered at the inner end of the last car in a position of high-profile privacy, with a special hinged barricade preventing the public from using the single-leaf doors and compromising his important calling. When the train reached the terminus, driver and guard changed ends, and the formerly private guard's 'lobby' was returned to the travelling public who were now prevented from using the inner-end single-leaf doors at the new rear of the train.

Door controls were duplicated on each side of the car-to-car communicating door to act as a visual reminder to the guard to open the correct set of doors – the buttons on the panel only operated the doors adjacent. At stations with short platforms, he could isolate the doors at the extremities of the train, and passengers unfamiliar with short stations would have to hastily force their way through the throng to the centre of the car to disembark. He also had the all-important bell-push to tell the driver to set off. The guard was in charge of the train.

When the trains were not busy, some guards would not even raise the bar, but would sit on the cushions between stops, invariably going to the correct panel in anticipation of which side the platform would appear. As a small boy, I thought this display of memory very impressive.

One night, shortly after I had started work and after a bit of enforced overtime, an unusually approachable guard was skipping left and right across the train in his practiced way and, between stops, earnestly reading from a thick paperback.

'What are you reading?' I asked.

'Tolstoy,' he replied in his neo-cockney accent. '"War and Peace". One paragraph at a time. One moment in the Napoleonic Wars, next punching buttons for Leicester Square, then Pierre again, then Covent Garden. I don't get much read between Leicester Square and Covent Garden,' he added ruefully. 'Too close together. I'm doin' all the Russian classics. Last one was Turgenev. "Sportsman's Diary". You read it?' he asked.

'Yes,' I said, relieved at justified affirmation, and suitably impressed.

''Good, ain't it! Liked that one, I did.'

'Yes,' I replied, as he jumped to his feet, opened the doors and looked out carefully as the last of the pretty typists, clattering on high heels in a haze of cheap perfume and backcombed hair, boarded the train at Russell Square.

'Pitman's,' he observed. 'A lot of beautiful girls is at that typing school learning shorthand and whatnot.'

He stood quietly watching while the last of the stragglers boarded the train. A quick swipe at the door buttons and then the bell push. The train set off with the guard keeping his own door open so as to ride regally down the platform until, with a clatter, we entered the tunnel as his door closed with a satisfying clunk.

'Best bit,' he observed of his technique. 'I'm a bit like the Queen, waving an' that.' He curled his hand over, palm up, and gave a fair impression of the monarch greeting her subjects from an open car window. He laughed and opened

Tolstoy at his piece-of-string bookmark and he was lost to the world for three minutes.

I left the train at King's Cross St. Pancras, reflecting on my happy encounter and knowing I would never forget the sight of that animated fellow moving left and right, sitting, standing, peering, reading, pressing his buttons, and whistling as he stood at the door waiting for 'time'. Yes, it was true, I had read many of the Russian authors. But I had done it during free periods in my last year at school, ensconced in the school library, the sunlight streaming in through the long windows, a haven of peace and studious tranquillity. That had been easy. Indeed, what else would I have done with my enforced idleness? How much more commendable, heroic even, was that guard, his jauntily-placed London Transport cap on a head filling with the Russian classics.

One paragraph at a time.

♦

It is Derby Works, the date being the 4th April, 1959. The weather is cool and sunless, but at least it is dry. Through the auspices of a model railway club, about twenty of us have shaken off the tour guide, who could not understand our preference for the 'old crocks', when there were so many lovely, shiny new diesels to admire, and are swarming over everything, like a cloud of locusts in a field of African corn. Most of what we saw, we knew about, although the detail and the significance of the moment would have been lost to us. At the time it was just a rare, treasured visit to a railway works. The day had already got off to a good start with a quick dip into Derby Friargate station and the reward of seeing a D16/3 pull out noisily on a short passenger train.

But it was so much more than that. It marked, in a real sense, the beginning of the end of everything we held dear. Here were Nos. D1 to D5 with only the engine of No. D1 running, the others described in my spotting book notes as 'being built' or 'brand new'. Here were Nos. D5014 to D5020 in various stages of construction, with No. D5012 out in the yard. Here was a gathering of the pioneer diesels, doomed by the optimism for the Modernisation Plan, languishing, their future distinctly uncertain. The Fell – No. 10100, ED2, 4 and 5, and No. 10202, as incongruous, now, as the steamers of old. There were large numbers of ugly, standard diesel shunters and a few older ones like No. 11127. But the diesels were outnumbered by dozens of steam engines and bits of steam engines – numbers, where identifiable, greedily put down in the spotting book.

We saw No. 40005, the first of the Fowler 2-6-2 tanks to be withdrawn a couple of months before from Willesden, but we didn't, really. We saw the smokebox door, carefully set aside, in case another member of the class could usefully use it in the future. The rest of the engine had already gone. We saw 'Compounds', in most cases for scrap, although 41000 was being slowly restored, the frames and cab, motion and unfamiliar pipework strewn around the workshop. It had been in the works in varying states of dismantlement for eight years.

In the old roundhouse, we found the 'Spinner', the Midland 2-4-0 No. 158, and 'Thundersley' looking very smart, but in far from exhibition condition. There were strings of other locomotives in for scrap including quite modern machines. It all seemed, even to small boys, quite random, like a culling of healthy deer on a Scottish mountainside – destroyed simply because they were there, because they were surplus to requirements, or because something had 'gone wrong' with them. A modern Ivatt 2-6-0, waiting for review, stood in the company of ancient Midland 0-6-0s and 2Ps and their LMS counterparts, while a lone 'Dougan', No. 49418, had trundled in from its home shed, Stockport, and, nobody knew what to do with it. It had joined one of the scrap roads north of the old roundhouse where it languished until November of 1959, when it was put to the torch. Derby was awash with condemned and threatened steam engines. In those days before British Railways sold them to private scrap-merchants, sidings around railway works soon filled up until there was nowhere to put them. The cemetery was overflowing.

To an extent, all this was sad but predictable. It was how all railway locomotive works functioned – mending the useful and discarding the rest. We knew all the types on show, the Stanier 3-cylinder 2-6-4 tanks from the London, Tilbury and Southend section, and a couple of Somerset & Dorset 2-8-0s, Nos. 53804 and 53807, which most of us would have never seen before, all going through works. But this passage might be entitled 'tales of the unexpected' and the unexpected that day was big, rusty, forlorn and dramatic.

Most of us knew what it was but we would never have thought we'd see it that day. It was, firstly, of a wheel arrangement that was, by that time, unique in Britain, and it was a survivor like no other. It had been usurped from its original purpose over fifty years before and had, somehow, survived. It was the Mersey Railway 0-6-4 tank, 'Cecil Raikes'. Immensely powerful, built to haul heavy passenger trains up the steep inclines from below the bottom of the River Mersey, several of the class had been snapped up by coal mining companies eager for a cheap slogger. Other locomotives from the Mersey Railway ended up doing similar work in Australia. 'Cecil Raikes' was the last in the UK and, by great good fortune, she had been set aside for preservation. Having nowhere to go, it stayed at Derby outside in the yard for a while and we saw it there, deteriorating gently.

Back home behind No. 73157, it had been just another immensely satisfying trip, full of great images that soon became valued memories. Nine and a half years later, it would all be over. Even the modern steam engines that had taken the place of the fifty year olds we had enjoyed that day would be gone. There is a sort of sad justification in old engines going to their Valhalla. We didn't want it, of course, but it 'made sense'. For two years we had all known steam was doomed. But that was without appreciating the true nature of that extermination. Besides, the blow had been softened by a supplementary plan to 'keep the most modern in the north west' – steam was to be with us for a long time yet.

It wasn't. The acceptable logic of scrapping ancient 0-6-0s with long chimneys was to be replaced by the tragic chaos of the sixties, when class after class of modern, efficient steam power was retired long before it was necessary, or even sensible.

No. 73157 wheeled us out of our innocence and into the gathering gloom of that April 1959 evening, to detrain in Luton and then catch the local home.

It was only later that the sad importance of that day dawned on us.

♦

Today's London is an irregular grand canyon of glass and concrete, threaded by a rabbit-warren of streets full of slow-moving traffic and railway lines retreating increasingly into the foundations of the multi-storey apartment blocks and offices they serve. Efficiency demands strict uniformity, and there is little room for the quaint. But, in February 1961, one could travel behind an N7 from Stratford Low Level to North Woolwich, winding through sun-lit docklands that still hosted ships, and then sail across the Thames on the steam-powered Woolwich Free Ferry. In our minds, this was the closest thing to the eccentric riverboats of the Mississippi available to us in the United Kingdom, even though the resemblance was slight.

Below deck, we could observe the beautifully-maintained steam engines driving the paddle wheels, so much more manoeuvrable than a more conventional screw before the days of bow and side propellers. The fleet at that time dated from 1923 and 1930, and the operator, the

London County Council, was justifiably proud of their craft. The memorable feature was metal plates attached to the big ends which, every time they revolved, struck a fibre swab installed at the bottom of each oil reservoir. By this action, a fine slick of oil descended to the bearings – simple but effective. Needless to say, all the mechanical parts were immaculate – copper and brass shone bright, with steelwork burnished and, in some areas, carefully painted.

The Free Ferry still operates, but now it is roll-on, roll-off and diesel-powered, although the craft were built at the Dundee yards of Robb-Caledon whose data processing tabulators I later supported. But one can no-longer arrive at North Woolwich behind an N7 or take the trolley-bus. Now, it will be the centipede of the Docklands Light Railway diving under the river that has rendered pedestrian traffic on the ferry a non-essential novelty.

♦

My father was excited.

In his context, that meant an occasional smile, extremely-understated levity and a slight but nevertheless discernible spring in his step.

It was 1953, a momentous year, with a new Queen on the throne – the dawn of the new 'Elizabethan Age' bringing a sense of excited optimism, and the family goldfish buried in front of where the big tree stood just as the Queen was crowned. It was the year of the presentation mugs at school – I still have mine – and the parade around the village with every child from my school representing one of the Commonwealth communities. I was 'Hong Kong', with a solution of custard rubbed into my face and a couple of discarded paint-pots clothed in corrugated cardboard suspended from a bamboo cane to help me to resemble a Chinese coolie, and wearing baggy pyjama trousers, a white vest and bare feet. Additionally, I had to carry a sign with the name of my newly acquired but temporary origins on a long pole that imperilled anyone who came within a yard of me – the risk of losing an eye or being bruised by my crazily-swinging buckets high on the list of potential consequences. The fact that I had another bout of my recurring tonsillitis and was probably running my usual 'sickness temperature' of 102 Fahrenheit just added to the possibility of disaster. I remember my mother ruefully suggesting the custard was probably unnecessary as I was already sporting a skin-colour far from my natural pasty Caucasian.

But this abnormal Sunday was much later than the June, 2nd Coronation, and the celebrations for that auspicious occasion were long past. This was the 20th September, and quite early in the day. Two buses took us from Harpenden to Hatfield, via St. Albans, there being no suitable Sunday train service on the line from Harpenden East that would have accomplished the journey in little more than half an hour. My father suffered from the need to arrive early for everything (a trait I have inherited), so I am sure we were on Hatfield station long before 10 a.m. on a day that was dry and sunny.

My father did not tell me why we were going out until we were on the bus. But when he did, I could hardly contain myself.

Dad loved 'Atlantics'. To him, their symmetry was unparalleled, and he saw few situations where anything else could possibly be an improvement. For instance, he particularly frowned on the proliferation of 4-6-0s, with their narrow fireboxes, rigid inflexibility, inferior steaming qualities, and hardly-improved traction. Of course, a 'Pacific' was just an elongated 'Atlantic', and he appreciated the retention of the potential for a wide firebox in what was bound to be a more powerful locomotive. But he was an LNER man in his head, and a Gresley man at that, and he would explain the virtues of 'Pacifics', the V2s, V4s and the late-lamented P2s for hours to his enthralled son.

But, of the 'Atlantics', he had personal knowledge of

the North British and North Eastern examples from childhood and saw the Great Northern ones when they worked infrequently to Edinburgh, and then the Great Central engines when, newly married, my parents moved to Pinner in Middlesex and my father began commuting on the Metropolitan and Great Central joint lines – by then LPTB and LNER. He thought the Great Central 'Atlantics' the best looking of them all, closely followed by Nos. 730 and 731 on the North Eastern.

He never spoke of the Lancashire & Yorkshire ones and, when I showed him a picture once, he just shook his head and raised his eyes heavenwards.

But, the centenary of the Doncaster 'Plant' was being celebrated with a resurrection of two 'Atlantics', Nos. 990 and 251, and we were going to see them. As we were so early, I had time to draw a picture of a Great Northern / ECJS six-wheeled passenger van sitting in a bay at the south end of the station (E941534, for anyone who is interested – yes, even at eight years old, I was *that* sad!), but a shriek on the whistles broke my artistic concentration and we watched as the two locomotives – a flash of bright green and burnished brass – roared through. Fate was on our side with nothing obscuring our view. An uninterrupted vision of Great Northern magnificence in a world still teeming with steam trains.

With the Great Northern and the LNER, there was a locomotive 'family resemblance' I believe to be unique on the railway scene. Patrick Stirling came to the GNR as Locomotive Engineer in 1866 and down all the years, through Ivatt, Gresley, Thompson and Peppercorn, a cursory glance at the front ends of all their products bore characteristics that, in humans, would render the need to take DNA samples to establish parentage unnecessary. Even the later Sturrocks – and we are talking about the age of coke firing and steam tenders here – looked like the ancestors of all the others. The fact that Stirling rebuilt so many of the Sturrocks with his own details and boilers helped with this family feel. There's a humanity about the

Great Northern look not found everywhere. They didn't look belligerent and tough like the products of Fowler, nor complacent like a Stanier, self-important like a Collett, or plain weird like a Bullied. Even a mighty Peppercorn 'Pacific' looked friendly and unthreatening.

And, for all the amazing technical wizardry of the engineers who followed Stirling, none had an ego that tried to reinvent the general appearance of the locomotive fleet. Stirling had put himself on the world stage with the famous 8 foot singles, and railwaymen appreciated his work with suburban tanks, big goods engines and the like, but Ivatt had his 'Atlantics', 0-8-0 and 0-6-0 goods engines and, arguably, the first modern suburban tank engines, Gresley was probably one of the finest locomotive engineers ever to walk this earth, Thompson – who often gets a mean press – took an aging fleet on an impoverished railway and standardised with his B1 and other simplifications that probably saved his employer from bankruptcy, and Peppercorn gave us a Pacific that won accolades for being the most available, most efficient, most appreciated express steam locomotives in the UK, plus an amazing class of go-anywhere 2-6-0s. And yet, they kept the flavour and ethos of the line – kept the family going for five generations – arguably six.

No other railway achieved this in the UK to my mind.

The Great Western had a grandfather, father, son dynasty with Churchward, Collett and Hawksworth, but that was only three generations. Each LMS engineer had his own views, so we have the Hughes and Fowler vastness and worrying numbers of bolts to hold the smokebox door closed and airtight, Stanier with a pleasing front end all his own, followed by imitators Fairburn and another Ivatt and, into the British Railways age, Robert Riddles. And on pre-grouping railways, as soon as they got their feet firmly under the draughtsman's table, each new engineer tended to take on the persona of a fashion designer and fulfil his role but, at the same time, zealously make his mark.

Not so on the East Coast lines. Here, family mattered.

So, around that corner wheeled the two racehorses, both by Ivatt, out of Stirling, with their children, grandchildren and great grandchildren still around in large numbers – all looking 'of a one'. I didn't know that the men on the footplate included drivers Bill Hoole and Ted Hailstone – two legends of Kings Cross shed – or the fact that No. 990 was only required because they had disabled No. 251's superheater in order to restore the locomotive as far as possible to original condition and a brisk timing had to be maintained. But I was aware of how very small the cabs looked – it was as though the crews were 'behind' rather than 'inside'. And I was impressed by the fact that the train was going quickly – there had been a permanent way check at Potters Bar, apparently, and there was probably time to make up.

And then, as soon as they appeared, they were gone. The last ex-Great Northern 'Atlantics'. Only the Brighton ones remained for a few more years. All that long torturous journey by bus, much appreciated of course, for a fleeting glimpse of one Sunday train.

Shades of what was to come.

Today, I still go down to the station to wait for half an hour to watch the passage of a single steam engine. Waiting in the sun or rain for an isolated experience, gone in a trice and then nothing more worthwhile to see.

On that late summer's day in 1953, there would have been many other trains at Hatfield, but my thoughts then would have been just as they are now, over sixty years later.

Plenty of trains, but only one mattered.

♦

Anyone interested in railways in my time, other than those who embraced modernity, probably suffered a little from clinical depression. Every new monthly magazine, every encounter with 'those in the know', would bring news of closure and withdrawal, destruction and dereliction, and faded glories consigned to the fire and the torch.

And if not actual depression, a certain pathos, an almost permanent sense of sadness and grief, that could only be shared with a select few. Most school friends were not in the slightest bit enthused by railways – to the point where one spoke as little as possible of one's curious passions for fear of derision and reprisals, sometimes, surprisingly, of a physical nature. Indeed, even writing this is, to some extent, cathartic, a purging of the effects of repressed thoughts, a 'laying bare' of hitherto concealed character and the occasional consequences of careless revelation.

Whether or not those closest to me will nod sagely and say, 'Ah! That explains why he is what he is,' I don't know. And it probably doesn't explain how I am, in the slightest. But it does explain, to a degree, what I am.

So, while President Eisenhower was enjoying his inaugural ball at the White House in the early weeks of 1957, being frightfully 'cool' by employing the services of Pat Boone singing 'Don't Forbid Me' and 'Why Baby Why' in front of his distinguished guests, and youth in the UK was embracing their new world of Bill Haley, Frankie Vaughan and Little Richard (and eschewing the likes of Harry Belafonte and Norman Wisdom as being 'past it'), we were opening Page 4 of the 'Daily Express' for the 7th of March to read Sir Brian Robertson's fateful fifteen words – 'It is virtually true to say that we are not building any more steam locomotives'.

I remember, I wept. His urging us 'spotters' to 'take heart', as it would take twenty years to scrap them all did nothing to calm troubled minds. The fact that they did go on building them for another three years, but his prediction of extinction was reduced to eleven years was, of course, information not yet available to us. There was another revolution going on in the transport industry unbeknown to us all that would shrink the railway and make it irrelevant to a whole range of traffic types, while concentrating the dubious products of the Modernisation Plan on the work-

categories and lines that remained after that revolution. This was eventually capped by the cowardly employment of an industrialist, Dr. Richard Beeching, to do the Government's dirty work.

But there was an inevitability attached to it all. All over the world, railways were bowing to the flexibility of the modern, powerful and reliable bus, car and truck, so why should Britain be different? As a consequence, we were presented with those most pathetic scenes, the 'last train' with its wreath on the smokebox (and, quite often, latterly, the front of a diesel railcar, as modernisation did nothing to stem the slaughter), railway cranes tearing up the track with indecent haste, station buildings with their glass smashed and paperwork strewn across tattered floorboards, and grass-grown platforms, graffiti on the civil engineering in and around cities, and the arrival of a new branch to our hobby, espying the remnants of railway lines.

Generalised railway industrial archaeology was born.

♦

Most of us became expert, whether driving a car, sitting on a bus, or cycling and walking in a city or the countryside, at spotting the tell-tale evidence of former railway activity. A bridge parapet; an off-its-hinges collapsing gate; a bramble-strangled wooden staircase up a jungle of an embankment; scarred and wounded countryside revealing empty cuttings and embankments that resembled an industrial-age Offa's Dyke; the fear-inspiring mock-horror of a gloomy tunnel mouth; a fine railway viaduct we knew to be trackless; proud, empty warehouses and yard buildings gradually succumbing to the vagaries of weather and vandals, and, never forget, the row upon row of withdrawn rolling stock, old and new, steam and even diesel. In short, the arrival of a brave new world we found so barren and lacking.

Hundreds of miles of line had closed before we were

born, and we knew about them – could justify their demise on the basis of extreme remoteness, closure of old, rural industries, the convenience of the urban electric tram (usurped, in their turn by shuddering 'oilers'), even commercial failure – but now it was thousands of miles of not-so permanent way, and it made no sense at all. Those earlier closures may have been sad, and many of us would look at pictures of the Welsh Highland (now, with us again), the Fort Augustus line, Campbeltown, Wantage, Walton-in-Gordano and the Valentia branch in south-west Ireland, and talk about them amongst ourselves – imagining old locomotives with tall chimneys pulling a motley collection of pensioned-off rolling stock, proud railway servants attending to passengers leaving an arriving train from this place or that, or a self-conscious group of railwaymen standing on the track and platform while their photograph was taken. Sad though those lost memories were, they didn't prepare us for the wholesale closure of whole networks of railway lines – Brecon to everywhere, north Norfolk, the Waverley route, the Great Central, the Port Road to Stranraer, the Midland route to Manchester through the Peak District, and a hundred branch lines, some short, some long, some matter-of-fact, some stunningly beautiful, mostly useful, some essential. We began to think they were closing lines simply because they were difficult to operate.

Phoney promises of bus replacements that often proved temporary and unreliable, and the dubious economics of closing an unremunerative branch-line while retaining the adjacent main line, only to find that the disobedient public did not get in their cars and dutifully drive to the former junction, but just carried on in their cars to their final destination, making no contribution at all to the railway's coffers, were soon proved to be the nonsense they were.

In no time, the former junction station would probably close too.

♦

Do owners of pleasure craft ever think about the effect of their naming policies on sensitive children, I wonder?

Back before the days of the Forth railway bridge, there was a celebrated ferry that plied between Granton, near Leith, and Burntisland in Fife. A curious railway, with its terminus at right angles to Edinburgh's Waverley station, mostly in tunnel and cable-hauled at its southern extremity, conveyed passengers and freight down to the harbour. From there, paddle steamers would churn drunkenly across the firth, some actually carrying rolling stock and making the passage the one with the first public train-ferry in the world, dating from 1849. Another train would collect passengers, in whatever state of dignity they retained after what could be an extremely choppy crossing, to take them across Fife to their eventual destinations.

The most famous ferry of all was the 'William Muir', which plied the waters until 1937, having swapped its role from being an essential conveyance to that of providing pure pleasure after the Forth Bridge opened in 1890. Nothing could match the sheer joy of what was virtually a sea crossing on a calm summer's day for Edinburgh folk, and even in the early 1950s, my relatives would talk nostalgically of the 'William Muir' with its spinning paddle wheels, the flash and glint of water cascading back into the foaming waves, the views up and down the broad firth, the huge ugly beauty of the Forth Bridge, and long lazy picnics on the Fife hills, before sailing home as the sun set red in the western sky.

So, when there was a plan to revive the service after the Second World War, there was much excitement in the family. Sadly, this eager anticipation cannot have extended to the world at large, as the new ferry only operated for a bit over a year. So, it must have been the summer of 1952 when we made that memorable crossing.

My problem was with the naming of the boat, which was nothing like as large as the 'William Muir'. I don't even remember its name, other than that it – or was it another boat alongside, I don't remember for sure – was blessed with a number as well as its name. It could have been 'Maid of the Forth', or something. But then they added VI – 'six' according to my Latin primer. Actually I am not even sure it was a 'six', but you'll get the idea in a minute.

'Why is it Number 6?' I asked.

Being of a nervous disposition where boats were concerned, the answer I received only reinforced my trepidation.

'I expect the previous five sank,' my uncle said.

I did not see the twinkle in his eye.

So, my otherwise pleasant boat trip was somewhat spoiled by a fear that 'No. 6' would join all its predecessors in Davy Jones's locker. As far as I know, there was never a 'William Muir 2' and, with nervous passengers, that is how it should be.

♦

We padlocked our bicycles on a forlorn overbridge in the middle of nowhere and scrambled down the embankment to walk for miles – much as my father had insisted we walk along his beloved canal banks years before – each bend and curve, each rising embankment, each bridge and gulley, each forgotten mile or gradient post, beckoning us on. We looked for clues of what had gone before. We listened to the birds chattering in dismay, frightened by our passing, rising on a fluttering of agitation, we now their only disturbance. We could sometimes smell the faint aroma of oil around severed signal pulley-wires and admire a forgotten signal-post, deemed too firmly stuck in the ground to be worth uprooting for scrap. We would explore a modern concrete trackside cabin reeking heavily of urine and now devoid of all legitimate purpose. We would see the widening of the track-bed as we arrived at a long lost junction – a closed branch off a closed branch. We would see the sprig curving away and then straightening so as to be at right-angles to us, striking bravely, for a mile or more, towards a clump of trees or the far-away detritus of an abandoned quarry or coal-mine – another open wound that would gradually heal as the years went by. And we would arrive at a one-time station, uncertain of the reception we would enjoy at the sight of an agricultural engineer or jobbing builder who had taken a lease on the property and erected a wonky, tumbling fence with unfriendly privacy signs and protected by a ferocious dog threatening to tear itself from its chains to make a meal of us.

And the sky would suddenly darken, in contrast to the weak sunshine we had been enjoying, and we would decide to return to the bikes, our passage hastened by the inevitable start of light rain that turned heavy. Heads down, now, we ignored the junction, the abandoned cabin, the fine old signal, the birds whose short memories did nothing to alleviate their fear at our passage, and the old mile and gradient posts that measured our way back to railwayless reality.

We would not come back. No reason to. Virtually nothing left to see.

Memory, such as it is, fading with the passage of time.

♦

It was not the visual experience I had hoped for.

I had anticipated a bit of a jaunt around what was left of the Lothian lines frequented by my grandfather. I was trying to piece together his life and work, and thought a bit of a cab ride – say, with a Type 20 – would give me a nice 'hook' to a book I planned. I might see the Edinburgh 'Circle', a few freight workings, perhaps even a bash across the Forth Bridge. Anything, really, to suit the authorities, would be appreciated. There might even be a few anecdotes and the pointing out of the locations of old junctions and yards that would chime with my researches and my grandfather's priceless diary-notebook.

The Scottish Region of British Railways didn't do that,

unfortunately, but, by way of compensation, offered me a cab ride in a 'Deltic' from the Waverley to Newcastle. It was kind of them, I suppose, and I was grateful. But it wasn't what I had visualised.

So, the 15th April, 1981 dawned dry and mild, with a watery sun, and I stood at the front of the train to the west country beside No. 55021, "Argyll & Sutherland Highlander", awaiting the arrival of Harry McCathie, Haymarket's senior inspector, who introduced me to Driver Wilson of Gateshead, a jovial and agreeable companion for the morning *(see an illustration at the start of Chapter Six, 'Taste')*.

'We've twelve on, 408 tons behind the engine,' shouted the guard, before moving off towards his brake near the rear of the train.

'Sit down in the second man's seat,' ordered Mr. McCathie, who stood behind the driver for the whole journey. I'd have gladly stood, but I think he wanted me isolated from harm. Perhaps, brandishing my first-class ticket which was the price one paid for a coveted cab ride, he felt I was entitled to sit.

To that point, the only diesels I had ever 'cabbed and ridden in' were a two-car unit at St. Albans Abbey station which the driver let two of us drive along the platform between services, and a baby diesel shunter on Granton Harbour which was more about a short-skirted girlfriend of mine than any reward for a railway enthusiast. That day, we rolled about at walking pace on the harbour over crazy track while he held her comfortingly around the shoulders and then slowly half-lifted her down to the ground at the end of our journey.

So I really didn't know what to expect from a proper diesel locomotive ride.

A green signal-light and a lot of whistling and arm-waving from the platform, and Driver Wilson nudged the controller open a notch or two. What a disappointment! It really was about four-minutes on the quadrant, maybe a few more. No effort, no sense of accomplishment, no drama. No. 55021 rolled slowly forwards and cruised into the tunnel. Accelerating quickly on the downhill gradient, the Inspector reminded Wilson to shut off as we swung around a housing estate three miles out where the occupants of self-satisfied, frowning bungalows with neat gardens and granite-chipped drives had complained about the noise the 'Deltics' made. Clear of them, we hurried off across East Lothian, past the notorious level crossing to a farm where my aunt and her children were sent at the beginning of the war and where, much more recently, several people had died in a collision with a V2 – steam engine, not flying bomb – and into the platform at Dunbar. My long-term memory of Dunbar was of platforms, sidings, an engine shed, and busy-ness. Now, this was like a lay-by on an A road, one platform with track, the other deserted, and accompanied by litter-strewn, rail-less ballast.

Soon we were off again, and all there was to relieve the monotony were two passing HSTs and the novelty of seeing sights such as the sea, now turning grey as the sky darkened, Berwick station, and the Royal Border bridge from this strange and unfamiliar angle. There were no goods trains at all, no junctions until we reached the Newcastle area, few intermediate stations, and none we stopped at after Berwick.

We talked about the numberless crows and how neither of them had ever hit one in spite of their dare-devil games of 'last across' as they picked at the carcasses of their less wary avian brethren – not to mention sundry decapitated rabbits and foxes. They pointed out a bit of a 'cut-off' that was supposed to iron out a tight curve, and I was made aware of just how damaging a speed restriction is when we slowed to cross a culvert that had collapsed. One little drainage bridge about two yards long brought the train down from about 90 mph to 20mph and then back up to 90mph, but the effect on the train was felt for at least three miles as first we slowed down and then regained train-speed. That must have cost us more than five minutes, I estimated. All the time, Mr. Wilson was tweaking the controller open and shut – delicate movements that required the pressure of one finger – and the big 'Deltic's' muffled roar responded obediently behind the firmly closed engine-room door. Sundry enthusiasts standing on bridges and embankments took photographs as we passed and I wondered if I'd ever see a picture of 'my train', other than the ones taken by me and a friend who saw me off at the Waverley. Mr. Wilson and Mr. McCathie were very happy, to the point where Mr. McCathie offered me a return cab-ride to the Waverley in one of the new HSTs. But my car was in a car park in Newcastle, I was living in Yorkshire at the time, and I had to decline. Besides, my first-class ticket was a single.

And I had done it – the diesel cab-riding thing. Don't get me wrong. I was grateful and told them so. I bought a nice little lunch for Mr. McCathie and I, in a place just outside Newcastle Station, while Mr. Wilson prepared himself for a return trip to Carlisle in a DMU before signing off. One minute in the top-link, the next on a rural railcar. I expect the authorities had done their utmost to make the controls as similar to each other as possible – helping train-drivers, pilots of aircraft and car-drivers alike to feel everything is familiar. All the same, all predictable, all manifestly ordinary, and no sense of occasion or majesty.

But think. Only two passing trains in all that time! A line once punctuated by stations, junctions, yards, signal boxes and a myriad things of interest, swept aside and now the same all the way. And a job where the stress of time-keeping, worrying about touchy neighbours, and (normally) being all alone is really, otherwise, a non-job of twiddled controllers, scanning trip sheets and matching the train's speed to changing speed limits.

I should have felt exhilarated. Instead, I knew why I had lost interest in 1968, other than the eccentric activities of the preservation scene and my increasingly passive studies restricted to the printed word.

♦

It is summer, 1951. Teignmouth, Devon.

It has been a long walk over the viaduct from Shaldon. It is very hot but dad is on a mission, and he strides briskly, clutching my brother's hand, while I try to catch up after pausing to watch a flight of swans cruising along the estuary about one hundred feet over our heads, their wings whirring rhythmically, necks stretched forward, feet tucked away neatly like black undercarriages on snow-white aircraft.

We are holidaying in Shaldon, at a caravan park next to the road. We have a very small caravan that, before the war, must have been a tourer, as its towing gear has already grazed my shins during careless, giggling pursuit of my two-year old brother. The caravan is newly painted dark green, perched on piles of bricks, and is called, wittily I thought, 'Noname'. It was advertised in the 'Evening Standard' as an inexpensive holiday destination for the unwary and inexperienced, so, naturally, we are here – our first complete family holiday, other than visits to relatives.

We have received a letter from my grandparents addressed to 'Noname, Shaldon'. It makes me wonder if we are going to live here forever.

But, the reason for our walk? Dad, my brother and I have been banished from the van.

My mother is trying to prepare a dinner and is clearly upset by the tiny kitchen and the gas cooker that always ignites with a huge bang that frequently blows the flame out, necessitating a further brush with danger. We are having many meals in restaurants and cafes during this holiday – perhaps the terrifying stove is the reason why.

On the whole, I prefer eating out because I have just been introduced to the magic world of Heinz Tomato Ketchup – a hitherto untasted delicacy that I already know I will love forever.

I am sure this will be the last caravan holiday of my childhood, even though it has never been discussed.

106

Children sense these things.

We reach the other side of the estuary and enter a small park between the railway and the road. There is probably a bowling green and some flowers and, of course, we have the run of the children's playground with its swings, sick-making roundabout and a long slide approached by a metal ladder rooted in unforgiving tarmac.

But these entertainments are not uppermost in our minds – certainly not where dad and I are concerned.

We perch on the fence alongside the railway and wait for the passage of trains.

When a goods train arrives, dad gets very excited. He tells me it is an ROD 2-8-0 and, as it lumbers slowly by, he points out the Great Western safety-valve bonnet on an otherwise Great Central design. As the grubby, unloved engine heads off towards Newton Abbott, he explains what ROD means and I know I must now share the abbreviated version of my name with the squaddies of the Railway Operating Division.

Dad is often taciturn, and he can be very intimidating, but once he gets started on trains, there is no stopping him. There are 'Castles' and '2251's, 2-6-2 tanks and some absolutely new 'Britannias' – they even smell new as they pass. As it is summer, there is a lot of traffic – trains of holidaymakers peering excitedly out at the estuary and lucky locals ignoring the commonplace, vegetable vans and cattle trucks, 'loco-coal' wagons and white-stained china-clay trucks with flapping tarpaulins. The late afternoon stretches on delightfully, train after train, more swans beating their way seaward, and fresh sea breezes – novel and exhilarating to a family from land-locked Hertfordshire.

Reluctantly, dad calls a halt to proceedings. Time to go back. Dinner must be ready.

Horrors!

No sign of my little brother.

He is not with us. Not in the playground. Not scrabbling about in the bushes. And certainly not watching trains.

He has vanished.

After a frantic search – and dad could easily be very frantic – he adopts a new but unexplained plan. We head back over the road viaduct at high speed, my arm virtually hauled out of its socket as he hurries me across. The sun is beating down on us. Perspiration stands all over my dad's balding head.

My mother is far from happy and voices are raised about 'responsibility' and my father's excessive enthusiasm for trains. I have rarely seen him lost for words, but he is now.

With me left in the care of another camper, my mother and father set off for Teignmouth – dinner forgotten by all, I assume, apart from me.

After an hour or more, they return with my little brother in tow. He had been found, aged two, wandering around Teignmouth, where he was picked up by a man in a car (this was 1951, and people were very different then!) before being taken to the police station where he stayed until my parents went to report his loss after a fruitless search of the park.

At two years of age, he knew his own name, but very little else.

I have no doubt the policeman on the desk had a few words to say to my father to add to my mother's condemnation.

I thought I saw an 'outside swinger', a double-framed 4-4-0, as I turned back to watch the railway on my forced march back to the caravan that evening.

But I cannot be sure.

Tomato Ketchup and sunstroke were two new experiences that holiday.

♦

When I first became a railway enthusiast, British Railways had hardly been born. My earliest memories, as you will have read, were from pre-nationalisation days, but I seriously became interested when, to all intents and purposes, we were witnessing the 'Big Four' (London North Eastern Railway, the London, Midland and Scottish Railway, the Southern Railway and the Great Western Railway) as they had been before the gentle (and probably fortuitous!) hand of the Atlee Government had been felt on the back of the private companies' necks. One major aspect of this Nationalisation 'false dawn' was the virtual segregation of motive power into their respective territories.

If I buy a modern railway magazine, such as the excellent "Rail", the trains illustrated are of a highly uniform appearance. Most are multiple units of one sort and another – very hard to tell apart – and where locomotives are to be seen, the pictures could be taken more-or-less anywhere in the country. A diesel class '66' could be in proverbial Land's End or John O' Groats, with only the livery betraying different ownerships. Even that would give no clue as to the traffic the train is pulling since locomotives are often hired to other operators.

In the early fifties, an enthusiast living in Plymouth with shallow pockets might see dozens of Great Western engines, a smattering of Southern types and the beginnings of an influx of Standard steam classes. But he would never see anything in the forty, fifty or sixty-thousand number sequences. Similarly, living, as I did, only twenty-five miles from London, while the LNER and LMS lines were easily accessible, the Great Western and Southern were not. And, being in touch with a region did not give one access to anything above a small slice of what could be found in our spotting books.

In the fifty-thousand series, we would occasionally see old Midland 0-6-0s, but that was it. Holidays in Cheshire brought me within reach of Lancashire & Yorkshire locomotives, while an annual return to my Scottish roots revealed the products of the Caledonian and North British railways. And I counted myself lucky. For reasons of not wanting to carry a proliferation of spares, not to mention the prejudices of the crews who didn't like unknown engines on principle, there was no good reason to try 'foreign' things out, just to see if they were better than the incumbents.

The Locomotive Exchanges of 1948 were supposed to compare like with like from the constituent companies to see if something magnificent was 'hiding under a bushel'. The theory went, if a class was expanded upon, it could form the basis of new construction in the brave new world of the nationalised railway. While the Exchanges were very interesting (and, incidentally, briefly brought 'foreign' engines to many parts of the country), the way forward was with a bewildering variety of what were, essentially, stripped-down LMS types, described as 'Standards' to confuse regional railwaymen, who probably had their suspicions about the subterfuge.

As a consequence of this understandable parochialism, spotting books of the period would be well-thumbed in one area and, at the same time, practically virgin in another, according to residency. I saw every one of the LMS 'Garratts' in time, but never saw the LNER one that was still bashing its ponderous way up Worsborough Bank, near Barnsley. I saw any number of LMS 4Fs but none of the LNWR 'Cauliflowers' that would have been familiar if I had lived in Penrith. I knew the LMS 2Ps and 'Compounds', but never saw a 'Dukedog' until the preservation era. I knew the N2s and N7s but never saw a Plymouth, Devonport and South Western Junction, or Brighton 0-6-2 tank equivalent. I saw a few Great Eastern 2-4-0s, but their Midland and South Western Junction sisters escaped me. Only the much-travelled and dishonest had spotting books with engines crossed off in volume on every page.

But, as the years went by, some infiltration took place. Like birds blown off course by freak winds fetching up on our shores, these migratories would suddenly appear and, after a short while, return to their far-off lands. This is not about the infrequent visits of well-known classes of engine which the more knowledgeable of us could identify – a Nottingham 2-6-4 tank transferred temporarily to make up for a shortage at St. Albans, for instance, or a Scottish-based Thompson 'Pacific' burling through Welwyn Garden City on an up fish train from Aberdeen, or a B1 turning at Blackpool North after bringing in a train of excited holidaymakers from Lincoln.

This is about odd-ball machines from other regions or parts of the country, rarely advertised to anyone who didn't need to know.

♦

On the 23rd September, 1956, my family went to Bedford for the day.

And so did the Southern Region's ex-South Eastern & Chatham Class 'D', No. 31577.

While we went on the river, where my father fumed at me for dropping an oar which took a long and fairly dangerous period of clutching and wild rocking to retrieve, the little 4-4-0 pulled a train called the 'Woburn Park Special' from Waterloo station in London to Flitwick and Harlington. The organiser of the trip, a Mr. Lockie, a retired dispensing chemist who was both a rambler and railway enthusiast, earned a reputation for this sort of thing. He had a passion for rare track, apparently, and this brought the old lady to the Midland Main Line. My father obviously knew about this and reasoned it was bound to be turned, watered and coaled in Bedford, a little beyond Flitwick.

Uncanny, that. Dad always knew about these things.

On our return to Bedford station after our long day out, there, just north of the platform and barely in view, stood the pride of Harry Wainwright and its train of green coaches. On the way back to Harpenden, by hanging out of the window, we could see it coming up the goods lines. We lost it when it turned in behind us onto the fast lines to

111

pick up its happy ramblers at the stations nearest Woburn Park and, by the time we reached Harpenden, it was dark. Dad, of course, wanted to see the stranger go through, so, with mother and little brother despatched to the warmth of home, we waited. Sure enough, the next train signalled on the up slow was the special. I have a clear memory of those big driving wheels with the sensual curve of the splashers, the drawn-back, elegant smokebox – a sight increasingly rare to the observer since the advent of the superheater – and the crew perched against the firebox. She was probably moving at about forty miles an hour, so she was gone in seconds. That excursion was her swansong after a career of more than fifty years. She was withdrawn in December of that year and broken up. Her sister, carrying its old South Eastern & Chatham number 737 and looking pristinely different, is in the National Collection.

Why do some brief images stay with us for ever? Who knows, but we are so very glad of them.

♦

Bedford was a place of surprises. At the back of the shed in amongst a host of railway wagons, stood a very unusual sight. Stored – dumped would be a more precise term – was an ex-Lancashire & Yorkshire 2-4-2 tank No. 50646 *(see illustration at the start of Chapter Three, 'Hearing')*. She had been sent south to work on the Bedford to Bletchley and Northampton branches, and was a victim of that railwayman parochialism of which I have already written. No-one on the Midland (or the London & North Western, for that matter) wanted the old foreigner.

In those days, it was quite possible for a shed master, sensing resistance and unrest amongst his men, to quietly dispose of a stranger in the long grass where it could easily be forgotten. Built in 1890, she was an early Aspinall tank, so successful on their own territory that one of their number warranted preservation. I may have seen her in

1958, the year she was withdrawn, unlamented, from Bedford shed, after a long time in store. It even resisted the general return to traffic of a number of stored engines during the petrol rationing of 1956. Perhaps it was truly forgotten, only visible to a small boy from a long overbridge close to Bedford station, so obscure that the number couldn't be seen and the 'experts' on the railway embankment in Harpenden had to be consulted.

No. 50646 was part of a tentative L&Y 'invasion' at that time, as its sister, No. 50650, also came south from Royston in Yorkshire – to Wellingborough, this time. It was to act as spare engine on the Higham Ferrers and Northampton branches. Wellingborough's Ivatt 2-6-2 tanks held off the dubious delights of No. 50650, while Bedford got a railbus for its Northampton services – modernisation was on its way, even though that line closed shortly afterwards.

♦

In the harsh winter of 1962 / 1963, I was commuting to London daily from Harpenden. It was the first really severe test of our comparatively new diesel multiple units that had been around for a year or two.

The weather was extremely cold, so much so the diesel fuel gelled in the pipework running from the tanks to the Rolls-Royce engines. So, 8-coach trains were frequently reduced to four and sometimes trains didn't run at all. Now, I may be accused of seeing my memories through rose-tinted spectacles, but I remember few cancellations in the days of steam. Trains could frequently be late – sometimes very late – but cancellations were, it is true to say, rare.

The morning of the 1st of February, 1963, nine days before my eighteenth birthday, dawned freezing cold. The whole year had been so unusual in terms of the weather that a whole new dictionary of words had been invented – 'frain' for frozen rain, 'snice' for a lasagne-sandwich of ice and snow that was extremely treacherous as it could be as much as a foot deep and collapse under the weight of an adult, and many other terms I have now forgotten. Even the BBC radio weathermen started to use the new argot. I remember our cat, always fastidious, looking plaintively at us as he gave up the hopeless struggle to reach soil for his would-be ablutions. Instead, he performed, shamefaced, in a deep snow-hole of his own creation.

As the Inuit say, 'beware of yellow snow'.

A day or two before, we had been turned out of the diesel multiple unit at Cricklewood due to the aforementioned fuel problem and we had to wait for a following train. One commuter collapsed on the platform due to the temperature and had to be helped by his fellow-passengers. Nowadays it would have been ambulances and I don't know what else. Then? It was encouragement and a helping hand that saved his day.

That season, the snow rarely melted in spite of frequent days of sunshine – it was like a coal-effect fire with the heating elements turned off permanently. The station platform at Harpenden Central was strangely quiet – most sounds muffled by the coating of snow and ice that even dulled the hiss and clap of gloved hands rubbed and slapped in chilly impatience. The only possible topic of conversation shared by all and, therefore, unspeakable. The track had virtually lost its sleepers and ballast, the rails running through a sea of glistening, eye-straining white. Teeth chattering and noses dripping, we pleaded for salvation in the form of a train to take us to town. We knew nothing of what was going on. Like most places, there was no tannoy in Harpenden – the only announcements coming from helpful station staff bellowing across the tracks if they had been advised by head office or a thoughtful signalman. And, that day, there were no announcements.

Eventually, a welcome but unusual sight greeted our eyes. Instead of the normal multiple unit – we'd have happily settled for four cars – a very smoky Type 2 diesel rounded the bend under the Carlton Road footbridge – smoky, not just because they were as a rule, but because it was pulling an LMS 4F, No. 44327, and a rake of our beloved steam-age compartment coaches. Either No. D5414 had no heating boiler or it had broken down, for the 4F was there to provide the steam heat – and that alone. A colleague and I settled for an unused brake van and travelled standing up while the diesel rushed us up to St. Pancras at record speed.

The poor old 4F, a temporary transfer to Bedford shed – she was only there for seven months, possibly to provide additional help during the adverse weather – was in a bad way when we arrived in Platform 7 in St. Pancras. In spite of its sole purpose to pass steam through the heating pipes, the ride must have been frightful with the crew holding on for dear life. The fireman looked relieved but tired as his steed provided us all with a brief moment of heat as we passed along the platform. The smell of very hot bearings greeted us. 'I don't think she's ever moved quicker than that!' the fireman muttered, as he and the driver anxiously checked her over. And he was probably right.

Had a 4F ever run at more than seventy miles per hour before?

♦

If we bunked off games at school – and I had a friend who had a sick note that gave him permanent retirement from the pleasures of cross country running, football or rugby, lucky dog – instead of the usual local at around 4:47 pm, we had a choice of two earlier trains. One was the 3:53 – the 3:20 from St. Pancras to Kettering although it was the responsibility of Leicester shed and we always thought it was a Leicester train – and the other, the 4:05 arrival in St. Albans, all stations to Luton. The 3:53 was the main attraction because it was a hotchpotch of a train – three items of compartment stock on the front, and up to five LMS corridor coaches behind, usually with an unoccupied brake on the end.

My memories of the motive power are of Standard Class 5, 4-6-0s, although I must have been unlucky because at that time, 1957, 'Compounds' were still regular performers on the train. While Nos. Nos.41095, 41078 and 41181 were noted frequently by the aficionados, I can only remember the 'Standards'. Still, travelling in a corridor coach with the guard marooned in the non-corridor brake third near the front of the train gave us free reign to sit in the ducket seat and peer along the train, watch the brake gauge with its needle bouncing as the driver applied the brakes on the approach to Harpenden Central, and enjoy the superior run behind a Class 5.

If we missed that, there was always the 4:05 which only ran to three coaches (although there was a coffin van added to the front to spice things up on one occasion) which might be hauled by anything that was available. A Stanier 3P 2-6-2 tank or even a 2P 4-4-0 were quite common fare. Sometimes, if the 'fast' was running late, this gave an excuse for a bit of a race, and if the 'slow' had a 2P, it could easily outrun the Standard with its heavier load, although our triumph might have been aided and abetted by the screamed encouragement to the crew from the first compartment! The spectacle, viewed from the 'local' as it stormed away up the bank with the 'Standard' Class 5 in hot pursuit, was one of the high-spots of those days. And with both trains having to slow for Harpenden station, it was a fairly evenly-matched race, although the local had a shorter brake-pipe to bring speed down. This could mean we would enter the station at a velocity guaranteed to take us to the very north end of the platform. I remember once getting off only by dropping onto the slope of the platform, with the loco crew apologising for our necessary alpinistic descent!

♦

On the whole, we were not party to what was going on.

Oh, some people with contacts in St. Pancras Chambers would get pre-warning of unusual events, but we spotters in short trousers were almost always surprised by peculiar workings. I remember walking along Carlton Road by the embankment one day in July, 1956, when an LNER O1 moved quickly along the down slow on a coal empties. An O1? Deep in the heart of Midland territory? Admittedly, we were on the point of losing our amazing 'Garratts', but we already had Riddles 9Fs to fill in the gaps on the roster. I didn't know why the Thompson rebuild of a Great Central Railway Class O4 was there, and my revelation a day or two later to the spotting fraternity was met with incredulity and not a little doubt.

I had a reputation for exaggeration, even in those days.

It was only later, when it turned up again and again, that I was vindicated. But we still didn't know why. Could it be possible that the Thompson rebuilds might replace Stanier's 8Fs? Whatever I might have preferred, that seemed hardly likely. It was only much later that we heard No. 63725 of Annesley had been swapped with No. 48678 in an effort to compare corrosion in the boiler tubes of the two engines as a result of the different water supplies. Annesley water was, apparently, better, as the 8F suffered nothing from its temporary transfer, while the LNER 2-8-0 started to corrode rapidly, relying partly, as it had to, on water from Toton.

The tests lasted until December of that year and, after that, LNER engines never returned, except on specials, and certainly there were no more goods engines. But, while unusual visitors were rare, they did sometimes appear.

♦

One of the lingering images in my mind is that of an Edinburgh tram rounding the corner at the foot of the Mound before it climbed the steep gradient and swung around the tight S-bend before heading south into the suburbs. It must be something to do with the rigidity of

117

rail, wheel and tram body when compared with the uncertainty and infinite variability of a rubber-tyred vehicle that never exactly repeats the trajectory of its fellows. When the cars were in a procession, they would roll along in a delightful string, like bottles in a bottling plant – each one repeating exactly the actions of its predecessor, nodding into and out of 'dished' rails as they occurred.

A character in one of my novels recalled that Edinburgh tram-scape as a result of a combination of disease and finding himself in modern Manchester.

'From time to time, his view is obscured by large single-deck trams that pass with an easy-going hiss and fold themselves around the corner at the top of a slight hill before disappearing. He remembers other trams in another city, trams that were day-to-day, matter-of-fact. They had been taken from him when he was about fifteen years of age, victims of supposed progress, but until then had been an essential part of life; his journey to school, weekend visits to that other city centre or down to the sea. Just normal and everyday. From the focus on the trams and the essential difference between the ones plying their trade in front of him and those lurching through his memory (the vehicles from his past were double-decked), he nevertheless recognises similarities; the way the vehicles move in straight lines on their tracks, their sway as they grow closer, the slight whine of their electric motors, a faint smell of hot oil mixed with warm brakes, a biting, discordant squeal as the flanges resist the change of direction on the tight curves, the hiss of the overhead wires.'

Of course, the distinctive sight of a tram on a city street is, thankfully, still with us, as trams make their comeback all over the world. Alas, not with double-deckers, as any resurgence of that configuration seems highly unlikely. This is probably down to the relative cheapness of Continental-style single-deckers where controls over vehicle length have been relaxed and novel methods for fare-collection have largely banished mobile conductors to history and museums – although, happily, they are still to be found in Blackpool.

The predictable trajectory of a tram made things easier for the passenger preparing to disembark. It wasn't going to swerve and, with a good anticipatory driver, it would come to rest evenly. A recent ride in a local bus reminded me of how good things used to be. Even with a modern single decker bus bristling with grab-rails, seat-back handles and even straps hanging from the ceiling, the swing towards the pavement, the presence of speed bumps, the irregular deceleration, and blunt automatic gear-changing, made a dignified exit impossible. I stood up and approached the side of the driver's cab in a form of weaving, drunken disorder, wildly reaching for anything that would prevent me from collapsing. The driver turned his head and grinned. He'd seen it all before – probably several times that day.

I still thanked him. He'd done his job absolutely at his best, given the circumstances. And my gratitude might make up for all the smooth stops on trams that went unthanked in my youth. With the decamping passenger and driver at opposite ends of the vehicle, appreciation could not be expressed in those days.

♦

1953. Salisbury. Easter.

My cousin was on tenterhooks.

She'd made the journey before and knew how long it could take. Things were getting tight. Her father seemed untroubled and went about his pre-trip motoring checks before reminding my cousin of the need for petrol en-route. She moved from impatience to exasperation.

Eventually, we nosed out of the drive in Bemerton and headed for Salisbury city centre and that necessary petrol stop – a leisurely, time-consuming occupation in the early fifties. We had to wait patiently for the attendant to come and serve us, followed by my uncle paying in cash at the car, with change proffered from a leather bag not unlike the type used by bus conductors at the time, before taking the slow and winding road to Southampton and, eventually, onto the New Forest side of Southampton Water, at Hythe.

My cousin was annoyed, frequently looking at her watch and sighing.

When we made our leisurely arrival at the small harbour of Hythe, my cousin was triumphantly and, it has to be said, just a little self-righteously, furious. There is a keen pleasure to be won from being right, even if acute disappointment is the consequence. There, over the water, long visible on our approach, towering improbably over trees and houses, the 'Queen Mary' was already in harbour and the tugs had practically finished their work.

Living in Harpenden at that time, the sight of any ocean-going liner was reward enough, but my cousin had wanted the trip to be special for us inlanders, to see it come up the Water with all the hullabaloo and spectacle that complicated manoeuvre promised.

She was deeply disappointed.

'A tied-up ship is all very fine but it doesn't compare with the thing sailing along,' she fumed, 'and how would *we* ever see that, other than coming up Southampton Water? It wouldn't have taken much, getting petrol the night before, leaving a little earlier …'. Etcetera…. My cousin was in full flight.

We clattered along the pier on that bizarre little train that is, precariously, still with us … an essential conveyance in the past that has become practically unique in the UK, the pier 'boat-train'. From the end of the pier we could see it properly – absolutely huge and magnificent, the pride of the Cunard transatlantic fleet, and British, too. Still in deadly competition with the French and the Americans, but surely the best?

In a few years, the idea of crossing the Atlantic on a ship would be as old-hat as riding on a horse-drawn bus –

until, of course, the arrival of the cruise liner brought it all back in a wave of simulated nostalgia and, for most, a brief moment of luxury. Already, planes were filling the skies between New York and London, with occasional refuelling stops on the way – only the demands of tradition, elegance, the ever-present gaggle of press photographers at the Southampton Terminal, not to mention a fear of flying, inhibiting their relentless advance.

So, there was the 'Mary', smoke still billowing from one of its three funnels. We sat and ate sandwiches, throwing crusts to the aggressive swans and looking at the resented 'Queen' over in Southampton, when attention turned to another and unexpected arrival. The 'Mauretania' came up the Water at the speed of a taxi with two or three tugs in attendance. Quickly, she turned and tied up.

My cousin was somewhat cheered by this unexpected development, but I was left slightly disappointed. How could such a large ship be so unimpressive? I don't know what my younger-self expected, but it wasn't this high-speed, undramatic landing. Having seen yachts tying up in St. Tropez harbour in more recent years, the 'Mauretania' seemed no more animated or exciting than the big, white, gin-palaces with their privileged clientele on the Mediterranean. Just hoving swiftly into view, round a corner, stop, tying up, done.

What was that?

♦

Another ship story.

It is the 19th of September, 1967, and I am out with my then girlfriend. She knew someone who was acquainted with Sally Carr, the lead singer of a then-obscure group that metamorphosed into the more familiar 'Middle of the Road', and they were giving what would now be called 'a gig' in a Clydebank pub. Clydebank is to be found at the western end of Glasgow. It was cold and already night-time when we arrived, but the menacing bulk of Ship 736 stood surreally over the tenements next to John Brown's shipyard. Those tenements were tall, probably four storeys, and the angle looking up towards the vessel was acute, but it towered over them easily as it reached upwards into the obscurity of the black night sky. Parts of the vessel were floodlit – I suppose they were still busy on board, building the thing – but the stern seemed to be clothed in darkness away over facing the Clyde and the south bank of the oily, sluggish river. The launch was planned for the next day and no-one in the public domain knew the name it would carry.

There were guesses and there was endless speculation, but no-one knew.

So we went into the smoky pub with a few other fans, completely outnumbered by the regulars who knew about Ship 736 well enough – many of them, doubtless, worked on her. They seemed to be somewhat taken aback by a bunch of strangers there for the entertainment and asking for 'children's drinks'. I remember enjoying the music, with Sally belting out her songs and dancing in that peculiarly Scottish way – left leg out about twelve inches, close with the right, right leg out about twelve inches, close with the left. For us Scots, that's about as good as it got. We knew our reels and country-dancing steps well enough – they were mostly about walking around and being indecisive about direction of travel, after all – but modern dancing was usually limited to bobbing the head self-consciously and returning to sipping the ale clutched in the right hand if we thought anyone was watching. And in that context, Sally danced extremely well. She could sing, too.

Next day, back teaching my primary school kids in Balornock, on the north side of Glasgow and therefore unable to witness the great event first-hand, Ship 736 was controversially named 'Queen Elizabeth 2' before the launch. Scottish Nationalists – and there were some even then – forgot that the Scottish yard was simply a contractor and that the owner could call their ship what they wanted. Also, they forgot that ships have their own numbering system that increments at its own pace – 1, 2, 3, and so on. So, they objected to a name that had never been carried by a Scottish Queen. To them, our monarch was their first 'Elizabeth', but, in the marine sense, there was already one of *them* sailing the high seas! The 'controversy' was over in a few days, in spite of being prolonged by the malicious press that is still with us today.

Like most things to do with ships, the launch, seen on television that night, was fairly undramatic. Having set the hull off by knocking out the restraining chocks way down below in the dry dock used for assembly, its progress was impeded by hundreds of tons of chains that roared promisingly along behind it before silence reigned again and the hull, nudged by a couple of powerful tugs, slowly turned . A ship being launched is put under tremendous strain, as part of the hull is still on the slipway – rigid and firm – while, in this case, the stern has to sink until buoyancy takes over and shoulders the weight of the craft. I have witnessed launches of smaller ships at Henry Robb's in Edinburgh and I can confirm the hull squeals in agony.

With tugs present, the 'Queen Elizabeth 2' quickly came to a standstill and the long job of building the superstructure and fitting-out could commence. She was practically the last ocean-going passenger ship built in the United Kingdom – the end of a tradition that commenced before records began. All that skill and talent – from marine architects to draughtsmen, from riveters to interior designers, from chain-makers to ship's painters, from boilersmiths to sailmakers, from ironmasters to carpenters – taken from us, never to return.

I might have learned to love ships, and I was certainly very sad when I saw the same 'Mauretania', seen at Southampton years before, being broken up in Thomas Ward's breaker's yard at Inverkeithing during the summer of 1966, but I enjoyed more drama in a Fairburn 2-6-4 tank barking out of St. Pancras on empty stock than those marine non-spectacles all those years ago.

But it is all about memory, and we hold on to what we love the best. Perhaps, indeed, we re-educate ourselves, constantly refreshing and, no doubt, modifying slightly in the process – like our own Vaughan Williams fantasia on a theme by Thomas Tallis. Visual memory can be unreliable and perjured, even to the point of fancying seeing something we would so wish to have seen. But I have tried to restrict these musings to certainties. Like a biographer, I have sought a second or third source to confirm mendacious recollection, so I have not spoken of a 'Remembrance' at the bufferstops in Waterloo, or an elegant 'Caley' 4-6-2 tank banking at Beattock, or of the time I fell down the stairs of a Manchester double-decker tram (only my mother recalled that one and she is now long-departed), or the little saddle tank proudly numbered '1' that I crossed off in my Western Region ABC, when it must have been just another industrial tank and not the legendary Ystalyfera Works locomotive, 'Hercules', having never, at that time, visited South Wales.

Other confirmed visual memories crowd the mind, however.

Changing at Craigleith to complete a journey from Davidson's Mains to Leith by train, a trip surely arranged for my benefit since it can hardly have been the quickest route. I remember the well-maintained Caledonian 0-4-4 tank waiting in Craigleith station, its air pump clattering and spoffling steam and oil, and the ride over the rooftops to the busy docks, before coming back in exactly the same way.

And I can visualise the curiously-profiled ferry wagons – long and low, sometimes equipped with a gently-pitched roof and covered in strange markings telling us of their French, Belgian and Italian provenance. Some had a ship's anchor painted on the side to confirm their suitability for the train ferry.

I can recall other 0-4-4 tanks moving smartly around the rails of the Isle of Wight, and the 'Crab' in St. Pancras heading the emigrant's train to Tilbury with crowds of tearful relatives saying their farewells – sometimes forever – to young couples seeking a better life.

I can still see, in my mind's eye, the 'H', yet another 0-4-4 tank, sliding though the Kent countryside, with my father sniggering at the station name, 'Ham Street and Orlestone' – why that tickled him I do not know, but as he wasn't a man who would have overlooked what he might have construed as a facetious enquiry, I remained forever ignorant on that score.

And there was the curiosity of the green 'Schools' class 4-4-0, No. 30909, slumbering behind the metal railings at the back of old Platform 4 in St. Albans with its train of green corridor coaches. Presumably, we assumed, conflating ideas, since it was a 'Schools', it had brought a party of schoolboys to some activity at St. Alban's School up near the Abbey but, on reflection, would they have needed a full train? Maybe it was more about a Kentish schools outing to Verulamium. Anyway, it seemed to appear about once a year and stayed put annoyingly in the sidings beyond our time for going home, preventing us from enjoying the sight of its departure.

I remember the tank wagons drawn up in Shrewsbury's Shropshire & Montgomeryshire Abbey station, and the roaring propeller-driven plane standing at the end of the runway at Manchester's Ringway airport with 'Aer Lingus' painted on the side, and marvelling at a real survivor – the station on the Southwold Railway, outside which we scrabbled with broken finger-nails to retrieve a lone rail spike from a discarded sleeper which was proudly taken home and then lost during one of my many house-moves.

They say one of the compensations for reaching a great age is a sharpened visual memory. I think it maybe more complex than this. Perhaps, we rely increasingly on memories of memories – a generational displacement that

125

brings me back to Vaughan Williams, hopefully, in these cases, not too wide of the authentic.

CHAPTER FIVE

SMELL

Vivarais Mallet leaving Boucieu-le-Roi 1998.

I trust I will be forgiven if I commence this chapter on a lavatorial note. But any male who visited St. Pancras Station's main gentlemen's lavatory (never a 'toilet') back in the fifties is unlikely to have forgotten it, even if it is rarely spoken about.

It was approached from the main concourse along what was then Platform 2. St. Pancras's concourse was largely across the end of the buffers – one might say the conventional location in any terminal station – but an extension along the platform and behind a make-do fence that prevented ticketless persons from boarding a train provided space for a number of offices devoted to public and non-public activities. At the far end, the stubby Platform 1 sidled in apologetically under Barlow's roof. At St. Pancras, 'Number One' meant the least important, most inconvenient, shortest landing place for a passenger train.

Readers of a certain age may remember the significance of that bastion of masculinity located at the foot of a flight of steps down which no woman would ever wish to tread. More club than convenience, it was an exclusively male domain. The combination of an infant bladder and natural excitement at a 'day out', especially with my rather stern, distant, but much loved father, meant that the end of a twenty-five mile journey from Harpenden was almost always concluded by a visit to the lavatory. The steps were, in my memory, wide, steep and ill-lit.

So my father, sighing at yet another delay to his plans – we would already have visited the bookstall for a long survey of the latest Ian Allan ABCs at my behest – would accompany me as we walked past the barber's premises on the right – vast, tiled, mirrored, stained-wood and sinisterly lit – and a boot-black who occasionally plied his trade on the left of the passageway. In my memory, there were other doors and other offices, but what these were I can no longer remember. The object of our journey was 'further on' and similarly enormous.

And the smell was unforgettable.

Don't misunderstand me. The smell was that of a particular disinfectant – wholesome, distinctive and effective. In those days, lavatories did not smell bad. They were cold, draughty places with a pervading sense of dampness but, to me, considerably more pleasant than their modern and expensive equivalents that are, in the main, warm, stifling and noisy – with hand-dryers, banging doors and the chitter-chatter of coin-operated admittance. Some of them even have piped music, as if that is imagined to be an aid to evacuation.

St. Pancras's men's emporium was quiet – the hallowed halls of this final extension of the erstwhile Midland Railway – and everything was large. The urinals were tall, chipped and private and, to a small boy, almost enveloping, with their tasteful graphics announcing the name of the specialist pottery-works who made them. The washbasins – plenty of hot water – were large enough, were it desirable, to bathe a small child, and the marble floor would have graced a roman villa. St. Pancras had another lavatory for men on the other side of the station where express trains usually arrived, but it lacked the sumptuous spaciousness of the one I have dwelt on.

As for ladies, I have no memory of where they 'retired'.

Perhaps, they didn't.

Speaking of lavatories, that at Kings Cross was, in contrast, long and narrow with two entrances, both off the legendary Platform 10 (now No. 8), and was also subterranean like its smarter cousin across the road. Whether they were still obtaining disinfectant from their respective headquarters I do not know, but the odour in King's Cross was quite different. It's not that I made a study of such things, and I cannot recollect any nasal analysis of, say, Waterloo or Paddington, but I daresay they were all dissimilar in those days.

Regional disparity was not restricted simply to rolling stock.

Even at an early age, I realised my father was a man full of secret fears and one of them was a fear of infection. So, while, as a young child, I was supposed to perform the necessary with minimal contact with myself, nothing else down there in those hallowed halls was to be touched at all. So the steep staircase had to be negotiated without recourse to the handrail, and visits to the 'stalls' would be discouraged with references to, 'we only left home an hour ago, why didn't you go there?', followed by many sighs and a highly embarrassing masking of the lavatory seat in yards of fresh, itchy, non-absorbent, disinfectant-impregnated, Izal-like toilet paper, that made the process fraught with a wide variety of potential disasters. A lifelong problem with haemorrhoids may have its roots in those days-out, assigning lunch, teas and sweets to bowels requiring emptying that was firmly and repeatedly discouraged until a return to the more hygienic and exclusive surroundings of home many hours later.

♦

Thinking further about 'being underground', it would not have been at all difficult, blindfolded, to distinguish between London Transport and, for example, the Waterloo & City or, at the other end of the country, the Glasgow Subway.

London always seems to me to be a toxic mixture of ozone and human bodies, but each line was different. Leaving aside the sub-surface routes that reflected the weather at the time, pleasantly warm in summer and bitterly cold and frequently windy in winter, with little to tempt nasal memory, the Piccadilly was cool and neutral, the Central line was warm and perfumed, and the Bakerloo always seemed to have an electrical smell as if something serious was shorting out in the tunnels. This was partly down to the rolling stock – the Central Line at the time I am thinking about being all pre-1938 stock with three or four heavy, hot, motor/driving cars in each seven or eight car train spitting fire and danger from the louvered or shuttered compartments that took up the equivalent of a quarter of a whole car. The Piccadilly Line was a mixture of these trains and the 1938 stock, still, at the time of writing, running in the Isle of Wight. The Northern Line was all 1938 stock and therefore not so interesting.

Today, the 'tubes' are less distinctive, with coffee and fast-food odours sweeping down the escalators from on high, but probably, overall, more salubrious than in the past. In fact they are 'royally tarted up' nowadays, part of the attempt by public transport officials to turn the process of being on-the-move into an extension of our living rooms and make it less and less like travelling by train. This all started, in my view, with the 'roman invasion' of

Tottenham Court Road, when Eduardo Paolozzi's pop-art mosaics, commissioned by the Greater London Council in a joint effort with London Transport, appeared in the 1980s. This amounted to a rash of colourful tiles that took an age to install and which had the effect of reducing the bore of the pedestrian ways by an overall thickness of cement and shiny irrelevance. They must love them, though, as they have been reinstalled after the Crossrail / Elizabeth Line disruption.

Incidentally, in the past, enthusiast and layman alike knew the difference between the Underground and the Tube. Now, nobody, not even the railway press, makes any distinction at all. This can lead to misunderstandings, as I recently read an article in a railway magazine announcing, in breathless tones, that the new rolling stock on the Metropolitan line could not be used on the Piccadilly line owing to its larger profile, as if this was an extraordinary revelation of a little-perceived complication. To us, it would have been blindingly obvious.

No one in the fifties and sixties would have entered into such a debate. We knew the Tube was bored, often at considerable depth, through London clay, with a tunnel diameter of only twelve feet, whereas the Underground was, mostly, 'cut and cover' – constructed laboriously by digging a trench in the roads which, once equipped with rails and roofed, enabled the road to be restored to its former purpose. Built in that way, normal profiled rolling stock could be and was used. Only the Elizabeth Line has complicated this distinction by being drilled like a tube line of the past but for trains of a normal loading gauge.

The Waterloo & City was not known as "The Drain" for nothing – it was as though a sewer diverted during its construction had been inadequately sealed. The old trains, I suppose, added to the olfactory experience, a breath of the Southern Railway in the modern age. Once again, by the time the scents reached either of the two stations, they were not unpleasant, but they were very distinctive. No doubt, modern train brakes, plus the inevitable Costa or

Starbucks, will have changed things now, but I wonder if it still enjoys the old sobriquet?

When I started to use the Waterloo & City, the carriages announced their former owner ('Southern Railway') on ventilators on the end walls above the emergency communicating doors. Through these ventilators rushed a constant wind while the train was moving and the change of smell announced not only our impending arrival, but also the destination for anyone with more than a lamentable sense of direction. Waterloo's was airy and cold, while Bank betrayed the presence of connections to London Transport and was noticeably warmer.

Glasgow's subway was only a few feet below street level, so it was more like taking a brief diversion under the road, apart from the smell of hot brakes as the little trains roared into the stations. For someone used to the London Underground where trains were mostly six coaches or more, and much statelier, Glasgow's two-car motor / trailer trains were a high-speed novelty. And, to me, the Mersey Railway always smelled of disinfectant, although whether this was just about Liverpool's self-regarding superiority, or a need to constantly clean up, I could not say.

Glasgow, in terms of subterranean transportation, did not, of course, only enjoy the delights of the foot-foot gauge subway. There were two other lines that went underground for several stations and, until the end of the 1950s, they were both steam operated. That means that, while steam on London's sub-surface lines had been banished for over fifty years (save for the goods trains from Paddington, and the passenger and goods trains from the St. Pancras and Kings Cross directions), Glasgow continued to experience smoke-filled tunnels and all the accompanying mess and inconvenience of steam haulage until comparatively recent times. Both Glasgow lines supported a service frequency that any urban line would expect to provide, so the smell and pollution were of heroic proportions. Both were east–west lines conveniently linking substantial parts of the former Caledonian and North British networks that otherwise warranted sizeable termini serving the city centre from the north or south.

Downriver from the centre of the city, ocean-going ships and the ship-building yards prevented any further bridging in those days. It is only now – with river traffic practically non-existent – that new road bridges can be thrown across the Clyde with equanimity. As the city centre is on the north side of the river, the low-level lines gave convenient access to the commercial and business hubs in a way that many conurbations would envy. Both lines paralleled each other from Partick in the west to Bellgrove and Bridgeton in the east. Central Low Level and Queen Street Low Level were only about a quarter of a mile apart, but they continued to provide a brisk service until electrification of the Queen Street line and abandonment of the other. Due to some serious failure of the electric trains, steam came back for a glorious swan-song but, by late 1961, the electrics were trusted and the steam trains were no more. In recent years, passenger traffic has returned so prodigiously to Glasgow that the Central Low Level lines have reopened. Of course, they are now smell-free – or nearly so. There is still that between-train air of the damp cellar about both tunnels, plus vomit on a Saturday night, of course, but you would have to have been there in the fifties to really experience the sulphurous magnificence of the Victorian underground railway.

◆

It may come as a surprise to many that smoking was permitted on main line trains until as late as 2005 on the Great North Eastern Railway trains out of King's Cross, although it had been banned gradually on other lines leading up to that time. And on the London Underground, they banned smoking on trains from July 1984, leaving the habit permitted on station platforms until the ghastly Kings Cross fire in 1987.

So I was brought up to tolerate the smell of smoking everywhere – not just on trains. And because it was permitted – normal, if you like – we never really thought much about it. One might *prefer* a non-smoker, but that is not the same as the histrionic arm-waving and pretend-coughing that accompanied the period of transition, and still persists where a luckless smoker hovering outside a block of offices is encountered by a (usually) female rising star who seeks to 'make a point'. Although I was never a smoker (other than in the back row of Harpenden's Embassy Cinema, before girls – who, on the whole did not smoke at all – became the attraction), I cannot remember being particularly bothered in the past by travelling in a smoking compartment.

It was only as growing intolerance shrank the provision for smokers on long-distance trains that it became really unpleasant. In the last days of their freedom, smokers on HSTs were restricted to one coach (usually, one from the end) which concentrated all the smoking into an eighth of the train on my then-line from Leeds to London. The air in that car would turn blue and the stench was quite extraordinary. On a full train, when choosing the ideal seat was impossible, a long-distance ride in that haze would leave the eyes running, nausea suppressing the appetite, and clothes impregnated for a week. I tended to prefer travelling in the front coach going north as there was less human passage, leading to a quieter journey, but any visit to the buffet car required a traverse of the 'cancer car' as we began to call it.

♦

And now, a confession.

Boarding my HST back to Leeds in the eighties after a long and exacting day working near Baker Street, I settled down with my collection of short stories by H. E. Bates and my eagerly-anticipated sandwich, coffee and Mars Bar nestling in a paper bag, courtesy of one of the burgeoning numbers of food outlets on Kings Cross station where originality is restricted to the name of the purveyors. It doesn't matter which one you use, the food all tastes exactly the same.

A perfectly nice, harmless, elderly gentleman sat down with his wife in the bay opposite and, after exchanging a few pleasantries with each other and dividing the Evening Standard touchingly between them, he proceeded to remove his pipe from the side pocket of an expensive Harris Tweed jacket, carefully filled it from a pack of quality Virginia pipe tobacco – which he lovingly shredded before forcing it carefully into the bowl – and lit up.

The coach was a non-smoker and I told him so.

I was courteous but firm – I valued my peaceful and reasonably fresh environment enough to speak out. Besides which, we had a long journey ahead of us. And I was eating, after all. And someone else would have said something eventually, I felt sure.

In fairness, he was overcome with remorse. He apologised profusely, to which I smiled and nodded, secretly proud of one small win in a day that had lacked them overall – it had, after all, been a hard day at the office – and he put his pipe into the side pocket of his expensive Harris Tweed jacket. I thought no more about it, opening my ham salad sandwich and sipping my coffee – with the coveted Mars Bar to follow.

I found the H. E. Bates story I had been reading and, after a quick scan of the previous pages to 'catch up', I started to read. Before many minutes had passed, however, I was aware of a strange smell followed by considerable agitation across the gangway. I looked up. The famous Harris Tweed jacket was smouldering well, fine wool threads wrinkling and curling in the heat. The luckless gentleman was frantically beating the fire out, broadcasting apologies around the coach to anyone who would listen. In no time, the conflagration was extinguished, and the pipe had been removed from his carbonised pocket, while the soggy contents of the pipe bowl were scraped into a tin he had secreted about his person. He looked at me and again apologised, but it was me who was wretched and felt a need for contrition. Keeping to the rules and being downright self-centred needs to be tempered by the personality of one's fleeting adversary.

With proscription comes intolerance.

Exaggerated health-warnings make us irrational.

Selfishness makes us speak out inappropriately.

Like sheep, we all follow and we all condemn.

♦

The big difference in the days of steam was the tendency for smokers to keep the windows shut more than non-smokers. One might think this would be the reverse of reason, but smokers enjoyed their fug, besides which, an open window would herald wind-borne ash swirling about and spoiling one's clothes and those of fellow passengers. In those days, too, smoking was a more variable pursuit, with cigars, cheroots and pipes mixing it in strength with the cigarettes that might be proprietary packets or hand-rolled, involving the deft manipulation of a tobacco pouch and the appearance of Rizla papers in a little flat pack, plus a small machine to do the job. Working men (it was mostly men) often made their cigarettes by hand, delicately thumb-and-fingering the components in a rolling action until the gummed edge of the paper was licked end-to-end before a final twist and the result could be enjoyed. But, when the hour I travelled arrived, either to school or to an office in London, the working men were already at work, so my travelling companions – the ones who rolled their own – had their little machines to reduce the nicotine-stains on their professional fingers and, at the same time, obtain a more perfect result.

One of my earliest memories is of my maternal grandfather, cruelly handicapped by a stroke that left him paralysed down his left side when I was about four years old, teaching me – on my holidays to Edinburgh – how to roll his cigarettes using his little silver machine. When he died, my grandmother made sure I got the machine as a memento. To my regret, I have, long-since, mislaid the precious device, but I still recall in detail what would now be considered a most unsuitable lesson for a grandchild! I can still remember the scents of cigarette-making in Davidson's Mains, and the rich odours of Senior Service, Craven 'A', Shag and Cuban cigars on trains linger in the mind.

♦

On buses, there was a general consensus that smokers restricted themselves to the rear on single-deckers – even when, in those days, the door could be installed at either end – while smokers were expected to be athletic enough to climb the stairs on double-deckers. This is a generalisation, and the less spry might brazen it out on the facing seats near the rear downstairs, or even hover on the platform, stepping politely off and on each time the bus stopped, perhaps winning brownie-points by supporting the arm of a shopping-bag encumbered woman or assisting in the removal of a folded pushchair from beneath the stairs.

One thing that was firmly prohibited, with a notice to that effect, was spitting, something one would have preferred not to smell at all – far less witness. I remember that restriction inscribed on a neat little transfer at the foot of the stairs on the STLs that operated on the Route 321 from Rickmansworth to Luton before the eventual dominance of the RTs. All the smoking that went on with practically every male adult was added to by chewing tobacco, a fairly obnoxious and, frankly, dangerous practice that has all-but died out in the UK (pun intended), even if it is still fairly common in parts of the United States. However, coal miners in deep pits in the UK chewed tobacco right up until Kellingley Colliery closed in 2015 for, wait for it, medicinal reasons. I think it was something to do with inhaling dust and stopping dryness in the throat!

So, smoking, chewing tobacco, and the prevalence of bronchitis in those days when antibiotics were not part of the nation's diet, caused the liberal creation of phlegm. Britain had to be educated about good manners concerning the disposal of catarrh and, judging by the absence of notices on subsequent bus fleets and the comparative rarity of seeing spitting in public (other than on the football field, where it is universal), one must assume that is a habit that has largely disappeared.

Of course, it is better that smoking is no longer permitted in and around public transport, but I do not like the want of forbearance that has come in the wake of its prohibition – even if I, on the occasion mentioned above, was guilty of overt bigotry.

Smoking went from being 'cool', even illustrated on greetings cards to convey a degree of sophistication, to being seen as akin to pitiful drug dependence in a single generation.

♦

Clever people could tell the difference between the types of coal used in fireboxes on the railways simply by inhaling the smoke. While I could appreciate the difference between Great Western engines burning distinctive Welsh coal and, say, a train on the lines out of St. Pancras that would be fired on fuel from Nottinghamshire or Derbyshire, I did not, otherwise, share this doubtful skill.

But it was more than simply a schoolboy game.

Locomotive designers the world over have had to know what kind of fuel would be used before taking pen to paper in the drawing office. In the United Kingdom, the earliest steam engines burned coke which, in an enclosed space, can be extremely toxic. That is one of the reasons why locomotive crews were reluctant to work in enclosed cabs and, in one instance on the Stockton & Darlington Railway, management had to remove generous, comfortable, all enclosed cabs on two engines used over the cold, wet, windy and often snowbound summit between Barnard Castle and Tebay after complaints about sickness and dizziness reached the ears of the Directors. Coke required different draughting arrangements from those required by a coal burner, as did oil burning.

Who can forget the smell and noise emitted by the Ffestiniog engines converted to burn oil in the past! They smelt and sounded, with their roaring burners, like badly-maintained diesel locomotives – so good those days are behind us. But locomotive design determined by the fuel burnt was a factor, too, in Germany, where some engines were designed to burn lignite, the stage in physical and biological development between wood (itself a fuel used in railway locomotive fireboxes, but not very much in the UK) and coal. Lignite was – is, since it continues to be burned in vast quantities in German power stations, a brown coal that burns with a distinctive smell and copious quantities of brown smoke. Calorifically, it is better than wood but inferior to coal, so a lot of lignite was needed to fulfil a given function, and German locomotives of the day that were going to be fed with lignite had large fireboxes and big tenders. A similar fuel is used in briquette form by the Vivarais metre-gauge line in France, and their 0-6-6-0 Mallet tanks setting off from Lamastre, (Ardèche) in the foothills of the Massif Central is a case of 'once smelled and seen, never forgotten' *(see the image at the start of this chapter)*.

Still, I envied that lad who could differentiate between an express arriving in Kings Cross from Leeds, Grantham, Newcastle or Edinburgh, simply by the smell of the smoke.

♦

When the HSTs started to operate on the Leeds to Kings Cross services, a distinctive smell would seep into the coach whenever the train was decelerating. These trains were a good deal faster than anything we had known before and the timetable demanded the demise, once and for all, of dignified slowing for stations. So, we could come down from one-hundred miles an hour to a station stop in a very short time indeed. This required new braking systems and new materials, and I took a certain amount of pleasure, when asked by uninformed fellow-passengers what the smell was, in saying it was asbestos pads acting on the disc brakes. At the time, there were a lot of scares about asbestos in the building industry, so I did point out that they were in no danger and that it was just a smell. At the time, I knew not whether I was right about any of the technology, but I enjoyed the look on people's faces!

In fact, it was more-or-less as I had described, and it is only recently that new compounds using ceramics and asbestos, and even steel fibres and asbestos, have been perfected for use in speed retardation on both rail and road vehicles. We all talk about train speed but it is worthwhile remembering that increasing speed adds to problems of stopping and the need for a greater distance between advising a train of a hazard and the hazard itself. In the days of semaphore signals and early high speed runs, the LNER in particular insisted that at least two signalling sections ahead be clear before their 'Coronation' or 'Silver Jubilee' trains entered section. This requirement was repeated when the high-speed diesel Pullmans of the 1960's made their entrance.

♦

When I was a child, I suffered a lot from tonsillitis. Antibiotics were not generally prescribed and doctors of mature years were wary of them. So, the response to my pathology followed a general pattern of my getting a very high temperature, an attack of speaking-in-tongues hallucination and nightmares, absence from school approved, two days at least of high fever with no improvement, a home-visit by the family doctor, a recognition that I would never get better on my own, a reluctantly-issued prescription for penicillin, a bit of a negotiation about having a loan of the one and only family radio after every breakfast times, and a further seven days of confinement to bed while I gradually regained my strength. This would happen seven to ten times a year until, at the age of ten, I was sent off to St. Albans City Hospital to have my tonsils and adenoids removed. Consequence? An end to a frequently-adopted excuse for being off school, and the commencement of annual bouts of hay-fever.

There were compensations for this highly-interrupted school regime – not the least being reading, one of my lasting pleasures. As well as the inevitable comics, mostly the 'Eagle', and magazines such as the 'Meccano Magazine', I read almost anything I could get my hands on.

Sometimes, when I was feeling particularly rough and reading was not a sensible option, and even 'Music while you Work' on the Light Programme grated, I would sleep and doze my way through the day. Lying there, especially in the summer, with the windows open, I would sometimes awaken to clouds of brown smoke drifting up through my bedroom window. Although we lived in Station Road, we were on the corner of Cowper Road which, unusually at that time, was a fully-paved turning off the main thoroughfare, and its intersection with Station Road was graced by a gas lamp-post and a strategically-placed water hydrant. There was always a lot of activity at our corner, what with the lamp-lighter, clambering up to light the lamp and, when necessary, replacing the mantles, before he set off with the ladder hanging off his bicycle, his right-leg permanently at an accommodating angle to clear the ladder and still remaining able to pedal, the Fire Brigade coming around and testing the hydrant by sloshing water all over the place, and the sucking-lorry periodically cleaning out the gully.

Although the hydrant was principally there to extinguish house fires, it had another valuable purpose. The steam-roller, which lived down at the gas works, would get as far as the end of Cowper Road before needing replenishment of its water tanks. I do not remember it ever negotiating Station Road which was steep and, even in those days, fairly busy. So, it would amble around the side roads from its home, taking the hill in easy stages, until it arrived outside our house. I suppose it was a particularly frequent visitor during the period of surfacing Harpenden's side roads – many of which were unmetalled when I was born.

The steam-roller had a long coil of hose hanging off the back, and the old chap who drove it would open the hydrant cover in the road with a metal lance he used to break up the clinker in the firebox and then fill the belly-tanks – a long and laborious process.

While this was going on, the brown smoke from the long chimney would curl into the atmosphere and roll over our garden fence where, trapped between our garage, the house and our neighbour's boundary, it would lazily accumulate, seeking an escape route.

It would have been a good idea, appreciating my condition, if I had closed the window. But I was often too ill to do the sensible. Besides, I rather liked the smell and the sounds. At the end of the task, the road often had a small pile of ashes in the gutter which would wait until the firemen came to test the hydrant again – the opportunity having been taken to clean and stoke the fire.

And in my room, the smell of the smoke would linger for hours.

♦

Partly because of almost universal smoking, plus the use of steam engines, and the fact that windows were under the control of the passengers, railway compartments had a distinctive smell. To me, it wasn't unpleasant, although its origins probably were a rich mixture of damp – especially if a window had been left open overnight by mistake – steam, coal smuts, body odours with every imaginable provenance, cigarette and other tobacco products, oil and dirt from passengers' clothing (remember, this morning's train full of city gents with pomaded hair and after-shave on their chins was yesterday's early morning service for workmen wearing their one-pair-a-week boiler-suits), stale perfume, Brylcreem staining the seat backs at head height, and the odd whiff from industry that the train passed.

Distinctive, but not unpleasant.

I know my mother used to talk so readily of 'filthy railway carriages' that the phrase became an unconsidered and extreme *leitmotif* to any conversation about railways. She even, evilly I thought, longed for the arrival of the diesel trains promised for the St. Pancras to Bedford services – a step her eldest son saw as a sort of death penalty – inevitable, unwarranted, unjust, and terribly final – on the grounds that suddenly we would be travelling in antiseptic splendour. When the diesels did come, some of the old smells disappeared for ever, but others arrived – predominantly the exhaust from the engines slung under the floor – but she wouldn't be swayed. Her opinions would not have worried me much but, rather like my father, it translated into a bigoted and acute fear of contamination from the 'filthy things' and, in her company, we had to develop scene-of-crime police officer's techniques for avoiding touching anything.

Fortunately, she believed her own myths, and the arrival of the diesels enabled us to be careless once more – as careless as we always were out of her company.

♦

Horses have been man's faithful servant from time immemorial. They were used throughout the world for transport and locomotion, and are as familiar to us as the backs of our hands. Humans have an enormous affinity with them – perhaps more so than with dogs which have equally enjoyed a long partnership as both servant and friend. My own contact with horses has been limited to pony rides and as an observer and, while their use in the scheme of things has changed, they have been remarkably adept at making themselves essential over the decades. In my childhood, they delivered the milk and coal, collected the rags and bones, ploughed a few conservative farmer's fields, and were even the prime movers in a corner of Fife where they drew carts that collected domestic waste into the 1970s.

I also remember seeing the wild-eyed, sea-coal gatherers scavenging for 'black diamonds' near Ashington in Northumberland. Into the surf they would drive their tough little ponies drawing ramshackle two-wheeled carts, using a contraption made of wood and netting to scoop up coal floating up from the piles of colliery waste that, in those days, was tipped directly into the sea. Coal, you see, floats.

It was odd to see this ancient activity – closely guarded and, when necessary, violently protected by whole families, dirt-black and wet from head to foot, living on the fringes of society like latter-day boatmen on the canals or itinerant didicoy scrap dealers – within shouting distance of 'Big Geordie', the 3,000 ton dragline walking grab (too heavy for caterpillar tracks or wheels) employed by the National Coal Board to remove the overburden for eventual opencast mining.

Local people would wink and grin when I asked where 'Big Geordie' was.

'Who knows,' they'd reply, as if they were talking about an acquaintance more feared than loved. 'He was here a four-week ago but now he's gang oop the coast, someways. If you drive up the coast road, ye'll see his jib over the hill. You cannae miss it.'

So I drove, and was rewarded by sight of that vast, swinging jib as it carved its way into a cavernous hole of its own making. 'Big Geordie', a 6,000 horse-power behemoth built by Bucyrus-Erie, came along at the end of steam and is, itself, now a memory – broken up because, since the British government turned its back on coal, it is no longer needed.

I guess the sea-coal gatherers may still be there in small numbers, as coal still surfaces today, long after the closure of the pits. If so, they will still be shouting gruff encouragement to their horses as the carts momentarily lurch to a halt on submerged, surfed rocks in the icy sea.

Some of them may even be redundant or retired miners with a nostalgia for coal. 'It gets into your blood,' they'll say. 'There's nothing like coal – or the men who cut the coal.'

In a book of this nature, it would be quite wrong to forget the contribution horses have made in the context of railways and tramways. Indeed, in the earliest days, everything was a tramway, upon which 'trams' laden with coal and rock revolutionised transportation. Horses were used to move the trams along unless the gradients were too steep and ropes or cables became necessary. Horses have been used on the railways since long before steam. Woodcuts, originating in Germany in mediaeval times, show wonky 'waggons' (old spelling) on primitive tracks made of iron or even timber being drawn by strong ponies, while horses were widely used on railways and plateways in the UK from the 18th Century right through to the end of the 1950s. The last proper horse-plateway was the Nantlle in north-west Wales which ran until 1963 and, unbelievably, was operated by British Railways – still with horse power – the last such operation by a Nationalised organisation in the United Kingdom. Shunting horses, too, lasted in certain railway goods yards until the 1960s, and no self-respecting preservation site dedicated to trams will not have an old horse-car and at least the capability of reenacting a scene that preceded their steam and electric progeny from time to time. Indeed, the Douglas horse tramway in the Isle of Man, devoid of all mechanical locomotion, is a National treasure – or at least it should be.

Horses are immensely strong, but they need a considerable amount of fodder to keep their vegetarian diet satisfied. This, in turn, makes a vast quantity of smelly horse droppings which presents their masters with a major disposal challenge. In the days of horse trams on city streets, thousands of tons of horse-manure had to be shovelled up and loaded into railed trucks to be moved out of the stable areas in a highly organised exercise. Fortunately, horse manure had a value in those days, and money could be made by selling it for agricultural purposes. Dead and dying horses were also a precious commodity in the manufacture of glue and other by-products. With a team of 3,000 horses for its modest 31 miles of track, Glasgow was just one undertaking that acquired and disposed of horses, and their by-products, at a prodigious rate.

To us, of course, horses are seen in ones and twos, and it easy to forget the vast industry that grew up around the business of horse power, or appreciate the speed at which it shrank when mechanisation took hold. But it is all very pleasant to ride a tram, or a Llangollen canal boat for that matter, behind the swaying rump of a horse and, yes, to smell the droppings – infinitely more acceptable than those of carnivorous animals. But it is still a distinctive smell, and more common when I was a child.

I remember, when the National Tramway Museum at Crich was in its infancy, they acquired a Sheffield horse car which, on high days and holidays, would be tethered to a local farm horse to give rides – long before they electrified the line. A case of preservation imitating reality if ever there was one. The horse was very large but extremely docile. There was, however, a noticeable reluctance on the part of some of the children to go anywhere near the animal. Children, brought up on

'Doctor Who' and blood-and-guts cowboy stories, were, frankly, scared of the horse. How far we have moved away from the commonplace of only a generation before!

♦

My first winter of working in London would go down in history – not, I add, because of my involvement or contribution, but because Mother Nature threw everything it could at Britain in terms of shocking weather, together with a phenomenon that had its last swansong in December of 1962.

Smog.

The word is often used inaccurately these days, being conflated with fog.

Smog was, and is, not fog.

Fog is grey in colour, smog was yellow. Fog is odourless, apart from a slight sensation of dampness. Smog had an acidic, rotten-egg odour. Fog doesn't catch your throat. Even as a seventeen year old, a run along the passages below St. Pancras and a two-steps-at-a-time leap up the wood-block stairs to reach the main-line station would leave me breathless and gasping in the smog. Others who retained their dignity and walked sedately from the Underground, but were older than I, often grasped at railings and coughed uncontrollably, searching for handkerchiefs which they would clutch to their noses, and holding their chests before bending down to recover themselves. When I did it, just as an experiment, a few indrawn breaths would leave a round, yellow stain on my handkerchief. Smog hung under the graceful Barlow roof to the point where even the yellow glow from the suspended lamps rendered the tops of the arches invisible. Smog swirled like a mist – a very heavy mist.

Even though steam had largely disappeared from the London railways, there were still vast quantities of coal burned in the capital. From Thames-side power stations to the many terraced houses with their comforting coal fires, under normal conditions the smoke simply went away up into the atmosphere, and we were certainly not measuring pollution as we do nowadays. But smog was dangerous and it snarled up the traffic – both road and rail. I remember policemen on traffic duty carrying torches, courageously stepping in and out of the traffic to bring some degree of order to a Euston Road that resembled the traffic conditions in Karachi. No-one knew when to set off, when to stay still, or even where to go. And at about that time, I saw a fireman on one of our few steam passenger-trains shinning up a signal-ladder and, using his hands, confirming to his driver, by feeling for the arm, that the signal was pulled off.

It was that dense.

Smog was not a condition peculiar to Britain. They still have it in China and, once again, coal is blamed. The hidden killer, carbon monoxide from road vehicles, is probably worse, but we have our Clean Air Acts, coal is gone, so we sleep easy in our beds.

♦

Passing trains, during the time of which I am speaking, often left their calling cards in terms of smells. I remember 'Earl Marischal', one of the rather ungainly 'Pacific' rebuilds of Gresley's P2 2-8-2 locomotives, rushing through Welwyn Garden City on the up-through lines pulling a fish train bound for, we supposed, a yard near Billingsgate. Those trains, now but a memory, were vital to both the railways and the fishing industry. The fishing fleets followed the shoals in the days when 'herring was king', and the old LNER dominated the trade from Peterhead and Fraserburgh on the north-east coast of Scotland to Harwich, by way of Aberdeen, Dundee, the Fife fishing villages, Fort William, Mallaig and Silloth in the west, and Leith, Eyemouth, the north-east ports, Hull and Grimsby and all the way across East Anglia.

Every coastal town worth its salt had its fishing

community and a branch line or siding to serve it. When one realises the LNER experience was repeated by the LMS all down the west coast of Scotland and England, and the Southern and Great Western further south, fishing was a huge and important industry in which railways played an essential role. Many enthusiasts nowadays might do a double-take at the thought of an express engine like that rebuilt P2 working what, at first sight, was a goods train, and they sometimes cast aspersions on the merit of the Thompson 'Pacific' rebuilds, citing their frequent employment on such trains as evidence of their supposed shortcomings. But that would be to discredit something unworthily. Fish trains were scheduled at express train speeds, and many were fitted with vacuum brakes or were, at least, 'piped' so that any braked vehicles on the train could be used effectively. When one considers that all fish wagons were four-wheelers, it will be appreciated that the crews who worked these trains were extremely skilled. A smooth 'pull' was needed to get forty or fifty fish-vans on the move – a broken coupling and its ensuing delay could prove disastrous for the perishable load – and every change of speed had to be handled very delicately. But, of course, the payload was fish, and, in spite of the vast quantities of ice loaded in great blocks into each wagon, there was quite a smell attached to the process.

Many of the vans will have started their journeys five hundred miles and more north of the capital. They will have stood on the quayside while they were loaded, by hand, fish-box by fish-box, and then coupled up to the local branch goods train, to be wheeled into a junction on a far-away main line. Then, perhaps, into a yard in Aberdeen or Dundee, where the train for the south was marshalled and a big 'Pacific' coupled onto the front end. Normally, the engine would have been changed once or twice en-route, all the time the ice melting and the fish warming gently. So, banging through Welwyn Garden City as quickly as it could go, No. 60502, was reaching the end of the journey, its wagons oozing quantities of melt-water onto the tracks and filling the station with the scents of the sea.

Spare a thought for the guards in their vans at the end of each of those long-lost and lamented fish trains. You can be sure the front door of the guards van would have been firmly closed!

♦

In Harpenden, just before the little chicane on the approach to Platform 4, the station box's up slow outer home signal sometimes held up a goods train. Normally, the signalmen would try to get the line cleared before progress was impeded, as a sharp up gradient stood in the path of the train that had, in all probability, been slumbering in the permissive block section that ended at Harpenden Junction. Trains could spend an age in that permissive block section. Besides, by the time the goods train reached that home signal, it was onto the tracks shared by local passenger trains and a slow departure could disrupt the timetable.

Sometimes, though, things wouldn't go according to plan, and the 8F would ease to a halt at the signal and whistle impatiently for the road while, maybe, the Hemel Hempstead branch engine would complete its shuffle into the goods yard ahead of it. So, the big goods engine stood and waited. If the first ten or fifteen wagons were cattle trucks, the relative silence of a stationary steam-hauled train would be interrupted by impatient and unhappy cattle lowing and shuffling their feet on their meagre bed of straw. This was not placed there for the animals' comfort or even sustenance. It was to aid cleaning the cattle truck at the end of the journey. But, in the meantime, one heard the endless shifting of feet and intermittent mooing, while what might well be their last meal worked its way odoriferously to the floor of the van and we, subsequently, reaped the benefit on our Sunday dinner plates.

Nowadays, few, if any, animals travel by train, other

than pampered cats and adored dogs. Even the racehorses have abandoned rail – the highly-valued beasts swaying and surging up and down the motorways instead.

Now, all we have are containers from China, stone from the uplands, and nuclear flask trains safely carrying their deadly load. Which smell of nothing at all.

♦

As an aside, in the years leading up to the early sixties, cars really were cars.

That is to say, they were unreliable, draughty, slow, noisy and chiefly black, but they proudly bore a British ancestry, with Austins, Morrises, Standards and Hillmans to the fore. Even the Vauxhalls and Fords, American in terms of ownership, were stubbornly British in appearance. No self-respecting American would have been seen dead driving a Ford Popular. Of course, they lacked any sort of mechanical or personal refinement, but they were, nevertheless, characterful and fun, and there were things one could do with a car to create unusual smells.

For some reason, our humour in those days was often about creating and being aware of unusual smells.

It didn't matter which make one bought, under the bonnet everything was always much the same. There would be the radiator – usually wedged with araldite in my experience in a vain attempt to reduce the effect of leaks – a fan, a sizeable iron cylinder head, the block running front to back, four (usually four) spark-plugs screwed into the top of the block and a distributor that put a pulse of electricity into the spark plugs at roughly the right time for ignition of the fuel to take place. There were other bits, of course, but they were hidden away and didn't really concern us. My first car had its petrol tank under the bonnet, right in front of the windscreen. It was well caulked up with araldite, too, as fuel dripped intermittently from it onto the exhaust pipe which, when hot, caused small puffs of smoke to rise, distinctly noticeable on the nose, even while travelling along the road.

We liked to live dangerously in those days.

When Japanese influence hit the streets and engines became more secretive about their working parts – the complete opposite of hemlines at the time – the vicarious fun was almost over. But before then, the car to tackle above all others was the wedding car. If one was wealthy, the wedding arrangements would include limousines and liveried drivers having a crafty fag dawdling on the pavement while waiting for the bride and groom to emerge from the church, so they were practically impossible to 'doctor'. The chauffeurs even took a strong objection to a string of baked bean tins tied to the rear bumper, so what we really wanted to do would have been impossible. Sometimes, when the wedding was a 'rich' one, they would still be there at the end of the reception, ready to wheel the happy couple off to the airport. In those instances, there was nothing to do but get drunk, smile weakly at the official photographer, and take compromising pictures of the bridesmaids. But if you were reasonably poor, and most of my circle were reasonably poor, the limo was restricted to the home-to-church-to-reception legs, and the new Mr and Mrs would rely on the Best Man to look after the groom's polished-up jalopy on the gravel outside the hotel or church-hall.

Oh, what a mistake.

It was then, during endless speeches, the pacification of moment-spoiling page-boys, and the embarrassing and dubious pleasure of a whirling Gay Gordon, that an opportunity could be grasped.

The string of cans was traditional, and paint-etching shaving cream or toothpaste on the bonnet were quite common, but access to the 'going away' car usually meant availability of the car-door keys and that meant all precaution was rendered ineffective.

In those days, when the cast-iron head was the highest point on an engine (I looked inside the bonnet of the car which I bought recently and I was astounded at the acres of plastic and unrecognisable gubbins that met my eye), anyone could see that it was tailor-made for a kipper. So, someone was detailed in advance to acquire such a fish and place it on the block while no-one important was around. Any number of crazy-hatted aunts, and in-laws with oversized and tasteless outfits, would have taken a dim view. And, of course, it was a more subtle trick than the cans rattling along behind the car or even the potato up the exhaust pipe that, usually, prevented the engine from starting, but just occasionally, when the car was really old, split the exhaust pipe with a thunderous roar, somewhat adjusting the first few days of honeymoon arrangements.

With the kipper, one had to be content with one's imagination.

No doubt the happy couple drove off, thanking their lucky stars they had got off lightly. A moment's pause by the side of the road to unhitch the cans? That would be fine. But, twenty-five miles in a from-cold car and the engine would warm up – and so would the kipper.

If a gently-warming fish was recognisable as just that – a gently-warming fish – the hapless couple would have recognised things instantly and the new groom, swearing under his breath and planning justifiable revenge, could have rectified the situation. But, in the dizzy, swirling, charged atmosphere of a post-wedding wedding car, excitement, and the smell of nail varnish, perfume and cheap aftershave, dull the brain. For mile after mile, with the piscatorial smell gradually increasing but hugely adulterated by many internal and external influences, the kipper would reach a state of culinary perfection.

On a plate, with an accompaniment of hot buttered toast and a glass of Buck's Fizz, it would be memorable. But, equally memorable was the scene at the side of the road after the new bride had insisted that her beloved check where that dreadful smell was coming from. A well-cooked kipper, skin-side below, sticks permanently to any cylinder head and, due to its readiness for the mouth, it disintegrates to the blunt touch of a hastily-applied metal spanner. And, however much one chips and scratches at the fish, little is removed, other than to fly in uncontrolled flakes to the bridegroom's going-away suit.

Maybe modern motoring, antiseptic and dull though it is, has its compensations.

♦

When they reopened the underground station at King's Cross after the dreadful fire which took place on the 18th of November, 1987, we were glad. After all, King's Cross, with its warren of tunnels linking the Piccadilly, Victoria and Northern lines, and its stairs and escalators up to the two mainline termini, the Circle Line, and the thronged streets, was a busy place. And, although the Circle Line platforms reopened the next day, it took four weeks to return the rest of the station to a fully operational state. Thirty-one died and a further 100 were injured, some of them terribly. I was at the station at about seven o'clock that evening, half an hour before the fire broke out, as I was travelling daily to Oxford Street at that time and had a habit of working late.

I consider myself very lucky to have avoided that fire. The flash-over was so sudden and so utterly devastating that even a railway enthusiast – whose instinct would have been to turn back down towards the platforms and try to find another way out – would have had no guarantee of survival.

When the station was reopened and I could use the Victoria line again, the price of my survival and the legacy of all those who died was an unforgettable smell which lingered for weeks and which I can accurately bring to mind thirty years later. It was probably more about the imagination than anything, and a lot had burned down there – wooden escalator steps, oil, paint, hoardings, varnish, rubber seals, and electrical equipment – but one couldn't get the real or imagined smell of burned flesh out of one's mind.

Small price to pay, you may say, and you'd be right. And perhaps it is appropriate that those of us who escaped it by a whisker should be reminded from time to time of our good fortune. But as I write this, that rich, sickly, uniquely distinctive smell assaults my nostrils again.

♦

With the signalbox door firmly shut against the cold and gusty night, low lights over the instrument shelf and the booking desk, and no other illumination save the winking signal lights beyond the glass showing red and white atop their posts outside the wind-rattled windows, I turned to the signalman as he rubbed his hands together.

'So, what are you going to do to earn your keep?' he asked. He had already forbidden me to tread any mud on his spotless lino floor and warned me about touching any levers or catches without a duster. Sweaty hands quickly dull burnished steel, and that signalbox was cleaner than the average operating theatre and, sorry, late-mother, much cleaner than home.

I hesitated before replying, feeling I was walking into a kind of trap. 'Well,' I murmured, 'I could make a cup of tea?'

He laughed. 'What? Dish-water like last time? No thank-you! Tell you what,' he said, 'you get yourself down the steps and fetch a bucket or two of coal from the bin by the track and *I'll* make the tea. Have you been eating plenty of your mother's carrots? You can see in the dark?'

I answered in the affirmative, hoping I wasn't lying too obviously. I thought I could place the coal bin in my mind's eye, although I knew it would be pitch dark out there. The outside lamp used to identify locomotives in the night was at the other end of the box, and so of little benefit. Bucket and stove-shovel in hand, I tottered down the flight of stairs with curses ringing in my ears. I had not closed the door properly and it had blown open with a crash before I had descended half a dozen steps.

It was a 'Dad's Army', 'stupid boy' moment.

Scrabbling about in the dark, I located the bin and, with eyes adjusting to the lack of light, shovelled up a few usefully small lumps until my bucket was full. Returning to the warmth of the box, I realised how pleasant the smell of burning coal was. It crackled in the stove, hissing and whirring as hidden pockets of gas burned brightly for a moment before extinguishing, to be replaced by another, deep inside the fire, the smell catching the back of the nose, inexplicably forcing one to inhale deeply and breathe out again contentedly, like a smoker with the first cigarette of the day.

The signalman walked along the box, two cups of tea in hand. No mugs for that fellow. 'Want a biscuit?' he asked, more conciliatory as I made an exhibition of wiping my feet on the mat and closing the door more carefully than last time.

I thanked him and went to take a sip from the scalding tea.

'Not so fast!' he bellowed, indicating my bucket with a nod of his head. 'That's not enough! When you are at home tucked into your cosy bed, I'll still be here working! And how would it be if I ran out of coal on a night like this? Here,' he said, passing another bucket to me. 'Get him filled, too. *Before* your tea!' he added.

I didn't want to ask what he'd have done if I hadn't been there. I was eternally grateful to be allowed up into the box, after all.

I made for the door.

'And try to shut it properly this time,' he bellowed.

♦

Just occasionally on my journeys to and from school, our usual string of compartment stock would be replaced by a train comprised of corridor coaches. Around the bank holidays, rolling stock normally kept for months-on-end in sidings near Cricklewood might be required to form cheap excursions from Bedford to the south coast while, in the other direction, the up-coming need for trains to carry emigrants to Tilbury might result in a special movement London-bound. These kinds of events were extremely rare, of course, as normally balanced working for the locals were thereby disrupted and complicated arrangements to restore the status quo had to be instigated, but circumstance meant that they were not unheard of. Whilst the normal commuters probably tut-tutted at the hugely inefficient provision of coaches with a maximum of three doors that restricted ingress and egress instead of the more normal nine, we liked the change and the endless opportunities for mischief these incidents presented.

On one occasion, a particularly antisocial compatriot of ours rose to the occasion when I made reference to the fact that it might be awfully fine to have a corridor compartment to ourselves, without any hope of my dream ever coming true. What I hoped to do with that moment of brief privacy on the up-train – so different from the homeward journey in which privacy was almost guaranteed – I do not now remember. It might have been restricted to hanging out of the window or even, horror of horrors, putting our feet on the seats, but Mr. Antisocial had the proverbial bit between his teeth. Having forced our way onto the train first – the days of standing back for our elders and betters while doffing our caps were firmly over – we scooted down the corridor and slid the door open on an empty compartment, pushing the door shut behind us. Adults bound for St. Pancras followed us eagerly down the corridor, knowing that our departure at the next stop would make the compartment just that little bit more desirable. There were four of us boys in an otherwise empty six-seater. You could see the attraction. If they could keep the compartment to themselves after St. Albans, they would be able to complete their Times crossword uninterrupted until the train slowed down after Kentish Town and found an empty platform at the terminus.

But Mr. Antisocial had other plans. He no sooner sat

down but searched in his schoolbag and, with a gleam in his eye, produced a crumpled cardboard box and extricated a small glass phial which he proceeded to throw to the floor. This was followed by at least three more of what were, obviously, stink-bombs.

'This'll keep grown-ups out!' he muttered in triumph.

Those businessmen must have thought we'd eaten baked beans for breakfast, or, worse, were all suffering from a form of gastric 'flu that induced diarrhoea so severe that a need for an immediate change of underwear was imperative. The smell was atrocious. Indescribable. The door to the corridor slid open and just as quickly slid shut again – our businessmen resigned to completing crosswords standing up. Our eyes watered and the skin around our noses started to itch. As it was late spring, I went into a fusillade of sneezing, as any irritation set my hay fever off a treat.

Our problem was no longer one of repelling boarders. In that objective, we had been impressively successful. No, survival for the ten minutes or so of our journey was now our greatest challenge. The little sliding window above the main area of glass was opened but, even as we gathered speed, the flow of air was pitifully weak. An opening of the door onto the corridor to encourage a through-draught drew angry shouts from nearby passengers clutching their noses and wagging newspapers dramatically, so we quickly closed it again.

We suffered alone.

It was a long ten minutes.

At last, we arrived in St. Albans and beat a hasty retreat. My guess is that no-one entered that compartment in the cathedral city and it travelled empty to St. Pancras where the emigrants would have had a lasting reminder to take with them to Australia.

Trouble was, Mr. Antisocial, who was not a very popular boy and who, with this single act, had drawn considerable attention to himself, did the same thing on the way home one day when we were riding in one of those delightful old Midland coaches with the half corridor leading to a lavatory compartment. In those trains home, we usually got the first coach to ourselves and that day was no exception. So, whatever we were going to do, simply study our unfamiliar surroundings, mull over our homework, or play an extended game of 'carriage he' or 'tig' throughout the two compartments – the lavatory was 'out of bounds' according to the rules appertaining at the time – in he popped and, with a mischievous grin, bombed the floor again and again until we really wanted to die.

Windows opened to the full, and a summary punishment of having his trousers removed, with the added threat of having them thrown from a window, successfully stopped the little tyke, and that was the last time practical chemistry was applied in our train. Soon after that, Mr. Antisocial left our school, never to be seen again, and, only noted for being a pest, he was largely forgotten.

But the nasal memory lingers on.

♦

From: 'The Boy in the Train'

There's a gey wheen boats at the harbour mou',
And oe! Dae ye see the cruisers?
The cinnamon drop I was sookin' the noo
Has tummelt an's stuck tae ma troosers ...
I'll sune be ringin' ma Gran'ma's bell
She'll cry, 'Come ben, ma laddie',
For I ken mysel' by the queer-like smell,
That the next stop's Kirkcaddy!

Mary Campbell Smith (1869 – 1938)

Kirkcaldy was only one station that was characterised (and, in this case, immortalised) by a 'queer-like' smell. I remember Kirkcaldy, and the reek from the manufacture of linoleum for which the town became famous. Linoleum was one of those clever, almost accidental, inventions that the British became lauded for. Who would think to combine linseed oil, cork dust, pine rosin and wood flour, and then pour the mixture onto a backing of woven burlap and canvas to form a flooring material that was unsurpassed for almost one hundred years? The same man went on to invent anaglypta, which adorned our walls and is still seen in old-fashioned pubs to this day.

Clever man, Frederick Walton.

Such a strange combination of ingredients was bound to make a very distinctive smell, and so it did. Indeed, it is almost impossible to describe – a hot, oily, vegetable smell dominated by the linseed, high on the register of scents – almost like sandalwood. Barry's, and in another district of Kirkcaldy, Nairn's, made linoleum in vast quantities from their towering factories that employed half the town and gave the station goods yard reason for its extensive sidings and rows of vans that, once loaded, would travel the length and breadth of the country. Although it was an English invention, Nairn's became the largest producer in the world, and there were at least another four manufacturers of the stuff in the town besides Barry's who dominated Kirkcaldy station. Lino was incredibly hard-wearing, but after years of being trodden on and washed – it was particularly used in kitchens, bathrooms and halls – it began to curl and crack. I remember how treacherous it became, and how children's bare feet would cut and bleed from contact with its brittle, scratchy hessian, and unforgiving deterioration. But that smell? It's gone now, I suppose, but some of the buildings were still there last time I passed by. Perhaps Kirkcaldy now makes that more flexible, plastic alternative – convenient, but lacking the universality, originality or romance of its predecessor.

♦

Travelling in the old days, one was constantly assaulted by special odours. Beer brewing, whisky distilling, unfortunately-located abattoirs, carpet-making in Wessex, huge coking plants adjacent to every steelworks, and many gas manufacturers. Becton was one, in east London. Enormous, and threaded by a network of railways with fussy little green tank engines – some built to run under retorts and no taller than a man. Scotland had some, too, in Granton and Glasgow, with one or two surviving to this day in preservation – some even on the narrow gauge.

Trains by the sea meant salt on the wind but, in some places, it meant the overpowering smell of fish, already alluded to, where the fresh-caught had been through the auction and carefully boxed for transportation, while the guts and offal, scavenged by a plague of argumentative and aggressive gulls, were the provenance of most of the odours that met our nostrils.

Cake and biscuit baking in north Manchester, jam-making in Dundee and Liverpool, the barf-inducing sickness of margarine in west London, bloody meat in the tunnels on the way to Smithfield, chocolate in Chirk and Bourneville, paint-making in Lancashire, and lanolin from sheepskins in the West Riding of Yorkshire – washed out in such volumes that a special plant had to be built at Esholt Sewage Works in the Aire Valley before the water could be returned to the river. The separated fatty wax was turned into soap for domestic and industrial use, and the distinctive smell along the valley from Shipley, and below the satanic woollen mills of Bradford, could be reproduced in your own kitchen for sixpence. Esholt had its own little branch line that crossed the river and climbed up to the main line where exchange sidings sometimes meant the sight of the little 'pug' assembling its wagons of we-knew-not-what before ambling back to precisely we-knew-not-where. Esholt was a mystery behind wire fencing, permanently-closed gates and strong scents, with the incongruity of TV film crews wandering idly around their fantasy Emmerdale.

There are still some smells from manufacturing processes, for we still make some things here in Britain.

Chemicals and oil products in the Wirral and North-West Cheshire, stone dust from the quarries of Somerset, Derbyshire and the Pennines and, yes, some beer making here and there. But most of the distinctive smells are gone, and with them the peculiar trademark epitomised by the poem that prefaced this piece. Now, only the smell of money pervades the railways in and around Liverpool Street, London, and that, though subtle to the point where it is hardly noticed, affects us all.

♦

Locomotives are prodigious users of oils and greases. They are, after all, a mass of moving parts – steel rubbing against steel, iron against iron, brass bearings against brass bearings. When two materials of approximately the same strength and density come into contact with each other, they will wear each other out roughly equally, but if the two components behave differently or are made of different materials – perhaps one is taking the strain while the other is simply a passive bracket, perhaps one is iron, the other steel – wear will be unequal. In every event, to prolong life, the rubbing surfaces need to be lubricated. As a consequence, a rich variety of materials – tallows, animal fats, greases, and oils of different viscosity – have been available to the railways since the very start of mechanisation. As the years went by, technological developments, such as the introduction of superheating, made considerable demands on the ingenuity of manufacturers of lubricating materials, and an elaborate science built up around this aspect of railway operation. The introduction of internal combustion engines and electric motive power broadened the demand for clever solutions still further.

However advanced it all became, the lasting impression is of the boiler-suited driver carefully going around his engine, oil-can in one hand and a cloth or fistful of cotton waste in the other, carefully topping up the considerable number of reservoirs and greasing around the back of bearings. The terms 'oil' and 'grease' were used indiscriminately, in my experience, although the materials are distinctly different – oil 'runs' whereas grease tends to be more glutinous. What was put into the oil reservoirs was, invariably, oil, but my grandfather's earliest locomotive work, after carefully cleaning the beasts, was known as 'the greasing' and usually meant 'going underneath' to lubricate near-invisible bearings.

Whichever, they all had a not unpleasant smell, and that altered as the machinery started to work. Hot oil or grease is fairly pleasant but experienced crews could identify a myriad of ills from the smells the locomotive gave off. One of Nigel Gresley's little known inventions was an additive that went into the oil reservoirs on his high-speed, streamlined 'Pacifics'. This gave off a smell of rotten eggs and was designed to alert the crew to a developing and serious lubrication problem – particularly in what was known as the 'middle engine'. The inside cylinder, with its mechanically-operated valves operated by rocking arms situated between it and its outside counterparts, was particularly prone to greasing problems and the eggy smell certainly alerted the crew to a potential problem.

It wouldn't have been possible on the air-smoothed exterior of an A4, but many a bearing running hot has been lubricated by a member of the crew, realising an issue was developing, clambering out of the cab and along the running plate to tend to the malfunctioning component while in motion. No professional driver would set off on any journey without first preparing his engine, so these antics would normally be necessary when a problem occurred. Pipework can block, and the little corks used to stopper an oil-reservoir could sometimes be lost.

Suicidally-courageous French railwaymen during the war would drop small coins into the top of the reservoir and then set off to collect their train, only to break down spectacularly in some remote location as the recalcitrant franc impeded oil flow and the bearings seized. At best, this would delay the train and disrupt the service. At worst, this could result in the locomotive's motion fracturing and causing considerable damage to it and even the track in the immediate vicinity.

But, if the crew could not get to the coin and remove it before a suspicious member of the Gestapo or a French informer appeared on the scene, the ruse would be discovered and summary execution was inevitable.

♦

A few years ago, I visited the transport museum near Belfast where one of the things I dearly wanted to see was 'Blanche', a 2-6-4 tank engine that formerly worked on the County Donegal. The engine is lovingly painted but it is not restored. The smokebox door is rusted through and the whole thing is as it was the day it was withdrawn from service – neglected, battered and shabby. But wonderful. I hope they don't ever replace half of what it is, in a mistaken project to 'make it like new'. I don't know why I did it, but a third of the way along, under the side water tank, there is an orifice made available to the crew for filling the oil reservoir. Casting around me, I realised no-one was watching, so I put my nose hard up against the locomotive.

There it was, the unmistakeable smell of locomotive oil. That was in 2006, and the line closed in 1959. Forty-seven years later, the oil was still present and, I assume, able to perform its function just as before. Of course, occasionally moving the locomotive around the museum site might have warranted a more recent grease-around.

But I'd rather visualise some flat-capped Donegal railwayman, unlit dog-end drooping from his bottom lip, walking around his steed on that last day in Strabane or Stranorlar, performing the ritualistic tasks that have been repeated time immemorial since the beginning of railway time – loosening the corks or lifting the reservoir lid, directing his 'pourie' into the reservoirs and behind the bearings, lifting the can skyward and watching carefully as the liquid slugged fitfully down into the darkness, wiping the excess expertly away, pressing the corks back into place and pushing them home once, twice, to ensure they would stay in place, or closing the reservoir lid with a satisfying clunk. Then, back to the footplate, knowing another task was well done.

Fortunately, with steam railways in abundance, this activity and these smells are still with us!

CHAPTER SIX

TASTE

With Driver T. E. Wilson before a run from Edinburgh Waverley to Newcastle on the 15th April 1981. Locomotive No. 55021, 'Argyll & Sutherland Highlander'

It became a joke – a sure-fire laughter-winner for stand-up comedians. Even those who had never tasted one felt an affinity – an 'oh, yes' at its mention, a shake of the head, and an uncontrolled belly-laugh if the gag was well told. Somewhere between the mother-in-law jokes, 'I won't say she's a big woman, as I am not known for understatements', and the rambling and insulting stories that began with the words, 'Take my wife'…. and the aside, 'I wish you would', invariably employed when audience response was flagging. It was enough to say 'British Railways sandwich' to gain an oft-misplaced titter – misplaced, because the amused had rarely partaken of the aforementioned delicacy and, after all, given the times, were they so bad?

It was called a British Railways sandwich because that was what it was. Not 'Prêt-à-Manger', not Marks &

Spencer, not Bagel-u-Like, or the product of any such concessionary. They were made on the premises, usually in the Refreshment Room or buffet, and sold at the station, and, sometimes, to passengers on a train from a chariot pushed dispiritedly up and down the platform as a long-distance service paused on its journey. They were comfortingly predictable and required little or no explanation. Cheese was cheese – very yellow, very mild, very brittle, very cheddar; there was luncheon meat – a kind of processed concoction made up of tasty fat and tasteless flesh, sometimes substituted by corned beef; there was fish paste – a thin spread of a vomit-like substance with no accompaniment to tickle the taste buds; there was boiled egg – sliced thinly with a curious blue tinge to it; and there was salad. This last was predominantly lettuce, with perhaps an accidental hint of tomato, well-past-its-best cucumber (limp and practically liquid), and a few shreds of cress. The bread was pure factory and as white as the driven snow, with margarine, when strictly necessary, spread lavishly – the only generous ingredient to be found.

Its limit for staying fresh was probably in the region of five minutes and, in those days before vacuum packing, it stood no chance whatsoever in the steamy atmosphere of the station buffet or exposed to the pollution of the railway platform. If you bought a sandwich that was older than an hour, you would need a cup of railway tea to assist you in the process of swallowing as they had an uncanny propensity for sticking to the roof of the mouth.

Perhaps, after all, they were pretty bad, even for those days.

The British Railways sandwich died a death sometime around the abbreviation of 'Railways' to 'Rail' in a misplaced attempt to save paint and become 'hip' in one simple move. The railway found it more practical to rent the former refreshment room space to any number of outlets with fancy French names, more adventurous fillings that would stay fresh for an alarmingly long time, and with the added convenience of a triangular plastic container that not only told you what the sandwich contained but gave comforting advice about when your sandwich was made and, sometimes, by whom, in the form of scribbled initials. Since you probably bought it in Crewe, with any dissatisfaction discovered near Lockerbie, knowing that 'CJ' made your sandwich an improbable ten minutes before you bought it became purely academic – part of the growing trend to provide more and more useless information that now fills our heads and reduces our ability to discern what is important from what is not.

Having mentioned railway tea, this needs to be expanded upon. Yes, it was proper tea – not tea-bag tea. And, as it was poured into heavy, thick, white, pottery cups from a tea pot of eye-watering heaviness, the last pint or so proved its provenance by its ferocious strength and a shoal of tea leaves.

Once, when I rashly asked which cup contained the sugar, the plump Beryl Cook character behind the counter thought for a moment, hesitated, then plunged her finger into the cup she suspected before licking it and confirming her choice. 'Thought it was that one,' she smiled triumphantly.

I was too young to complain.

Noel Coward was an acute observer of human nature, and his script for the David Lean film "Brief Encounter" encapsulates the character of those long-gone refreshment room attendants who, invariably, had too much time on their hands, such that they could indulge their curiosity in their customers and respond, on the one hand, with sycophancy to the businessman ordering a 'Double Diamond' who might leave a threepenny bit in response to a kind word and a toothless smile, and, on the other, authoritarian suspicion at two or three schoolboys swinging duffel bags and carrying their tea and chocolate marshmallows to a table up against the window that looked out upon the fast lines. Crumbs dropped, tea spoons accidentally swept to the floor from the robust matching saucer, and loud exclamations at the passing of a 'Royal

Scot' heralded a tutting and sighing from the Refreshment Room attendant that could be heard five tables away, and she had an air about her that demanded the table be left tidy, in contrast to her, 'don't you worry about that, sir, I'll deal with it,' as she advanced, soggy cloth in hand, on the businessman preparing to leave, with his empty glass and drained bottle abandoned on the puddled surface.

We learned to avoid eye-contact in the presence of adult-injustice, but felt our ears burning long after we returned to the platform.

But now, over all that, a sense of nostalgia remains. Those refreshment rooms, buffets and cafeterias, mostly licensed and all things to all men, were everywhere. They were on many medium-sized stations, at junctions, in county towns, in the industrial north and the rural west and, of course, at every terminus. They were relaxed and quiet – no music or coffee machines that whooshed and spat in their attempts to resemble the sounds of the steam engines we had come to see, no train announcements (or not often), and no mobile phones with daft ringtones whose owners seem to be under the illusion that we need to hear at least ten bars of their choice of attention-seeker before picking up. Children were, on the whole, better behaved in those days, so no trade-union negotiations carried out by liberal-minded parents who prefer long drawn-out discussions, usually followed by some crazy incentives, such as, 'would you like some chocolate to reward you for being a perfect pain in the neck?', to using phrases like 'be quiet!', 'wait until I get you home' or 'that's enough!'.

Those establishments had a form of shabby dependability about them. Nothing changed, not even the name, which could be heralded by a robust cut-lettered board hung at right-angles over the door, sometimes with the word 'Room' added, other times pluralised and shortened to 'Refreshments' and using the same style and font as all the other station 'offices' – 'Ladies' Waiting Room', 'Gentlemen', 'Station Master', 'General Waiting Room' and 'Porters' Room' – invariably punctuated correctly. There might also be a 'Lamp Room' and a 'Parcels Office', although access to them was usually prohibited. (I often wondered where ladies "went" as, peering through the 'Ladies Waiting Room' windows, it resembled nothing more than a waiting room, whereas our establishment was entirely and solely a lavatory. Little doors, discreetly placed in corners of the ladies waiting rooms, managed to avoid my gaze and, conversely, stimulated my curiosity.)

A refreshment room visited in 1958 had probably remained substantially the same since 1938, or even 1918. They were rugged, you see. Durable. Built to last. The doors were thick, heavy and ornamentally panelled, and they were often fitted with those piston-and-bracket door-closers that could maliciously remove the fingers of the unwary. The tables and chairs looked as though they had been made by ecclesiastical furnishers on an off-day. The mirrors on the walls were ruined by years of steam and damp and the memory of thousands of ladies peering inquisitively at their reflections, precisely adjusting their hats and discreetly patting at powder-caked cheeks. The counters – often marble, but mostly wood, and chipped by careless travellers with Gladstone bags or shooting sticks placed proprietarily on the surface while ordering – managed to remain sticky in spite of being wiped incessantly. If the refreshment room was also a bar, jolly reminders of the pleasures to be gained from alcohol lifted the spirits as well as encouraging their consumption. Framed posters of animated birds discussed the merits of a glass of stout with the famous slogan,

'If he can say as you can,
"Guinness is good for you",
how grand to be a Toucan,
just think what Toucan do.'

'Good Old Johnny Walker' strode vigorously towards the observer, proudly displaying his comfortable but not excessive paunch, while more sophisticated tastes were attracted by slices of lemon and bubbling tonic water awaiting a shot or two of gin poured by an improbably handsome waiter, whose eyes engaged lasciviously with a female customer, so delicate that she might have been nothing more than an apparition, and seated before a small, round table that bore no resemblance to the sturdy and stained realities of the railway station bar, while her husband, oblivious to the sexual chemistry being played out before him, sucked contentedly on a long, fat, rather suggestive, cigar, its smoke curling lazily to the lofty, chandeliered ceiling – a contrast to the reality of grubby strip lights hanging from chipped and peeling gloss-painted plaster – and voluminous enough to form a convenient advertising speech-bubble.

Nowadays, to find somewhere even to sit down would be a challenge, and who wants to sit, '*al fresco*', on a tin chair behind a plastic curtain on a station concourse? 'In full view', as my mother might have said, her face twisted into a grimace at the thought, always keen on discreet anonymity. And even if one came to like a favourite corner, 'in full view', away from the throng and where watching the world go by was still possible, when one returns the following year, it will probably have ceased to serve improbably expensive coffee in an unrecyclable take-away cup, to be replaced by a sushi joint or an authentic New York Burger Bar where the staff look blankly when you express a need for gluten-free buns or a garnish that excludes onions. And the old refreshment room will have been boarded up, knocked down, or turned into an expensive and rather dirty pubic convenience, eager to swallow your thirty pence and, at the same time, prevent entry if you so much as press timidly on the patented gate.

But that, as they say, is progress.

◆

For a few years, and with customary good planning, I pursued a career that took me to London on extended day trips about once a week while I lived near Leeds, a couple of hundred miles away. This was towards the end of the diesel locomotive-hauled era and just as the High Speed Trains came into vogue. So, I started with Type '4' Brush diesels, then 'Deltics' as they were displaced from the Anglo-Scottish trains, and then the all-conquering HSTs became the norm. I travelled up on the red-eye from Leeds to Kings Cross after I had to admit the unreliability of the connections to and from New Pudsey or Guiseley, and would sit in the non-smoker nearest the buffet car.

Leaving home before five-thirty, breakfast in the house was a somewhat rushed affair, to be followed by one of British Rail's cheese toasties that were microwaved in the cardboard box they were served in. This was accompanied by a coffee, brought to my seat by a very obliging steward who had served aboard ship before entrusting his career to dry land and the railway. He reached the stage where he would see me from the platform at Leeds City as he walked up and, with arm gestures, know that 'the usual' was required. This was very convenient as I was served before anyone else and before the bar was opened, which could delay things beyond Wakefield if there was a crowd on.

I remember that sandwich as being delicious, but I don't quite know why. It shouldn't have been. It was, as I have said, microwaved in a cardboard box! It was made with white bread cut into long triangles and entirely lacking in any form of garnish. Some of the cheese would ooze out of the bread and congeal on the cardboard where it could either be abandoned or scraped up using a fingernail, to be chewed endlessly on those long miles to London. The latter was favoured because it was, I kid you not, so delicious.

British Rail also did a bacon toastie, but it was rather mean in the bacon department and almost impossible to bite through without great care, or the teeth of a Bond baddie. The usual consequence was a quick mouthful of the entire rasher, followed by several munches of pure bread. And it wasn't as tasty as the cheese.

What I wouldn't give for another cheese toastie and hot steaming coffee served by that friendly attendant as an HST ground its way around the curves at the west end of Leeds City and pointed its streamlined nose in the direction of Wakefield on a pre-dawn Yorkshire morning!

♦

Everyone who is interested in railways enough to follow web sites and Facebook pages will have seen images of breakfast being prepared on a washed-down fireman's shovel.

I have to say, I view these with a certain degree of amusement and caution as to their authenticity and hints at implied universality. Did railwaymen really cook their breakfast … or any other meal, for that matter … on a shovel? On long hauls, or on express trains, there would have been no time from beginning to end of the journey to rustle up a hot meal on the swinging, rattling, surging footplate, besides which, the fireman's shovel would have been too busy shifting coal into the firebox to be used for a leisurely breakfast. For many railwaymen, when they set out for work in the morning – or afternoon, or evening, or in the small hours – they knew not what they would be doing or where they would be at whatever mealtimes coincided with their shift. The unpredictability of the days' work for many would have meant planning the ingredients for an eagerly-anticipated shovel-meal coming to naught.

The other thing mitigating against fry-ups on a regular basis was the sheer cost of the ingredients. It was only in the years following the last war that footplate men were in a position to lavish even modest sums on feeding the inner man. The 'nine to five' nature of the preserved railway lends itself to the idea of breakfast from a shovel, but my grandfather, like most railwaymen, worked unsociable shifts and, so far as I can tell, while tea was made in a can filled with hot water from the engine, and sandwiches (a 'piece', in Scotland, where he lived and worked) were invariably brought from home, I can find no record in his much treasured 'diary' of food being prepared on a shovel.

For the in-excess-of twenty years he kept records of his daily life, he worked on 'pilots' (yard shunting and trip working) and goods trains, and there were occasions when it was possible to make something warm in the brake van where the guard's stove lent itself to basic culinary pursuits. The juxtaposition of a lay-over in a yard, and crew members one was happy to spend leisure-time with, could result in riotous goings-on in the van, sometimes involving alcohol and even, on regular turns, it is said, loose women, but my grandfather was a fully paid-up member of the Independent Order of Rechabites, a Friendly Society of a type very popular in the 19th Century, which combined a strand of mutual support (that is, life and accident insurance in times of hardship), with a non-conformist rectitude and discipline, and he had 'signed the pledge', so drinking would have been frowned upon. Furthermore, as he was happily married, as straight as a die and, apparently, a forceful character to boot, there would have been no loose women and no drinking in his presence.

But one thing he did do was coddle eggs. If you look at a recipe for coddled eggs, it involves placing the egg in warm water for about ten minutes and this was normally done before the shell was removed – lightly boiled, if you like. Some coddled eggs are hardly cooked at all.

If you also look at photographs of certain types of 19th century steam engine, the safety valves, usually two, were placed on the top of the dome inside a pair of ornamental 'pots'. These were, coincidentally, of a diameter that enabled the egg to be placed inside the pot and on top of the safety valve, and, once prepared, still retrievable with a piece of cotton waste to avoid scalding. Unlike modern safety valves of the Ross 'pop' type that go off with a sudden roar of steam, old-fashioned lock-up valves reached the steam-release point gradually and tended to leak a small amount of steam most of the time – ideal for coddling eggs. On some railways, this constant leak was so common as to be called 'the feather', and this can frequently be seen in old photographs.

The shape of the safety valve pots on their seating, and the nature of their performance, meant that coddling eggs in the manner described was extremely common on roads that used locomotives with the correct physiognomy. Thus, this was done on all the Scottish railways and those English lines with a Scottish connection in terms of their locomotive engineers, for example, Stroudley on the London, Brighton and South Coast, or Drummond on the London & South Western.

So, a couple of eggs from the hens at home – and most railwaymen until recently had access to hens – and an *authentic* railwayman's breakfast would be attainable. A brief layover at the end of a run was all it took, and my grandfather, and thousands like him, would clamber around the outside of the cab and pull themselves up to within reach of the safety valves. Then it would be down to personal preference – leaving the eggs bouncing gently in the safety-valve housing for five minutes or ten. Freshly coddled eggs, together with bread and butter from home? Those would make a fine meal, eaten at any time of the day and night. An 'all-day breakfast' if ever there was one.

Mind you, it needed the cooperation of the fireman or anyone else in the vicinity. The status quo had to be maintained – just leave the engine precisely as it is. No turning on the injector, which would reduce steam release to nothing, and certainly no coal on the fire.

There was a story that a shunter who worked at one of the yards in Leith saw my grandfather on his pre-meal, boiler-clambering escapade, knew what he was up to and, out of devilment and while my grandfather was otherwise distracted, threw a couple of shovels of coal into the firebox. At first nothing adverse happened. When coal is first thrown into the box, the temperature slightly reduces as a result of the cold, unburned coal being added. But once the new coal was burning well, things changed. The boiler pressure rose, the valves blew, and grandfather's happily-anticipated meal was consigned to the heavens, while the urchin-shunter legged it, roaring with laughter.

I have no doubt that in times of comparative prosperity – mostly since the Second World War – the preservation society breakfast was enjoyed by many railwaymen, and diesel and electric locomotives certainly had electric rings upon which drivers could prepare something to eat, but lack of money and the impracticality of shopping for and then preparing a generous fry-up in the past surely determined a simpler regime?

♦

With the proliferation of food outlets, train spotters on, or in the vicinity of, large railways stations today – hardly worth that name as they scribble the numbers of railway carriages, multiple units and the occasional locomotive down, or even recite them into their mobiles (!) – can always peel themselves away from the excitement and grab a burger and chips. But, let's raise a glass of Tizer to the train spotters of yesteryear who had to rely on the kind offices of their parents to provide lineside sustenance.

Why 'Tizer, the Appetizer'? Tizer was the drink of choice in my circle. As part of my research, I bought a bottle not long ago. It didn't taste the same at all. Sweeter and more ordinary than I recall, and the Tizer of old had a unique smell when one took the top off, as far as I can remember, by means of that flip-top stopper-thing that has recently enjoyed a bit of a resurgence. The flip-top was certainly common with Corona, but it was the better-off children who had their gaily-painted lorries calling every week, which is probably why my teeth lasted longer. We never threw the flip-tops away, as one could get the money back on the empties when returning them to the shop.

176

Depending upon adequate notice of a spotting trip being given, a kind parent would ensure their offspring did not starve. Pork luncheon meat was one of my mother's staples for these adventures. Sometimes it was cut in the round by the butcher – thin, pale-pink, circular slices – and at other times it came in a tin with vicious, sharp edges, cut more crudely, and, it has to be said, more generously by said parent. We were a butter household, so this was liberally spread before applying the filling.

Cheese was sometimes used, but this was always grated – I suppose for economy – and fraught with difficulty in the 'real situation'. A grated cheese sandwich eaten from a plate at home is practical, but sitting on a railway embankment in wild, scrub-like grass desperately in need of the later-summer burn-back, was about as comfortable as a stretch of the African veldt. Carelessness, while shuffling about to crush a small area for sitting on, in the manner of a member of the cat family in the wild, could easily result in the greaseproof wrapper unravelling, with the consequence of the cheese spilling out of the bread and descending into the flattened grass, to the instant delight of thousands of ants.

After bumping about in my bicycle saddlebag for ten miles or more, my mother's signature sugared-banana sandwiches turned quite black, assumed the thickness of a sheet of paper and oozed moisture when unwrapped. This, too, was welcomed by the ants, with the added disadvantage that the critters were not discerning, and dripping banana transferred to the grass was as welcome to them as that on our sticky fingers. Sitting on the embankment and staring into the middle-distance watching for a passing train, propped up on one's palms, a curious sensation alerted one to a veritable swarm of the blighters crawling hungrily over spread fingers. Frantic rubbing and wiping while uttering adolescent oaths could easily result in the Tizer bottle being spilt – all the worse when the ants were of the red, biting variety. Jam sandwiches were an equally flawed form of sustenance.

If the outing was to be a long one, we might have a pork pie, uncut and full of unwanted jelly that had to be disposed of somewhere, and, joy of joys, a packet of Smith's crisps – the ones with the little twist of blue paper containing salt – not the hermetically-sealed pack of more recent nostalgic revival. There were no chocolate biscuits on hot days, but there might be a few 'Rich Tea' or 'Digestives', still in the truncated remains of the factory wrapper.

The banquet would be finished off with an apple, usually a Cox's from a friend's garden and, after the aforementioned journey by bike, liberally bruised so that the incautious among us threw the incompletely-eaten fruit into the long grass.

No wonder those ants awaited our visits with eager anticipation.

So, the carefully-prepared picnic frequently ended in slapstick chaos, with much of it abandoned and forgotten. But, those railway embankment lunches were, I suppose, more nutritious than today's 'same the world over' outlet-equivalent and, giving way to the onslaught of the hungry insects, snoozing in the grass and burping contently, they remain an inescapable part of my boyhood memories of train-watching at Bourne End, Boxmoor, Bushey, Welwyn Garden City, or Three Counties.

♦

Having mentioned the paucity of chocolate biscuits in the spotters' picnic, it should not be assumed that chocolate was in any way a rarity. On the contrary, we ate a lot of chocolate – although, in the context of today, this has to be tempered by 1950s and 1960s moderation. In my memory, chocolate was not often brought from home and, it is true, if the day out involved a long cycle-ride and a soot-stained, grassy embankment miles from civilisation, chocolate there was not. But, for every bike-ride spotting occasion, there would at least be one involving a train ride and long waits on railway stations – sometimes curtailed abruptly by station staff irritated by our undisciplined antics. Of course, armed with a return ticket, we had a legal right to be on the station, but we probably pushed that one a bit since a day train-spotting might mean missing fifteen trains we 'could' have caught home.

Welwyn Garden City was a very welcoming station. I do not remember any trouble thereon and the station was well-equipped with slot machines that vended chocolate as well as those curious metal strips that, by means of a dial and a large pointer, could be 'impressed from underneath', like raised type. After inserting the money, we would swing the pointer around and, having located the first letter of one's name – the most popular subject – a lever would be pulled, to be followed by further swinging, pointing and pulling. At the end of the task, the guillotine-feature was applied and the piece of metal would emerge from the slot below the dial. The dial was very elaborate, with letters, numbers and a range of punctuation marks to choose from. Having obtained one's own name, other subjects could be attempted – girl's names, the names of favourite locomotives, rooms at home. My mother, I remember, reacted rather unkindly to a punched-out tin sign advising people of the presence of the 'bathroom'. For some reason, she thought the sign unnecessary and, well, rather indiscrete.

That, then, was the theory of the metal printing machine. Money in. The pleasure of selecting. Tin strip out. Sadly, those machines were practically guaranteed to disappoint. There was no relationship between the entry of the coin and the ability of the machine to work satisfactorily. In fact, there was often a complete absence of virgin tin, and after laboriously swinging, pointing and pulling, the guillotine would be triumphantly applied to nothing more than fresh air. Alternatively, the emerging piece of metal strip would be about an inch long – enough space for two letters at most as, until you cut it to indicate completion of your type-face literature, each letter would have been superimposed, one on top of another. Instead of one's name in full, complete with spaces and a neat full-stop at the end, the short piece of metal resembled the consequence of firing a pistol at a tin can.

Better, then, to spend our modest funds on chocolate.

The chocolate machines, however, were also malicious and unreliable, but an improvement, on the whole, over the metal type printer. Most machines had a choice of bar with a slide at the bottom of the glass-windowed column. In theory, one put the money into the machine and pulled smartly on the tray of one's choice. In practice, it eagerly gobbled up the coin but, at that point, the contract was often terminated. The experienced would check the column of chocolate bars before making a choice. If they were not lying completely level, a blockage could easily result. Pulling too gently on the slide might trigger the coin-dropping before vending took place. Equally, too rapid a pull could scrunch the bar of chocolate up in the mechanism with a sickening, ripping of the paper and 'Fry's Five Boys' spread like Nutella all over the exit. This meant the tray could not be returned to its rightful position and misery would ensue. The safest approach was to wait until another traveller chose their chocolate successfully before we attempted to emulate both choice and operational actions to the letter. But even that would not guarantee success, and nobody really wanted the mature traveller's 'Cadbury's Whole Nut' anyway, so the practical lesson was, largely, academic.

Fry's seemed to be the greatest providers of chocolate vending machines in my youth. If it wasn't 'Five Boys', with its message that, however miserable the self-centred youth felt, finishing a bar would restore his spirit, there was a Fry's Chocolate Creme bar – dark chocolate containing white fondant – and the 'Crunchie', although, being thick and narrow, they were probably the most hazardous in vending machines. Flat bars were safest, but still not entirely trustworthy.

Although a sound stock-control technique, 'first in, first

out', was determined by the technology – new bars inserted into the top of the column by the vendor, oldest spewed out on the pull-tray for the buyer – the relative freshness of the chocolate was entirely dependent upon popularity and its position *vis-a-vis* the sun. If demand was high, the chocolate would be in reasonable condition, but the location of the machine would also be an important factor in all this. The Welwyn Garden City chocolate machine was conveniently placed on the down main-line loop platform, so the brief but distinctive pull on the chime-whistle chain of an A4 could be positively responded to without abandoning the machine or missing seeing the train. This was in contrast to the metal puncher which stood on the branch line platform – an inconvenient dash away from passing main-line traffic. On the other hand, the chocolate-bar machine faced east and was carefully positioned to absorb the morning sunshine. It was also well to the south end of a platform that was only used by London commuters getting off the train. As most passers-by would be on their way home to supper, it was hardly placed in an ideal position for brisk trade to ensue. In no time at all, the chocolate in that machine, bleached by the sun, frozen in winter and positively antique in terms of 'sell-by date', assumed a marbled effect, such that great streaks of white albinoed the normal dark brown. Those areas of chocolate that remained correctly tinted also lost their lustre and became dull. The taste was distorted by the bar's experiences – rancid, waxy and guaranteed to stick between the teeth for an age. So, why, you may be asking, did we use machines that spoiled chocolate and were so unreliable?

I suppose it was a simple case of infantile lust. One forgets previous disappointments when desire takes hold.

♦

In a previous chapter, I mentioned the wild games of off-ground or carriage 'tig' or 'he' that took place in otherwise-empty compartments in steam days. Rarely athletic, I nevertheless took an active part in those games of wild abandon and would swing in and out of the racks, whizzing along the seats and falling to the floor in an attempt to avoid the pursuer. On one occasion, a particularly spectacular leap along the rack, about which, otherwise, I would have been very proud, coincided with the train suddenly slowing in an unusual spot. Sandridge signalbox stood at the side of the up-slow and it was often switched out, with trains, even on the slow lines, having a clear run from Harpenden Station box through to St. Albans North, and vice versa. But, this day, I was in the middle of my sliding *luge* on the south-most rack of a north-bound train when there was a sharp brake application. Suddenly, the safe and familiar tangle of luggage rack string mesh was no longer below me and I fell via the edge of the seat to the floor below.

Whenever I taste blood in my mouth, I am reminded of that day when I bit a neat hole through my tongue and cursed the Sandridge signalman.

A few weeks later, on the same train, I got myself into a fight with a boy from a rival school who was not only more privileged than me – a mere 'Grammar Grub' – but both stronger and freer with his fists. More blood and permanently shortened front teeth were the result. So, blood and trains are always conjoined in my memory – fortunately, not seriously.

◆

I am sure the fortunate and well-heeled passengers, travelling first-class on the Belmond Pullman or any other special train providing a full sit-down meal, are well looked after. They will certainly know that they are taking part in a tradition that has been going on for a very long time indeed. The practical need to feed travellers whose journeys exceed a couple of hours or so precede mere train travel. Coaching inns and equivalent establishments bear witness to a widespread and international industry that meant from Kowloon to Chicago, from Auckland to Antofagasta, and for a price, the inner man could be satisfied and, if necessary, a bed for the night could be obtained. One such American catering chain, Harvey's, named after its British inventor, has even been immortalised in a 1946 Hollywood musical directed by George Sidney and starring Judy Garland.

On the railways, the idea of a meal served on the move was slow to appear, but railway hotels, conveniently positioned near main stations, arrived in the very earliest days. They were, after all, just a continuation of accommodation and sustaining services that are described in the words of Confucius and the Bible and, just as there was once 'no room at the inn', service has often fallen short of the ideal ever since. In Russian literature, a bed to oneself was only guaranteed in the context of human companionship, with cockroaches and bed-bugs literal 'bed-fellows' – a phenomenon that, apparently, can still be experienced in a number of unlikely places, such as fine hotels in London and New York.

The thing that has, as far as one can tell, been grudgingly well received has been the food, although that might be about diminishing expectations at the onset of hunger. So, the railways – first with their terminal hotels and later with hasty station-stops in remote spots – had a tradition of moderate approval to uphold. Before the days of restaurant cars, Swindon, Normanton and other places provided restaurants at which travellers could eat a lavish meal while the train paused on its long journey. Normanton was one of the more interesting as its environment was far from salubrious – surrounded, as it was, by colliery waste, railway sidings and a No-man's-land of scrubby grass and dank pools of brackish water – but wide platforms and extensive, deserted buildings stood as a nineteen-sixties testimony to a past where peace would be broken by a slowing Midland express bound for Scotland and the ensuing mayhem of hundreds of passengers making for the restaurant where pre-booked and *à la carte* meals could be partaken-of, not to mention the picnic boxes provided by the railway for consumption on the train. A whistle from the engine and the stampede would be reversed, the train would leave, and the sparrows and crows could descend from the skies to the deserted platform to polish off the remaining morsels, while the bolder birds could make a foraging expedition to the dining hall though a door carelessly left ajar.

When dining on the train, brought to us by the American, George Pullman, again on the Midland, but closely followed by the Great Northern, became generally available, it was obviously directed at the rich. Even modest travellers brought their lunch from home or, on rare occasions, partook of the railway-provided lunch-boxes already alluded to. So, from Mr. Pullman's sumptuous cars, the provision gravitated downwards only to first-class passengers to begin with and, even in recent years, the 'for all' restaurant cars were always placed nearest the First Class accommodation. Frequently, First Class passengers were served at their own seats, while Third Class (later, and more logically, Second Class and now 'Standard' Class) travellers were expected to vacate their tables at the end of a 'sitting' and return to their own compartments.

When my family used to travel down to Salisbury on the 'Atlantic Coast Express' from Waterloo, we used to travel Third Class and then, as soon as the summons to the restaurant car was issued, we beetled down the train, abandoning our luggage safely stowed on the generous racks of those days, and spent the rest of the journey having a leisurely lunch in the much more sumptuous surroundings of the restaurant car. My father was incredulous at the cramped seating provided by Messrs Maunsell and Bullied for Third Class passengers, judging this as evidence of a vastly inferior railway.

But, in my experience, the food was good (touched upon elsewhere in the context of travel by Pullman), prepared from fresh ingredients, and hot. Happily, this tradition is still maintained on the Specials and, oddly, on preserved railways, where a journey could legally be completed in twenty minutes. Clearly, the pleasure gained from wobbling through the countryside at twenty-five miles an hour while eating a four-course meal is attractive and a bit of a revenue-generator for them, and may it long continue, but it doesn't compare with the modern-day special or my own memories of sitting in a twelve-wheeler going over Shap or Ais Gill. That silver-serviced lunch or tea was dining to remember.

We felt like lords.

♦

In the country that gave us the TGV, where those narrow rails of steel provide a safe running surface at speeds of over two-hundred miles per hour in normal service (and over 350 miles an hour on world record-breaking test runs), where the only thing keeping the wheels on the rails is the Stephensonian flange of less than two inches and very precise engineering geometry, railways are at risk.

While thoughts of French railways turn to the familiar shape of second-generation, distributed power, double-decked trains on the LGV, and most cities have generous suburban services backed up, in more than twenty-five cases, by modern tramways, that statement might seem ludicrous. But if you live in the deeply rural areas of the south and west, as my wife and I did for eleven years, that statement might not seem so exaggerated. SNCF, the nationalised French railway system, has an unfortunate habit of taking long, meandering lines – some of them over one-hundred miles in length, winding sinuously over rivers, hills and deep valleys on their uncertain peregrinations from one main line to another – and cutting them in half. Not so much 'in half' as a cruel severance that leaves a couple of short stubs to small towns or a cluster of grain silos, with the centre portion that used to make sense of a connected, rural railway, closed and, in the fullness of time, torn up. This happened several times during our life in the Lot, and it still continues. Of course, it is deliberate, since much of the traffic is lost and the replacement bus between the two outposts will, inevitably be extended to the stub-junctions and then they can close the railway altogether. The original line from Bordeaux into the *Massif Central* is now a stuttering broken line on the map, with parts that are open with others closed, a small portion preserved, and other stretches converted to the French equivalent of a Sustrans cycle-track.

When we lose a railway, we lose so many things. We lose freedom of movement, since not everyone owns a car; we lose flexibility; we lose choice; we lose an element of democracy and, most difficult to justify, we lose charm.

Sadly, the insecurity surrounding railways in France is not confined to the National network, tragic though that is. During our period of tenure in France, we lost at least five preserved railways – a tragedy, fortunately unheard of in the UK. One, a narrow-gauge line, closed down because of a landslip, but most go because the preservationists do not have properly thought-out business plans and have no ambition beyond extending their professional careers by 'playing with trains'. Many of them are genuinely mystified when Joe Public does not beat a wide path to their door to ride behind a shabby diesel locomotive on a graffiti-tagged branch line, the view obscured by rampant, encroaching vegetation. Furthermore, most of the preservation groups do not own the track (which remains with SNCF) and annual inspections of the not-so permanent way by the landlord can result in an order to replace a thousand sleepers, the cost of which must be met by the tenants. In most cases, the plucky crew can only buy the diesel fuel by clubbing their credit cards together, so the bill for sleepers is prohibitive, and the line closes.

One line that very nearly closed down for good, and has now, fortunately, been revived, is the Vivarais in the Ardèche department of Central France. When my wife and

I first visited the line, it ran from Tournon, where it linked with the freight-only, right-bank SNCF line from Lyon to the south, but it has been truncated in recent years. Ironically, now that the Vivarais has had to vacate the station with its tunnel and almost-unique, shared, dual-gauge for a mile or so, to set up shop on its own land some distance from Tournon, the freight-only line is to have its passenger service restored. Future travellers, instead of enjoying a cross-platform exchange that would recreate what was present back-in-the-day, will be faced by a hefty walk or perhaps a bus link to the narrow gauge.

♦

France has fathomless charm. It doesn't quite know it, but it has. Our first ride up the Vivarais in 1997 brought out some of that spontaneous whimsy and crazy appeal. The train took two hours to get to Lamastre, the end of the line. This portion is only a shadow of the line's former self but, at over twenty miles, it makes a sizeable ride on a preserved narrow-gauge railway in anyone's book. An even longer fragment of this once 126 mile network has also survived to the north-west, but the Lamastre line is the one with the more spectacular scenery.

Returning to the subject of a railway's duty to provide at least the opportunity for passengers to obtain sustenance, after a twenty mile trip into the hills on a wooden coach pulled by a large 0-6-6-0 Mallet tank, we felt hungry and a little anxious about how we would be able to feed the inner man, and woman. But we were in France, the home of good food. We needn't have worried.

The timetable in those days allowed for a leisurely four hours to be spent in Lamastre and the town was bristling with restaurants to suit every pocket. After wandering around the station yard, during which we watched the tank engine being turned, by hand, on the turntable (everyone was encouraged to join in) and refuelled with small coal and a quantity of briquettes before being watered and left to slumber during the heat of the day, we walked into town to assess culinary opportunities.

At each of the many restaurants, the owners stood and encouraged people to come in with brandished menus or sometimes a sweeping gesture with a teacloth-covered arm. Some establishments were attached to hotels and looked very sophisticated, while others were little more than sandwich bars with televisions showing football matches and knots of locals coughing on their gauloises, sipping their '1664s', and placing bets on the trotting races held with enthusiastic frequency throughout the country.

We opted for a restaurant somewhere in the middle of the range of possibilities, with a narrow frontage half way up the main thoroughfare, and dined royally deep inside the many-roomed, shabby, and half-lit establishment, where the tables were covered in washed-down, patterned plastic tablecloths, the cutlery was far from clean, and all conversation was halted occasionally by the buzz and flash of an insect committing suicide on the blue-lighted exterminator screwed over our heads. The main course was a delicious rustic stew of generous slices of beef, and a formidable helping of potatoes and vegetables drowning in thick gravy, preceded by soup and followed by cheese and then a sweet *île flottante*. The bread basket was repeatedly refilled, so that the only way to stop the flow from the kitchen was to resist yet another slice of French stick and leave the basket full. Quantities of rough local wine served in a large glass carafe washed everything down very satisfactorily and, apart from having to master a hole-in-the-floor French *toilette* whilst heavily under the influence, all went extremely well.

At about a quarter to four, the engine began to whistle and, returning to the street, we joined the throng of happy, slightly tipsy, stomach-swollen tourists exchanging notes and quickening their step at the repeated whistles of the green Mallet, No. 403. As we had cut it a bit fine, I more-or-less broke into a brisk trot and was relieved to see the station clock saying ten to. Ten to what, was unclear, since the hour hand was missing. But I needn't have worried, and the unhurried progress of others in the street should have calmed my indigestion-racked body. This was France, the home of good food and bad timekeeping. No-one seemed in a rush.

No. 403 continued to whistle intermittently, but actually shuffled out of Lamastre a full twenty minutes late, billowing clouds of yellow briquette-smoke into the upper reaches of the town like sun-dappled smog drifting on soft breezes. Locals waved at every crossing – it was, after all, the beginning of the summer season. My wife and I gazed contentedly at the passing countryside, waving back, and, I admit, dozing, lulled to brief sleep by the rapid 'clack-clack' of the bogies beneath our feet. From time to time, we were pleasantly awakened by the locomotive's whistle and the singing of a spontaneous choir going through an impromptu repertoire of folk songs at the other end of the coach.

I felt a tinge of exclusion at this – a sense of missing out on something that was vital and, at the same time, not my own experience. My scholarly musical range was mainly limited to Christmas carols, and whatever other songs I learned in school had long since been driven from memory by years of listening to Radio 1. But these people were from another era, another place, another country. Unrehearsed, not even knowing each other, the songs kept coming, with smiling faces, the occasional timid piece of amateur conducting, vigorous head-nodding, and a fusillade of happy self-congratulation at the culmination of another ballad about goatherds and fair damsels, the song of a nightingale resembling a voice from heaven, or a patriotic anthem of courage in the face of adversity.

Soon enough, and with great care, we joined the tracks of the SNCF main line, a little locomotive hauling a string of wooden carriages facing the possible oncoming might of a pair of French electrics hauling a one-thousand tonne freight at passenger-train speeds. Across the river we had followed from Lamastre, over the fields, and into the suburbs of the town we wobbled, before hurtling into the tunnel – still 'wrong line', weak lighting in the carriages reflecting off the tunnel roof and reminding me poignantly of days gone by, of other steam trains and other carriages, of other smoke billowing fitfully along the cavern of sulphurous black, before we slowed down and took the curve into the safety of the Vivarais yard.

A vast range of memories were triggered by that little restaurant and its generous fare and the thought of the tummies full for the rest of that evening. I think that journey, that lunch, and that Mallet, with the bouncing wooden bogies following obediently around the endless curves, and the voices of the amateur choir, sowed the seeds that culminated in our move to France in 2003.

And nostalgia being what it is, a selective yearning, makes me, as I write this, want to go back to the Lamastre of those days ... and never return.

♦

Of course, the Vivarais was not just an end-to-end ride. There were many intermediate stations in years gone by, and there still are a few. The new 'Tournon' terminus is, in fact, near to one of those former intermediate halts, and Lamastre was but a wayside stop, albeit an important one, before services ceased in 1968. The Vivarais had been saved from the clutches of demolition after closure by the practical labour of enthusiasts and a host of local people, who coupled a certain nostalgia for *'Le Mastrou'*, their pet-name for the line, with a shrewd recognition that a successful preserved line might attract tourists with money to spend.

In a desire to take a few photographs and imprint images of the train in its natural surroundings on the mind, we took another day to scour the line for good photographic locations and to get a feel for the place. From our experience of the previous day, we knew the train paused at Boucieu-le-Roi to take water, so that was where we went first. We arrived in plenty of time, probably, knowing me, a good hour before its timetabled arrival, and came upon a scene of delightful chaos.

To explain, the station was a typical French rural establishment. A pretty little station house – accommodation for the station master above, offices below, a loading bank, a passing loop, a *pissoir* in its own little building to one side (no immediate signs of any such facilities for women, as usual, although they could be found if you had the skills of a Maigret), a water tower, two strategically-placed water cranes at the west end of the loop, and a long siding containing a few tumbledown wagons and a spare *fourgon* – a form of multi-use guard's van.

It should be added that what looks like a station loop in France is not always the case, even though that at Boucieu is now a useful passing place. With very sparse services, passing trains were a rarity – even in the earliest days. Often, the track furthest from the station facilities is the running track, whilst the one or two between are used as sidings. A gap is always left between any parked pieces of rolling stock so that passengers can easily join and leave the train opposite the booking office – the wagons for collection being marshalled at the appropriate end of the false 'loop' each side of the gap. This is why trains on local and narrow-gauge lines in the France of long ago took an inordinate amount of time to complete their journeys – they were forever stopping and shunting, depositing and collecting, before shambling off to the next station. This method of operation was perfectly reasonable before the First World War but, following that, and the arrival of lorries and buses (and the demobbed men to drive them), the rural French railway went into decline.

Because our visit was on a *fête* day at the beginning of the running season (which, in those days, only spanned the warm months between Easter and All Saints), the village laid on a welcoming party for the train and its passengers. Folk dancers in traditional dress spun and clasped, stepped back and forth, changed partners, and pirouetted to the sounds of an accomplished accordionist, while stalls served a huge variety of olives glistening in herby, spiced oils (a local delicacy), freshly-made croissants, baguette sandwiches with thick slices of soft cheese resembling brie coated in white rind, or slices of *saucisson* (undoubtedly tasty, but so hard it might have been called 'the dentist's friend'), and home-made cakes, each one sliced and priced on tickets pushed indelicately into the icing. The beer-stall vendors diminished the profits for the day in some frenzied sampling, while wine-corks popped happily in anticipation of the hoped-for throng at the 'by-the-glass' bar, the inevitable cans of Coca-Cola warmed gently in the sunshine, and a delicious variety of locally-produced sweets stickily fused in plastic packets. A few, served loose, seemed to be the exclusive domain of early wasps enjoying the convenience of a sugary takeaway.

There seemed to be stalls for everything – a kind of German Christmas Market in springtime France – animated, colourful and charming. All they now needed was for the few local early observers and tourists to be boosted exponentially by passengers from the train.

A distant whistle further aroused the already-hyperactive stallholders who ran around their displays in a last-minute attempt to improve their attractiveness. All, eventually, was ready. Before the invasion, we bought packets of *artisanal* honey *bonbons* that made the head swim with the sugar-rush.

The train rounded the curve, crossed the level crossing and ground into the station, moving slowly along the platform until the engine was opposite the water crane. Narrow (metre) gauge they may be, but a Compound Mallet weighs 44 metric tonnes in working order (compare with a GWR 14XX 0-4-2 tank at 41 Imperial tons) and, with an 0-6-6-0 wheel arrangement and the front low-pressure truck articulated (in a similar manner to a Ffestiniog 'Fairlie'), they are impressive indeed.

From one of the coaches, a silver band – which could

be heard long before the train arrived – blew a final blast on their instruments, partly to compete with the land-based accordion, we thought, and headed for a bar stall for a few much-needed beers. Hundreds of passengers stumbled off the end-balconies – the men heading for the *pissoir* while the women indulged in feverish retail therapy. The dancers danced on, regaining their superiority in the entertainment industry, their efforts and costumes being applauded appreciatively.

We sucked on our dizzying honey sweets and took in the scene, the engine now taking centre-stage as happy travellers sporting newly-purchased bags of provender wandered up to have their photographs taken, the men putting one foot possessively on the driver's step imitating the professional's unconscious stance, while the young girls posed hands-on-hips and blew kisses to their loved-ones' cameras, and the older women blinked shyly in the sunlight, seeking an elegant solution to the problem of the swinging shopping bag.

All too soon, No. 403's whistle blasted, and the passengers, now including the dancers who were going up to Lamastre with the band for a further performance, clambered aboard *(see the image at the start of Chapter Five, 'Smell')*. The ensuing musical battle, started before the train moved off, between a lone accordionist and a ten-piece silver band looked unlikely to reflect the outcome for the biblical David. But courage and inevitable failure can, equally, be bedfellows, even if they are rarely recorded for posterity. When the division between travellers and observers seemed to have been clearly established, and with some further whistling, the big engine lifted its long train away and up the line, giving a further blast to acknowledge the support give to the railway by the now-dead Countess of the Château de Chazotte, who always waved at the passing train from a lofty window. This tradition persists to the day. So, with whistle blowing, locomotive puffing hard, Piafesque accordion serenading, and silver band blasting raucously and frequently out of tune, the train-load of delighted revellers slowly rounded the curve outside the station and took to the hills.

Peace and quiet returning to the little station, the vendors quickly packed up their stalls, and we prepared to leave. The village looked inviting and thoughts of lunch were in attendance. But then, from down the valley, came the sound of a horn. I wasn't completely able to place the noise but the stall-holders went into a frantic *volte-face*, hauling food, drink and confectionery out of boxes and from the rears of a dozen Renault vans. Another train was coming!

It was only one of the funny little *autorails,* but it was full to bursting with passengers, each wanting to visit the *toilette* and part with their money. By the time it had throbbed to a standstill and the engine had been turned off with a sigh from the brakes, the retail operation was fully open for business again, as though the following train had been fully expected and the frenzied animation in response to the surprise arrival had been but a figment of our fertile imaginations!

When that bus-on-rails left, without any visible signs of signalling – a phenomenon on the French narrow gauge – the show was truly over. Another fine lunch was enjoyed and the afternoon was spent sitting on rocks beside the river before the down train could be watched and followed over the buttressed viaducts as, first, the steam train and then the diesel descended from the plateau to the Rhone valley.

The lunch was, I remember, extremely satisfying, but the lasting memory is of the honey sweets with their liquid centres, and those bring back images of animated and joyous people, the unexpected extra good fortune of the stallholders, the careless precision of the folk-dancers, and the blasting silver band, their instruments blending with the train whistle as it echoed off the flanks of the valley, with its forests of oak, pine and fruit orchards, dotted farms, and the silvery flow of the River Doux as it slowly meandered its way down to blended oblivion in the Rhone at Tournon.

And, after the cacophony, the near silence, broken only by a gentle breeze in the station's lofty trees, the occasional bleat of a tethered goat, and the intermittent barking of a dog a long way away.

♦

Taste, of course, has another meaning.

Personal taste.

In spite of the fact that most of my friends lived in or around Harpenden, we had differing railway preferences rooted in experience, nationality and that peculiar thing, artistic taste. As a Scot born in England and with most of my relatives still in Scotland, plus my late grandfather's place of employment in Auld Reekie, it was hardly surprising that my first love was for the North British Railway and, obviously, the London and North Eastern into which the NBR was absorbed after the Grouping. For some curious reason, I also loved the Lancashire & Yorkshire Railway, and bought books and read up about that alien world of black engines, short block sections and austere brown coaches.

There's no accounting for taste and juvenile enthusiasm.

Living on the ex-Midland Railway, there were many who loved the Midland. Its locomotives were still accessible in my childhood and there is a lot to love about the Midland. Others liked the London & North Western, whilst the Great Western was a terrific pull.

As people grew older, their interests diversified – into signalling, rolling stock, the Underground, the narrow gauge, and so on. Some even began to like buses, and we all had a soft spot for trams, seen in those days and with much regret as yesterday's form of transport. Oddly, with maturity, bigotry and intolerance reared their ugly heads, and we began to judge others' taste, intelligence and even sanity on their transport preferences. Harmless rivalries metamorphosed into hardened opinions that were largely baseless and did not bear close examination. I suppose it was all our version of football-team rivalries where one would prefer to die than have loyalties misunderstood. As in football, the greatest antipathy is felt when local rivals meet, and so our proximity to the lines out King's Cross, St. Pancras and Euston generated the most keenly-felt competition.

As with all such situations, there is always something to support a preference. Equally, there are always reasons to denigrate one's rivals. So, we 'LNER men' pointed at the neat efficiency of articulated stock – Gresley's patented method for resting four coaches on five bogies instead of eight, for example. Or, the sheer brute power of LNER engines and the railway's 'big engine' policy, so that an 0-6-2 tank was quite capable of doing the work of an LMS 2-6-4 tank. The presence of over two-hundred 'Pacifics' on the former LNER lines greatly improved the flexibility of traffic-management on that line, compared with the less than fifty on the old LMS, and so on, while the sheer style and romance of the LNER – eight-wheeled tenders on express engines (not the common-old six on the LMS), teak stock (rapidly disappearing at the time), somersault signals, the Royal Border Bridge that isn't on the border, the romantically-named express trains, the vast variety in the steam stock a consequence of corporate poverty, King's Cross station, York with its fabulous roof (still with us today), the tended shrubs beside and between the railway lines at numerous locations, the intersecting railway level crossings at Newark and Retford taken at high speed, the swing bridge at Selby taken at low speed, the view of the sea north of Berwick – everything supported the LNER's obvious superiority.

To me.

But, of course, St. Pancras was finer than King's Cross, the LMS was less ramshackle than the LNER (although we would have thought that a distinct advantage at the time), Glasgow Central was more imposing than Queen Street,

and the LNER and Eastern Region's access to Aberdeen –
one of its most prestigious destinations – was at the behest
of the lot in Euston who controlled the signalbox where
the two lines combined. The Great Western had been
reasonably profitable, so had undergone a policy of
updating its steam engines to a high degree of
standardisation – an advantage to the operating department
if not us, mere observers – and the Southern, even then,
was a rash of grumpy electric trains in most of the London
suburbs with their amazing steam curiosities living far
away in country areas rarely, if ever, visited by me or any
of my compatriots. You can tell that we still thought in
terms of the pre-Nationalisation companies, even though
British Railways ran everything.

One lesson we had to learn was to overcome bigotry
and see the best in every point of view.

But we rarely did.

CHAPTER SEVEN

TOUCH

Austrian electric locomotive at Bregenz-am-Bodensee,
Summer 1962.

It is an odd thing that, while all other senses are constantly
bombarded in the context of transport, touch is, perhaps,
the rarest. When travelling by bus, tram or train, one
grasps a door-handle or a handrail, steps up or on, gains
the comfort of a seat (if we are lucky!) and then, when the
journey is over, with the help of a door-handle or handrail,
descends from the conveyance. Whatever we were
travelling on will have left us with strong impressions –
visually and aurally – but touch?

Maybe touch is best treated as a composite sensation
and not one that invariably stands on its own. The cool
mass of an in-steam locomotive regulator, when cracked
open, reveals sensations of power and noise, vibration

even. A tramcar controller, when notched up, results in a surge forwards, a pressure in the back if one is sitting down facing the front, a delicious, expectant pause as current reaches motors and motors and gears mesh before the car moves off. You can even feel that slight delay on an electric train or a diesel railcar. So, it is touch, and more.

But not always. Climbing the three or four steps up into a dead steam locomotive's cab, as we often did as children on privileged official shed visits (and illicit ones), it was only the feel of the regulator and its stiff resistance that fed the memory. This was the control we all recognised and, therefore, the first great attraction, although it wasn't the last. An engine in steam takes some of the work away – the steam seeks release and helps with the task, whereas a dead engine is just a piece of machinery – reluctant, passive engineering – with its regulator as hard to move as a rusty hinge on a garden gate – not that that stopped us.

A steam locomotive, of course, was not just the regulator – be it fastened to the rear of the firebox across the cab and V-shaped so that, from either side of the engine it could be opened and closed, or a neat pull-out, duplicated on the other side, as with a Gresley 'Pacific', plainly not designed for repeated use during a shift of shunting, but available for slight adjustments of the speed as the driver used his skill to ensure he kept to his timetable despite changes in gradient, weather conditions, train weight and speed restrictions playing their part during long periods of forward running. There was also the reverser, sometimes a long lever travelling in a quadrant – a bit like a lever in a signal-box but provided with a number of notches that affected direction, plus speed, power and economy of operation as much as the regulator. Furthest from the centre point, where the engine would go neither forwards nor backwards, the maximum amount of valve-travel would be available for starting or when the load was heavy. The more the locomotive got under way, it could be notched back towards that centre point and,

199

although less power was available, economy improved and the fireman did not have to work so hard – besides, it is getting a train on the move that takes the most out of an engine.

Instead of a lever, prohibitively heavy on large locomotives, some were fitted with a wheel which could be operated easily by the driver from a sitting position, but reversing with a wheel was slower and, ultimately, more tiring – more suited to locomotives that would be going in one direction for a reasonable length of time. A quick wrench on a lever could reverse a locomotive in a second. Indeed, I have seen drivers of shunting engines move the lever over the quadrant to the reverse position while the engine was still happily moving forwards. In this way, and probably at the cost of the engine's welfare, shunting was achieved most expeditiously, almost to the point where perpetual motion was achieved. Fly shunting, so much a feature of my childhood memories, was very efficiently accomplished using an engine equipped with a reversing lever. The locomotive would set off pushing a line of wagons, only to stop suddenly and be on its way back to have another shove as the trucks broke free from the rake. Not so easy to achieve with a reversing wheel that required many turns to go from full forwards to full reverse. Of course, the reversing lever was directly attached to the reversing gear sitting between the wheels and valves attached to the cylinders, and on a large engine, the gear would be too heavy to be operated by a lever.

Goodness knows what could have happened if the shed staff during those unaccompanied visits were not particularly alert after we had gone, with reversers adjusted, gauge-glass cocks opened and shut, regulators on the second pull, injectors and ejectors activated, water scoops lowered, and anything we had no knowledge of examined with the hands rather than the eyes.

♦

Many drivers had the most calloused hands, and if they greeted you warmly in their bone-cracking way, it was like touching something alien, such as the footpads of some giant dog. There seemed to be no warmth in them, no tactile mobility, no sense of flesh and blood, and no response – the clumsy caress of a seal lion's flipper at a marine park. When they were in the timekeeper's office, where the men consulted the notices and signed on and off, it was something of an ignorant surprise to see those huge mitts grasping a pen and, invariably, writing so beautifully.

Those hands had been the victims of constantly operating the locomotive, with the plethora of levers, cocks, taps, hoses and wheels associated with its operation, and their endless exposure to running water, scalding steam, coal dust, oils and greases, the weather, and grasping the other equipment they came into contact with, from hand-lamps to water-tank covers, from couplings to the darts that held the smokebox door closed and safe. All those ultimately took their toll.

And the men's history came into play, too. Every driver had put long years into being a fireman and, before that, started out as cleaners. Every task associated with locomotives made its contribution to a locomotive man's pathology – bad backs, damaged legs, ruined lungs, frequent bouts of pneumonia, gritty eyes, rheumatism, arthritis, loss of hearing, endless bruising – but the only thing that was obvious to a stranger was the handshake.

No wonder the old drivers at St. Margaret's grinned as they absorbed the sight of Black Bob Low's soft grandson! One of the most obvious features in the few photographs of my grandfather that I possess is the spectacle of his huge hands, and this brings back the memory of brief physical contact with more recent men working in the same profession.

♦

When I started to travel by train, the suburban stock I

mostly rode in was of the compartment type – six-a-side with a door at each extremity. First class compartments were five aside and more luxuriously upholstered, but they were rarely used by us as, to be caught in there with what was always a third-class ticket, would have encouraged raised voices, humiliation and, perhaps, an interview with a policeman, resulting in a clip around the ear or a possible fine. Occasionally we did break the rules and were puzzled by the need for wealthy people to have access to more seating space. Clearly, in those days, it was the wealthy who were more usually overweight.

Each door contained what was known as a 'drop-light', a glass window that could be lowered into the door. The glass was held in a beautifully-shaped and jointed wooden frame (mass-produced steel or aluminium came later) and the window height could be adjusted by means of a leather strap which was attached to the bottom of the window on the inside. If the window was closed, the strap was almost entirely on view and the window rested on a ledge or lip accessed by lifting the window and, simultaneously, pushing the window outwards. A fully-open window meant the strap was largely hidden, away down in the depths of the door.

The strap was three or more inches wide, drilled with a few holes to adjust the amount of draught admitted to the compartment as a result of being placed onto a rounded hook (generally brass) on the inside of the door, and it was doubled-over at the end – often with a piece of wooden dowel inserted in a loop – and stitched strongly to itself. This served the ingenious secondary purpose of stopping the assemblage from disappearing down into the depths of the door when the window was fully lowered, never to be seen again. The business end, where the strap was flexibly attached to the door, was also usually doubled over and fitted into a metal recess, but, in this case, the dowel was often replaced with a riveted brass clasp that sheathed the leather.

♦

In the days of steam, every compartment was a smoker unless it said it wasn't. On our Midland lines out of St. Pancras, three coach sets – usually a brake-third in the middle (six compartments), plus a third, and a first / third 'composite' (nine compartments each, with three dedicated to first class passengers in the compo), there might be only three non-smoking compartments, clearly indicated by the presence of a red, triangular 'No Smoking' sign glued immovably to the fixed windows at each side of the compartment. This was not always the case, and I dimly remember 'Smoking' signs that, presumably, meant, in their absence, the compartment, by default, was a non-smoker. This approach was, apparently, reversed when people who liked to smoke had contraband signs that resembled those of officialdom printed – or maybe a few pence given to a railwayman with access to printed stocks in the form of a bribe could achieve the same objective. Apparently, on boarding the train, they would paste their smoking sign on the glass and happily light up. Eventually, smoking compartments outnumbered non-smokers, to the practical elimination of the latter, and something had to be done. Hence the arrival of the 'No Smoking' sign.

Incidentally, there might also be a 'ladies-only' compartment, usually placed next to the guard's van, where the more nervous and fragile members of the delicate sex might feel protected by the close presence of authority. Of course, in a nine-coach train, there would be three guard's vans, and, maybe, three ladies-only compartments, but only one guard. Fear of crime that may never happen can be compensated for by groundless faith.

All those mostly-smoking compartments needed to be ventilated and, depending upon the time of year, the window would be dropped and then raised at the approach of a tunnel. Courtesy demanded that someone in close proximity to the window did the honours and, be it Elstree, Belsize or Camden Road tunnels, the window would be raised and then lowered again once the tunnel had been passed. Some overly-conscientious coves would also make adjustments at what amounted to long bridges, and if the weather changed for the worse, or another train roared past, further raising would be desirable. In spite of this constant, attentive adjustment, and particularly in winter, the air in trains at that time could be quite blue and impenetrable.

Those straps were expected to last for the life of the carriage and, unless they were slashed off by dodgy barbers in need of a strop strap (or even the occasional domestic householder not yet enamoured of the safety razor), that's what they did. Starting out life in a stiff, pale, thick, leathery brown, they quickly softened to the touch and darkened until they almost shone. They felt flexible and permanent, almost sensual, and gave a unique form of contact to the traveller.

♦

Facilitating the opening and closing of carriage doors has been a challenge to rolling-stock designers from the early days of the Liverpool and Manchester Railway. The problem was to make it easy to open when required, but to impede this activity at all other times. The soft option was to simply lock people in, and, due to tight clearances, the Ffestiniog Railway still adopts this policy, but locking the doors has its challenges when accidents or fire rear their ugly heads. Some railways made passengers open the window and lean out to grasp a handle on the outside of the coach. In fact, this has been the most lasting technique, down to the advent of driver or guard-operated doors which came in with second-generation diesel and electric multiple units on the main line and rather earlier on underground trains. Before throwing in the towel and removing the inside door handle altogether, various designs were to be found in the UK.

The LMS favoured a simple handle which was vertical

at rest. In theory, one knew when it was properly shut, owing to its position, while its likelihood of getting caught up in clothing and opening unintentionally was slight, but not impossible. Children were very good at opening these doors, usually causing momentary but considerable panic on the part of their mortified parents. Most railway carriage doors of the period had a double-latch which meant it could not open, even by leaning on it, so long as the first snib was still engaged. An attentive member of the station staff would espy a door on its first latch and give the door a hefty push to engage the second snib as the train went by. It was this double-latch arrangement that gave the door its satisfying 'ker-clunk' sound as it was shut.

The LNER had a rather nifty sliding handle in a housing that framed the to and fro action. This was perpetuated by British Railways in its earliest years – even on electric multiple units and diesel trains. I think this type was also used by the Great Western. This design was a distinct improvement as it was even less likely to get caught up in any clothing, and was practically child-proof. Lack of maintenance, however, sometimes meant that the handle became very stiff, and opening the door involved broken fingernails or resorting to lowering the window and opening the door from the outside.

Closing the doors of slam-door stock from the inside almost always involved dropping the window and pulling on the frame. I was quite unjustly threatened with a number of frightful punishments by a porter at St. Albans Station on the way home from school one day, owing to pulling, perhaps too vigorously, on the window-frame to shut the door of a delightful old Midland coach.

We were lucky to have these odd-ball coaches on our train home which, unusually, comprised seven coaches – two three-coach sets and an extra on the front, which could turn out to be almost anything. One I was very happy about was a Lancashire & Yorkshire Railway 10-compartment vehicle, well away from its home territory.

To return to my cause for embarrassment, said window,

much to my horror, fragmented into a sickening heap of broken glass and splintered wood liberally scattered in equal quantities on the platform and inside the train, which quickly turned to relief at realising I had sustained no personal injury, followed by an acute sense of injustice at the tirade from aforementioned portery person. The fact that I may well have assigned a beautiful piece of rolling stock to the scrapyard added to my discomfort. In those desperate days, even a small piece of essential maintenance could sign the death warrant for an elderly coach.

Anyway, those door handles were fun and tactile, if probably smothered in germs. Oh, and I didn't get reported to the police, as the threats emitting from the porter's mouth were never conveyed to anyone in greater authority.

Lucky me.

♦

Many shops, especially those selling breakables such as crockery, display little signs begging visitors to look with their eyes and not their fingers, with a threat of charging for the item if it is broken. Notwithstanding the injustice in this threat – the shop would undoubtedly try to extract the full retail price for the item and thus make a profit out of one's carelessness – we used to touch everything.

It comes back to the long hours of inactivity when in the pursuit of trains, but we touched the curly-legged Midland Railway platform seats, tracing the bumps and bends on those knobbly legs. We touched the framed pictures in the carriages of idealistic pre-grouping trains (LMS constituents only, of course, on our line) by Cuthbert Hamilton-Ellis, or the sepia photographs showing threatening skies over Buxton or Pitlochry in a wishful attempt to turn us into tourists. We examined the little tubes through which the emergency communication chain travelled from one compartment to the next and dared each other to touch the chain whose wrongful use would result in a fine of forty-shillings and, no doubt, a clip around the ear. We touched the luggage racks and climbed nimbly into them in crazy games of the aforementioned 'tig' or 'carriage he', in which the luckless pursuer had to keep his eyes closed under penalty of death. Even in a single compartment, it could take some time to be discovered, while the pursued giggled and gasped when light-fittings were accidentally kicked, and fingers became enmeshed in the woven string of the rack.

When the British Railways standard suburbans, essentially the same as those that had gone before, came on the scene with their brushed aluminium roof racks, they didn't seem anything like as robust as the pre-nationalisation ones, and fear of causing lasting damage inhibited the clambering somewhat. But for us, the LMS stock was predominant until the diesels arrived, so the games continued until the arrival of the open, part-gangwayed, diesel-multiple units when, with the likelihood of discovery greatly increased, the death-knell to all pranks was sounded.

One of our school chums, who seemed at the best of times to be slightly deranged, one day took umbrage at something someone said and, announcing he had had enough, he opened the door and got out onto the running board. In order to set the scene accurately, and explain why this incident warrants inclusion in this book, I should add that we were travelling at a good forty miles per hour at the time and were fast approaching what we called 'Sandridge Tunnel' which was, in fact, an overbridge about 200 feet long and divided into two by brick arches, one for the fast lines and one for the slow.

He got out, nevertheless, thoughtfully closing the door behind him.

Seconds later we were into Sandridge Tunnel.

We all looked at each other, events moving more quickly than our brains. At the end of the tunnel we peered out but couldn't see him on the track, which would have been well-nigh impossible, given the rapidly retreating bridge obscuring the view. The next six or seven minutes must have been the longest in our lives. Having gone through the exercise of trying to remember who had triggered his hefty over-reaction, with accusations and denials as to the guilty party flowing back and forth, we arrived back in Harpenden, not quite knowing what to do. In situations like this, does one brazen it out, explain, confess, or simply burst into tears? At aged about thirteen, any response would have been understandable.

But, as we opened our door and shamefacedly got out, so did our adventurer. He had hung onto the grab rail outside our compartment and swung, we knew not how, along the side of the coach, presumably like that scene in the pre-war film version of the 'Thirty Nine Steps', and gained admittance to the next compartment which was, fortunately, empty until his somewhat eccentric appearance. For a short moment we waited on the platform to see if our antics had been spotted, but they had not – not even by the driver and fireman who were just ahead of us on their Fowler 2-6-4 tank. So, all ended well, but there had been a lot of 'touching' of the white-knuckle variety that day.

Nowadays, grasping door-handles has become a gesture of the past as it is almost always about pushing buttons or simply waiting for the things to open. The level of personal responsibility in train travel has diminished in recent decades, as have the opportunities for amusement.

♦

Many will be astounded to read that slam-door stock was in daily use on the London Underground until about 1960. The Metropolitan Line still used it, both locomotive-hauled and in the form of multiple units, on its Rickmansworth and beyond trains, as well as the line to Watford. Until they reached Baker Street from 'Metro-land', they resembled trains on many other lines in Britain but things became very unusual if they continued on to the city – to Aldgate, Liverpool Street or Moorgate. All the stations revealed bowler-hatted city gents, pretty typists and workers from a myriad other trades, opening and closing slam-doors by hand as a matter of course on what, otherwise, appeared like a normal London Transport underground station. The normal rush-hour procedure – all over the country when using such rolling-stock – was to open the door long before the train stopped and, stepping nimbly onto the running board, exit the train at just the moment when it had slowed to one's own personal walking pace. Facing the direction of travel and, with the door opened wide, the commuter would stretch the leg furthest from the train outwards, and transfer weight to it, leaving the door open for others to follow. The last person to leave, glancing back into the compartment to make sure a tardy individual was not still struggling to his feet and pulling his dispatch case and umbrella off the rack, closed the door behind him. Anyone leaving the door open, thus delaying departure of the train, would be loudly admonished, or accused of being inconsiderate. It was not unusual to see the door firmly shut for departure before the train actually stopped. There was something balletic and elegant about it all. Getting off and on whilst moving was perfectly normal with trams and buses, too, in those days, and accidents were rare.

The Metropolitan stock that survived for so long had doors with semi-circular tops to them. This ingenious design ensured that, if an over-enthusiastic bread-winner opened the door while the train was still in the tunnel, impact with the tunnel wall would slam the door shut, hopefully without too much damage to the commuter or the rolling stock. But this seldom happened. Commuters, in those days, knew their stuff. They were a part of the machinery of travel and performed their role to the full. They were expert, skilful and professional travellers, in a way that is not now necessary.

♦

Pullman cars were a delight. In an earnest attempt to rethink train-travel, the highly original George Pullman devised levels of comfort that were unsurpassed when he started in business in 1864. His first cars were sleeping cars in the United States and, to maintain quality, he did everything, from building the cars in his own factory to providing personnel of every trade, which extended to seamstresses to repair the shirts of wealthy travellers. His rolling stock first came to Britain ten years later and, until after the Nationalisation of Britain's railways, the company remained independent. Sumptuous furnishings were the order of the day, with every conceivable surface lined in upholstered material, patterned and soft to the touch. There were solid and rare woods to please the eye, and high-quality glass on lamp fittings. As trains universally became more spartan and 'practical', Pullman knew their best course of action was to stay firmly rooted in the past in order to cater for a wealthy and traditional clientele.

On the rare occasions my family journeyed by Pullman, it was like transportation to an earlier age of elite luxury, permanence and wonder. It was all rather humbling, as if the conveyance had an ecclesiastical mien and we had entered the railway equivalent of a cathedral that demanded hushed voices and, if we had been wearing them, doffed caps. We felt privileged and terribly superior at the prospect of Pullman travel, but this conceit evaporated as we entered the hallowed halls of polished wood, glittering brass, and timeless style, and encountered our first gloved Pullman attendant, instinctively stepping aside when he approached us in the open saloon, to be followed by apologetic shuffling as he, simultaneously, stepped aside for us. We were glad our shoes were freshly polished and had made our entrance in clean clothes and with our hair freshly brushed. To us, Pullman travel was only a small step down from an audience with the monarch, and it was certainly the grandest thing I ever did as a boy. Without wealthy relatives – only a rare few of mine ever even had cars – holidaying with family and, just occasionally, in boarding houses, and exclusively living in homes linked in one way or another to their neighbours, nothing we ever did in life could match this moment of rare entitlement. There was so much to gasp at and to admire, which provided another opportunity to touch and to ponder.

That one could travel for eight hours and more from Edinburgh and enjoy not one but two meals without leaving our seats, the fact that nothing was rushed – not even the journey, which took us on the pretty route through Ripon and Harrogate before a reversal in Leeds where we paused and looked down loftily at the sprawling city – all smoke, noise and tatty tramcars – and that anything one could possibly want was available, was an extreme novelty. At the press of a bell-push, or a cursory wave of the hand at one of the immaculately turned-out attendants who would periodically pass through the cars intimating the arrival of another repast with menus followed by another visit to take our order, the level of service was indeed a wonder. In a leisurely fashion, the table would be laid with decorum; inconspicuous, professional and silent. There would be white tablecloths and napkins, silver cutlery and condiments, with, as the meal progressed (three courses plus coffee drunk incredibly slowly, as my mother loved to smoke one of her Du Maurier cigarettes while sipping delicately from her cup), the arrival of silver serving-dishes engraved with the Pullman insignia.

These were not put on the table for us to serve ourselves, but were displayed respectfully by the attendant as he asked what we desired and my parents would point out the individual slices of beef, potatoes and vegetables that took their fancy, and where, precisely, they wanted their gravy to be poured. This had followed the soup course, sometimes mock turtle or brown Windsor, that the attendant managed to serve without spilling, pausing occasionally and in skilful anticipation as the train hit a junction or suddenly swayed at the passing of another train, To those proffered dishes and mumbled inducements, my parents very much entered into the spirit of the thing, any premature shyness quickly dispelled and a desire to appear anonymous requiring a rapid elevation in class and manners. For the Pullman, my mother had a silver-mounted cigarette holder which only ever appeared in public and when we had guests. Casting one's eye around, one admired the silver condiment set, the cut glass table-lamps with heavy bases to prevent them from toppling over, and enjoyed the superlative ride offered by the six-wheeled bogies on some cars that rode like a luxury liner. Even the name, 'Pullman cars', set them above all else we, who rarely frequented restaurant cars, knew on the railway, while that term 'car' became, curiously, everyday when in the context of urban transport – trams and underground vehicles were always 'cars' to us.

Bored by the slow curl of cigarette smoke, the endless requests for coffee cups to be refilled, and the adult conversation that seemed to consist of many verbs but few, if any, subjects or objects surrounding them to which one could attach any meaning, clarity or interest, a request to visit the lavatory was rewarded by the sight and touch of brass pipework, generously-sized vitreous china sanitary-ware, soap with a very distinctive smell and a wet stickiness that remained on the hands for hours, bevelled and monogrammed glass mirrors, a foot treadle that opened a door at the bottom of the lavatory-bowl affording occasional glimpses of trackwork at junctions and the anticipated thrill of sluicing water onto the lines, and stained glass in the windows designed to admit light but no prying eyes and arranged in a beautiful oval shape that reeked of luxury, reflected in the shape of the windows in the car's external doors.

The most obvious difference in a Pullman was those doors. They opened inwards, which enabled the train attendants or 'conductors' to open them long before the train stopped in the station. This was particularly satisfying on entering Kings Cross, after a long and torturous journey on the 'Queen of Scots' from Edinburgh in winter time. There we were, rolling through the smoke-filled, occasionally illuminated mysteries of Gasworks Tunnel, with a hand on the brass fittings of the open door, our exit securely blocked by the uniformed bulk of the attendant who knew, as if by magic, which side of the train would be nearest the platform.

None of the commuter panic for disembarkation was present here. The train moved regally into the darkness of a Kings Cross peppered with a hundred yellow lamps illuminating a scene of understated interest. Shadowy Gresley tanks, their cabs lit by an occasional flash of orange light from open firebox doors, stood like dispersed cattle in a field on a dark night. The cathedral silence would be rudely interrupted by the bark of a J52 or J50 goods tank engine emerging from the depths below the station with its string of empty meat vans from Smithfield, long open wagons with mysterious sacking-encased packages from the docks, or empty coal trucks from the Southern, tranquillity returning as the goods train gained the mouth of the Gasworks tunnels. Rakes of gleaming mainline coaches, empty, dignified and quiet, stood in long straight rows. Incoherent station announcements made to a public that listened not, because it could not comprehend, nevertheless squawked, sizzled and coughed in the still air. Platform staff, their hands on dozens of barrows, or lingering, cigarettes in hand, their backs against the brick pillars that stretched way up into the semi-darkness, counted away the hours to the end of the shift. A misplaced refreshment trolley with an irritated lady attendant directed to an arrival platform by mistake and now heading as quickly as her wrinkle-stockinged, long-before-Norah-Batty legs can take her to the concourse to miss the throng and locate a soon-to-depart, late-evening train, *sans* refreshment car, where anxious passengers with rumbling tummies awaited the arrival of her modest range of unimaginatively-filled sandwiches, Lyon's fruit pies and the warmish contents of her battered tea urn. A railway policeman, erect and spare, hands behind his back, buttons gleaming, and a PC49 moustache neatly trimmed, stood surveying everything and nothing. A dispersed knot of unintroduced members of the public waited to receive travel-weary relatives, perhaps with a Lanchester or a Wolseley parked just outside the station – no meters, no yellow lines and no fuss – before heading back to Hampstead or Kilburn. The welcoming glow from W.H. Smith's, emptying now, the racks for daily papers cleared for the next day's deliveries, a small pile of rubbish in the corner protected by a discarded long-handled brush. A breeze, bringing shivers and the sounds of traffic from Euston Road, threatened to disperse the newly-tidied floor.

The train would draw to a halt in the platform and our attendant would step regally off the train before turning to face us touching his cap as he helped with the luggage. If we needed a porter, and we always seemed to, he would step to the centre of the platform, arm uplifted. I do not remember if coins exchanged hands but I suspect they did. Barrow successfully laden, we would follow the porter as he marched quickly along, shouting for a clear passage until we reached the limit of his territory at the edge of the saintless Pancras Road, the incongruous detached house that people said had been an advertising gimmick for a long-forgotten house-builder at our backs. More touching of caps and coins definitely changing hands, the moment of luxury and class, which had commenced on the long curved platform at Waverley Station in bright sunlight, was suddenly and comprehensively over.

With the porter and his barrow returning to the lamp-glow of the station, it would be dad carrying the cases and directing events, while mother grasped my and my brother's hands in her gloved palms and we would struggle through the briefly-pausing traffic and up the flight of steps into the sainted St. Pancras station. In no time we would be boarding our slow local train home; the familiar, the ordinary, contrasting with what had been before. But, we were soon going to be home.

And home was, when all was said and done, best.

♦

Petrified with fear – driven more by fear of rejection than anything else – trains were good places to hold girls' hands if an empty compartment could be located.

I remember one girl who did not want to be seen holding hands in public – her trepidation was due to anxiety over possible discovery by one of her mother's wide circle of friends who, she imagined, would be lurking around every corner and only too eager to report any sightings of her daughter in, what ranked as 'compromising situations' that, nowadays, would be thought of as staggeringly innocent. Even for those days, her mother was a trifle prudish and extremely strict.

And she didn't like boys around her daughter.

With that girl, I yearned for dark nights and anonymous cinema seats, unlit walks home, and a quiet park bench under trees in the park, but trains played their part too. Armed with my scholar's season ticket, the cost of taking her out to the cinema in St. Albans – where the flea-pit nature of the venues in Harpenden were distinctly improved upon – was only increased by her 1/8d fare – quite a percentage of my modest pocket-money but worth it in terms of making a good impression. That would be about eight pence in today's money for a five mile return journey.

In those days, one 'took a girl out' in every sense – picking the venue (after ascertaining her current favourite film which was invariably dictated by her preference regarding the leading actor) and in a financial sense too – fare, if necessary, the cinema ticket of course, and the essential bag of sweets (I don't remember popcorn) consumed quickly before the main feature started and serious snogging could commence without interruption from latecomers, ice-cream usherettes with their wretched downward-pointing, flickering, invasive torches, and the risk of the house lights coming up as they did frequently throughout the preliminaries of advertising, newsreels, previews, cartoons and even the B-picture. Frustration was measured by the performance of the house lights and the inability in those days for cinemas to 'get on with it'; not like now where the film is followed as quickly as possible by a clearing of the theatre and repetition of the main feature.

The evening would end with a walk back to her house and a chaste kiss before the obligatory pause to see her walk up the path, open the door, and disappear inside. I would even wait to see the hall light extinguished and know she was safely upstairs.

We knew how to behave with respect in those days.

So, there we were, sitting on the train, her hand in mine, deep down beside the mysteries of her thigh, the rough material of her mid-knee skirt brushing my long-trousered leg, lips bruised, returning home, relaxed, happy … but cautious.

Always cautious.

Something must have warned me of impending danger as I picked up a newspaper from the empty seat beside me – a thing I would never normally do in a girl's company, the priority being to remain ever-attentive. Maybe a sixth sense came into play, as reading the paper would certainly not count as being attentive.

It was an "Evening Standard" as I recall, open at the crossword, impressively near-completion and fortuitously no longer in pristine condition – a shambles of a paper, folded and shredded like the paper in the bottom of a budgerigar cage. Her hand, warm and soft in mine, suddenly froze and then gripped me tightly. I turned to her and her expression was one of abject fear. I didn't know at the time, but the coated and trilby-hatted figure who had entered the compartment just as we were moving off was her father.

And this was an old-fashioned compartment with

nowhere to hide.

Knowing the house-rules, and having kept them so assiduously during the reign of that relationship, I could tell we were in some sort of trouble, but I did know the extent of our predicament as her father and I had never been introduced. She looked so frightened that I knew discretion was required Using my free hand, I spread the newspaper over our knees while moving slightly away and, rather clumsily, taking a pen from the inside pocket of my evenings-out Harris Tweed jacket.

Unfortunately, it was my left hand, and while I am ambidextrous and even left-handed in some regards, I was chastised into using my right hand for writing by my preparatory school which took a dim view of my odd habit of handing my pen from one hand to the other as it progressed across the page. This curtailment of my natural inclinations was undertaken aged five, while I was probably fifteen at the time of which I am writing. Yes, it was the last full year of steam trains and compartment stock, so I must have been fifteen – fourteen or fifteen.

So, with the object of my immature attentions peering at the crossword in a detached, 'fancy meeting you on the train, what a coincidence' pretence, we attempted to maintain the deception by my first somewhat rudely greeting her father without shaking his hand – my right hand still gripping his daughter, and left-handed handshakes unknown in Hertfordshire – and then earnestly trying to work out the clues in the crossword. The train moved off into the night, with that gentle fore-and-aft movement conveyed through the stock by the locomotive, smoke passing the window in a fleeting cirrus, with a brief view of the lamp shining from above the booking desk in the St. Albans North signalbox and the lights from the compartment dancing along the low cutting bank. We settled into our contorted pose while she exchanged a few words of greeting and innocent explanation with her father. I smiled, hoping that the worst was over.

All would have been well if the rest of the crossword

had defeated us but, as well as being very pretty, the girl in question was extremely bright.

'Four across, five letters, "a building of no obvious purpose", the word is 'folly',' she blurted out.

'Are you sure?' I questioned, anticipating the situation she was steering us into better than she, and praying for alternatives to her stated crossword solution – for doubt, for delay, for time.

'Yes, yes,' she cried. ''It is. It fits! Folly. F-O-L-L-Y' And then, the *coup de grâce*, caution thrown to the wind, 'Go on! Write it in!'

So, in my best five-year-old hand, a leftover from prep-school days, not advanced since the violence of the classroom, I scrawled the missing letters while her father, bemusedly, looked on.

The rest of the journey was spent looking for ways of uncoupling hands which was finally achieved by the girl herself, looking out of the window and distracting her father with an imagined flashing light somewhere in the north St. Albans darkness.

That night, I walked home alone.

A few months later, just after she dumped me on the grounds of needing to concentrate on her schoolwork, which was a lame device to let me down gently on the appearance of an older, better-looking rival for her attentions – he was even having driving lessons – she moved schools to one in St. Albans which entitled her to her own scholarly season.

I wouldn't have minded, too much, but if we had remained 'an item', I could have taken her to the cinema in St. Albans without having to fork out for her train fare.

♦

During a holiday at Rye Harbour in 1955, my family self-catered in a delightful cottage standing in its own pretty garden.

What a holiday that was! Ten years old and a greater

degree of freedom than I had ever experienced before. There were battered hulks to explore drawn up on the marshy mud-flats around the shore – one, I remember, was called the 'Alsina', an old, wooden fishing boat with a little wheel-house at the rear that smelled vaguely of fish, and a cavernous hold which holiday-making and local boys explored using an old ladder and a rope.

There were crabs and eels to catch, jelly-fish to beat to death with sticks when they became stranded on the harbour wall as the tide went out and we could get our revenge on stings inflicted as punishments for carelessness in the water, a wide variety of strange dwellings scattered around, including at least one old railway carriage which I would have preferred to the beautiful cottage we occupied, and, across the river, the remains of the Rye & Camber railway station with three foot gauge track set in concrete near the platform.

On the western side of the estuary, where the cottage still stands, just a little step to the north, was the end of a disused goods-only, standard-gauge branch line which, in better days, served the harbour. Now, long since defunct, it was full of what were known as 'crippled' wagons – a term that is probably unacceptable nowadays but which we all used innocently enough and without any disrespect in those simpler times – and these broken, unloved and, no doubt, doomed trucks stretched all the way back to Rye, well over a mile away.

When we had caught all the eels we needed, and kicked over the crab-pots into which we had deposited all manner of writhing and irritated livestock, nothing pleased us more than some wild games among the trucks. In and out of them we ran, ducking through the wheels, coupling and uncoupling them (well, that was chiefly done by a boy of about my age who was built like a boxer and who had a long piece of wood that proved most efficacious for this task) and, in our imaginations, turning that peaceful corner of Sussex into the lawlessness of the Texas panhandle. Hide, crawl, stand-up, wriggle through under the wheels, whoop and yell, hide again – we hoped our adventure would never end.

But then I misjudged the need to look before standing up.

I can confirm, a ten year old boy's head is no match for the buffer of a railway wagon. Up I stood, and that was the last thing I knew for a while.

I came to with my head cradled in the lap of our personal Rocky Marciano who, having mopped the blood, was on the point of calling for help. I knew a return to our holiday home would incur no sympathy at all. Instead, all sorts of inventive punishments and a ban on all exploits on the old railway line would come my way. So, I pleaded for more time, a continuation of the first aid, and more washing of the bump in Rye's brackish water, courtesy of the River Tillingham.

For once, due to my situation, people actually did what I asked – the underdog becoming overdog *in extremis* – and in no time I was looking very much better than I felt. As the wound was above my hair-line (and I had a good head of hair in those days), I was able to hide my situation pretty well; so long as I avoided being seen 'face on', in which case my resemblance to one of Francis Bacon's tortured portraits would have given the game away.

I could, in short, conceal my injury. A return to the cottage was achieved without discovery or any need to disclose the true cause of my bumped head. Indeed, kids are always bumping their heads, as I explained to my mother. No harm done. And in those days, Disprin were happily handed out for every ailment, so the headache soon went.

That was, however, a case of 'too much touch'!

♦

In 1962, my last 'family holiday' was spent in Bregenz-am-Bodensee, by the expanse of water we more usually know as Lake Constance. My mother was 'into opera', and she yearned to see a performance or two on the famous floating stage on the lake. The fact that the town was situated about four miles from the German border and a little further from Switzerland, with all of its railway interest, would no doubt have softened my father's resolve to avoid classical music, and especially opera, at all costs. So, we ended up staying in a house belonging to a young widow and her four children. In those days, it was quite normal for travel agents to book accommodation and all the travel documents as an early form of 'package', and it was equally common for the accommodation to be in a private house.

The house backed onto the railway line from Bregenz to Lindau in Germany as it skirted the lake on a low-walled embankment.

So, imagine the scene: house, small garden, single track electrified railway on the overhead system, low wall with a drop of a little under two metres, then the placid blue waters of the lake, skirted by a very narrow, tideless, pebbly beach.

We became firm friends with the Hershers, the Frau Doctor being a wonderful hostess who went out of her way to make us comfortable. The presence of her daughter was, for me, an added attraction. She was about fifteen, tall, pretty, and cautious. I was seventeen, plagued with a disfiguring outbreak of impetigo on my face, and very much attracted.

Whilst we often did the touristy things – climbing hills, visiting villages, managing to travel by train almost everywhere, and spending many, too many, evenings watching the Vienna Philharmonic accompany several operatic stars of international renown thrashing through Mozart – there were a few free afternoons where we would all end up on the rudimentary beach by the lake. This was approached by simply traversing the garden and then the railway track which had to be walked along for about two-hundred metres before a suitable point for dropping onto the beach could be reached.

The technique adopted by the Hershers was simple. Wait for a train bound for Lindau in Germany (which would just have left Bregenz station) and, as it was a single line, a good time would have to pass before another train would come from the German direction. They had it in their heads that there was always a balancing working – one to Germany, one back, one to Germany, one back, and so on.

So, off we went to lean on the flimsy gate in anticipation. In the fullness of time, the elderly Austrian boxy electric *(see the picture at the start of this chapter)* duly tottered past, whistling in uncanny imitation of a Caledonian Railway steam engine, as it prepared to make its international crossing. By that point, it was probably travelling at about thirty miles an hour. Our Austrian hosts, beaming from ear to ear and displaying knowing glances, set off for the beach, with the Low family trailing behind, travelling as Brits abroad surely did in those days with arms full of towels and swimming costumes, books to read, cameras, and my father's many guidebooks and maps for detailed planning of the next day's outing. Additionally, my Dad carried the smallest Hersher child in his arms.

I seem to remember a bit of a delay – perhaps we had forgotten the *Piz Buin* suntan cream, or the bottle-opener for the *apfelsaft,* I do not know, but I do recall that we took a long time to actually gain the trackbed. We started to walk, facing Germany, talking and laughing, watching the Hershers dropping off the wall far ahead, the pretty Christl walking straight into the lake like the water-baby she was, and turning to wave at us.

At me, I hoped.

I remember her singing like an Austrian version of a Lorelei siren as she stood there, laughing, up to her knees in the lake's warm water. I was smitten.

I have probably implied this already.

Then suddenly, too suddenly, the Caledonian whistle. From behind us.

We were not going to experience a reciprocated

222

working from Germany. A shout from my mother, a roar from my father, and the repeated screech of the locomotive whistle. My brother was propelled into inner space, followed by my parents – Dad still clutching the youngest in the pack. Surprisingly slow for my age, I chose to drop down to sit on the wall with my legs dangling over the narrow beach as the hot, oily axle-boxes of the locomotive's driving wheels passed far too close to my shoulders.

'Get down!' roared my father, but to propel myself off that wall would have required a moment of sitting up and that I was not prepared to do. While British trains had no hazards below the footboards attached to the bottom of the carriage body, other than the occasional additional one for the guard, continental trains had to be equipped to enable ingress and egress from a platform that really wasn't a platform at all. And that meant a small flight of stairs from very near ground level. So I crouched, and felt the hissing draught of the steps for each and every coach slicing past my ear as I bent forward and prayed I had done enough to avoid premature death.

I can still hear the cruel rush of air interminably pulsing past me.

Afterwards, I calculated the bottom steps on a train of six or eight coaches – two or three doors to each coach – can only have been about an inch from my cowering neck, an accelerating draught indicating the extreme proximity of those lethal steel and wood steps. Not touch, but certainly 'near touch'. Very near touch.

Even to this day, I give moving trains a respectfully wide berth.

A recent look at Bregenz on Google Earth revealed shocking and startling change. The house we stayed in has gone, replaced by a car park canyon between a low block of flats and some offices. The main station has upped-sticks and moved further into the town, leaving a small platform adjacent to a marina full of fancy cruisers. The little beach that we sat on amongst the flotsam of the lake, our backs to the walled railway embankment, has been turned into a promenade with flowerbeds and architect-placed designer trees, moving the lake a considerable distance away from the railway. And, of course, the adults in our happy party, living on a form of borrowed time after the near tragedy, have probably all passed away in the interim fifty-five years.

But I still think occasionally of the pretty Austrian.

♦

The Lancashire & Yorkshire Railway was a proud railway.

It displayed its name wherever and whenever possible. From the War Memorial at Victoria Station, Manchester, to the trespass notices at every level crossing and bridge, there was never any doubt about ownership. During the year Roger Bannister broke the seemingly impossible four-minute mile, a visit to relatives in Macclesfield was greatly improved from my point of view by a visit to Manchester conducted by my father. If we saw any of 'cottonopolis', I don't remember it, but we certainly saw a lot of trains.

Whilst Dad was an unashamed steam man, he took a passing interest in other things, so we managed to see the new electrification of the Sheffield line while shiny locomotives were tested and their drivers were being trained, we travelled on the Manchester, South Junction & Altrincham for a few stations and, most interesting of all, travelled out to Bury on the third-rail.

This was in the days of the L&Y stock, and the whole process of boarding and alighting from a train had to be re-learned by us as those trains were quite unlike anything else we had ever seen before. The vehicles, assembled in five-coach sets, were long and open with horsehair-stuffed leather seats that resembled those of a tram. At the end of the cars, there was an open platform roughly triangular in shape with the end of the coach forming a right-angle to the entrance and the hypotenuse containing the door into the saloon. It was therefore possible to board a train by stepping onto the open platform before opening the door into the saloon and for the train to move off with passengers clinging to whatever they could. This was deliberate, and anticipated their use in practice which was about quick-loading, short-journey, rush-hour services, where the predominant clientele would be regular commuters who would learn to cope with trains that were extremely fast off the mark. To my mind, the BR replacements seemed far slower.

We, of course, were not experts but, fortunately, we were not travelling in the rush hour, and a lot of grabbing and grasping the door fittings was not further complicated by frustrated regulars working around us. But we did set off 'on the move' and had to negotiate that door – my brother being only about five at the time – with much pulling and pushing before we arrived in the sanctuary of the saloon which resembled pictures I owned of American rolling stock. I remember the Lancashire &Yorkshire monogram on the racks over the seats and the strange ringing sound of the gears as the train accelerated away from Victoria, the third-rail encased in wooden boards, and the round spectacles in the cabs of Aspinall 0-6-0s dotted around in great numbers from Victoria to the sidings and sheds in Bury.

But I remember, most of all, the struggle with the door on the hypotenuse, another 'touch and more' memory.

♦

For a while in 1967, as already mentioned, I taught at Balornock Primary school in the east end of Glasgow. It is still there now, although many of its rather spartan features may have been modernised. The only real 'inside' there was at the school in my days was the classrooms – all access on both floors being in the form of balconies and walkways that ran the length of the building and, since the children were not admitted until the arrival of 'teacher', I would arrive outside the classroom to the sight of raggedy, wet children shivering and not a little resentful at my sometimes tardy appearance.

At the time of which I am speaking, Balornock Primary had a very mixed catchment area. There were many tidy, well-kept council houses with neat and loved gardens, but there was also a smattering of run-down and unhealthy tenements, all overlooked by the sentinels that were the Red Road Flats – then, new and optimistic, but now, disgraced and demolished. The scheme was still being built when I was there, and those allocated a Red Road flat felt superior to all the others in the neighbourhood, boasting of its claims to fame, notably the height of the, to be, eight blocks – at the time the tallest in Europe – and the eventual population which rose to thousands. Many of the children in my care were, however, very poor, with about a third on assisted lunches and the same percentage had to see the 'green lady' periodically on account of harbouring 'nits' – head lice, if you like. Or don't like.

Deprived, in many ways, but those kids had a spirit and an energy that that would put many more fortunate to shame.

My route, from where I was living at the time in Motherwell, took me all the way in to the Celtic Football ground, and then I would point my little Austin A35 van northwards to negotiate the infamous Blackhill before hitting the safer acres of Balornock.

Glasgow, in those days, could still claim to be an industrial city, and my route took me past Beardmore's steelworks at Parkhead Forge, a huge industrial site completely surrounded by human habitation. Diving under a wide railway bridge, there was a careworn, industrial railway line crossing the road at ground level on an acute angle, with a shambolic gate that was usually closed in favour of the road. But, at times, the gate, manned by flat-capped, skeletal workers dragging on hand-rolled cigarettes cradled in their tight-fingered fists, would be closed across the road traffic, and a huge billet of steel on a large wagon propelled by a small diesel shunter would appear moving at not much above walking pace.

Visually interesting, that was not the lasting memory. Sitting in my little van with the windows closed against the cold air of autumn and, frequently, avoiding the sting of wind-troubled rain, the heat from the billet would penetrate every orifice in the car. Suddenly, the ineffective heater was overwhelmed by a sensation that defied description.

The very air was burning.

The billet, all transformed steam engines and scrapped ships, old cars and the acetylened detritus of a passing industrial age, trundled slowly across the road on its way to the rolling mill – its passing welcomed on two counts. In moments, the temperature would drop to something more comfortable and, the little engine propelling its load of perhaps fifty tons having passed into the walled vastness of the rolling mill, the road would be reopened.

Parkhead Forge is now no more, its name retained for the inevitable shopping centre that it has become. Where the heroes of another age laboured in dangerous conditions for little pay; where a company that had reduced its activities from building the cars, taxis, aircraft, ships and locomotives of the past to the basic functions of steel making; where drawn-faced men held up the traffic for skin-peeling and pedestrian passage of red-hot billets over the road, lines of congestion now nose slowly into one of the hundreds of free car-parking spaces to binge on Primark, Asda and JD Sports, and to feed the inner man at MacDonald's, before collapsing into the popcorn-hazed multiplex for yet another mindless, forgettable blockbuster.

But I think again of the shabby workmen, the grubby little shunter and the heat from that steel billet. Was life then so bad, I wonder?

♦

I don't know who was more surprised, the Port Penrhyn

employees or us. Very little had been said about the afternoon's activities by our house party leaders back at the Bangor boarding school we occupied for a fortnight. There had been a lot of intense Christianity that week – the usual simple answers to complicated questions that young boys, I was about twelve at the time, normally settle for and accept with little or no question – and the mention of 'Bethesda', which had an Old Testament ring to it, gave no clue as to the content of the afternoon. The leaders, a well-meaning bunch, thoroughly enjoyed mysteries – well, it rather came with the territory – so we had to accept a number of 'ah's' and 'wait and sees' until lunch was over.

We set off on foot through Bangor to the port, a straggling crocodile swinging box cameras and 127s while, gradually, the news leaked out of the purpose of our sloppy route-march. And yet, how can you picture it, a bunch of schoolchildren from the Home Counties? A quarry? A narrow-gauge railway? A goods train journey?

The Science Museum in London, before it became a form of static Disneyland, had modest displays that required more than fifteen seconds of on-the-move observation. My father and I could spend all day in it – well, all day, other than a dip into King's Cross and a ride around the Circle Line – but there was nothing more exciting than the rusty remains of 'Rocket', dozens of glass cases containing beautiful scale models, a collection of cars, scientific instruments, motor bikes, domestic interiors – cookers, baths and so on, the chance to have millions of volts pass through you with a loud bang but no lasting injury, aircraft hanging from the ceiling, and a pendulum hanging from the roof that demonstrated how unstable Planet Earth was.

Very exciting, therefore.

There was also a number of dioramas – an art form probably largely forgotten now – where an attempt was made to establish a three-dimensional effect by building a glass-cased model on a concave curve comprising a painted backcloth with a foreground of gradually more complete features until, nearest the glass, the objects gained precise, scaled, intimate authenticity. There were several of these dioramas, but I remember only a few – an ocean liner, an airfield cluttered with flimsy aircraft beneath an airship, a landscape near the sea with what used to be called a *charabanc* drifting downhill towards an improbably blue seaside and, in an industrial section, the Penrhyn Quarries.

So, those of us who had had the good fortune to be swept into the Science Museum on occasions, knew what we were going to observe. A mountainside torn open like a mortally wounded animal, its interior bared for all the world to see, exploited, pillaged, stripped of its goodness, and ruined. A large number of tiers, clearly twenty or thirty feet apart, ran around the scarred surface like contours, and on each of them, the nearest beautifully modelled, those furthest away mere paintings executed with the precision of a Canaletto, men worked with the rock – blasting, cutting and loading blocks of slate into wagons sitting on a tracery of narrow-gauge railways. There were at least two tiny engines, cabless, tenderless and improbably dainty.

Our long walk to Port Penrhyn was rewarded by the dignified sight of the Harbour Master's office – a bijou industrial pseudo, country house, worthy of National Trust sponsorship, standing in the middle of a network of railway tracks, narrow and standard gauge – rows of wagons, and a number of coasters tied drunkenly beside the harbour awaiting the incoming tide. A standard-gauge 2-6-0 shunted the yard and, away at the far end, 'Linda', a large narrow-gauge Hunslet tank engine, was assembling the last of the afternoon 'up' train that included, at the rear, about three, small vehicles, rather like overgrown toast-racks.

The first thing that occurred to me was how big they were. They were heavy, four-wheeled, cumbersome things, each labelled with an identifying alpha character, painted in a form of dark, reddish brown, and coupled to the rest of the train with chains hanging below central buffers. There were no roofs and, as we quickly found out, no springing and no braking system operated from the engine. As the train comprised about a dozen empty slate wagons and our three little coaches, we soon learned about taking up the slack in order to get a goods train on the move. The wagons were all reversed until they clattered into our conveyances and then 'Linda' moved off smartly in a southerly direction. From stationary, we were instantly travelling at five or six miles an hour, schoolboy bottoms bouncing over crazy trackwork on unsprung axles. Touch does not necessarily imply through the fingers and, in no time at all, we were feeling every single rail-joint as though each one was the first. In no time, I risked reprimand by standing up, ostensibly to take a picture, but in fact to protect my coccyx. The banging wheel joints, coupled with the constant change of speed that caused the carriages to strike their neighbours before stretching away again caused one of the leaders to joke about Victorian train travel. And that is what it was. Open air, third-class, four-wheeled, smut-laden, and smoke in the eyes – like an old lithograph of the Liverpool & Manchester Railway. All we needed to complete the picture was the rain.

Then it started to rain.

'Linda' barked up the bank, slower than at first, before coming to a slithering halt on the greasy rail on one occasion and repeating its backing up and running away again trick. More bad backs and discomfort. And a sense of helplessness. Oh yes, we were enjoying the unusual journey, we really were, but couldn't it just end?

At Bethesda, biblical only in name, despite the omnipresence of non-conformist chapels as yet still performing their original purpose, 'Linda' came off her train which was then propelled to the bottom of the first incline. Some of the more adventurous of us climbed that first incline to see a number of the little locomotives on this authentic diorama, while the rest of us inspected the soon-to-be-famous 'scrap line' and looked around the railway works where 'Marchlyn' was undergoing a general overhaul. The odd thing is that the locomotives on that scrap line are, for the most part, now happily restored! That is the odd thing about works of reminiscence, like this book. Sometimes, what we saw fading away, is now on its way back!

We travelled back those long miles to Port Penrhyn, the rain thankfully abated and nothing further amiss occurred, save the sore bottoms and the unfortunate derailment of 'Linda' as she made her way around to collect a few more empty slate wagons.

We left the Port Penrhyn staff expertly levering her back onto the track and scratching their heads about the English lads with plummy accents who made a special trip just to sit upright in the pouring rain on their little train.

♦

A holiday in Germany introduced me to the dubious delights of a chairlift.

Even though the conflict ended a mere fifteen years earlier, Germany – recovering remarkably quickly from the devastation of a lost war – seemed to be a country full of interest and many surprises, not the least being the idea of seating people in a flimsy double-seat hanging under a steel cable and launching them unceremoniously into space.

My family, as already implied, consisted of my two parents, my brother and me.

One would have thought we boys would have been shared out equally – one child to each adult – on such a perilous quest. I was, after all, only fifteen, and my brother had just passed his eleventh birthday. To those reading this book who ski, or those who frequent pleasure parks where nausea and vertigo are the rewards for considerable financial outlay, the idea of plunging into a gravity-defying void will seem the most natural thing in the world. But we had no experience of this. Travelling fairgrounds were the pinnacle of death-defying pleasure to us, which meant nothing more than a sedate ride around in a circle on a horse that rose and fell rhythmically, or a helter-skelter so greasy and awkward that descent was made at walking pace at best – not much helter and certainly devoid of skelter.

My mum, you see, suffered from heights, which is probably why the decision was made to pair my brother with me, so that dad could take care of his apprehensive wife. I have no idea why the chairlift was attempted – the view could have been enjoyed more rewardingly if we had climbed the hill ourselves, a thing we often did – but attempted it was.

The chairs were rigidly attached to the cable, so one simply stood with one's back to the contrivances as they arrived around a horizontal wheel and unceremoniously clobbered us in the back of the knees. Guttural German – only heard rarely before that time and certainly entirely incomprehensible – together with frantic arm-movements, indicated the action one had to take and, to our credit, my brother and I managed to wriggle backwards onto the seat and pull the bar closed as we swung skyward.

I should add, there were no seat belts.

A chairlift is a novel form of transport, and one which I have subsequently repeated. The unstable chairs swung about in response to our every movement. They quickly took us aloft so that we were soon above the rooftops – a novelty for two boys who had never been in an aircraft – and jiggled in a frightening and hesitant way as the cable crossed the pulley wheels that doubled as pylon supports and subtle direction changers. Up the hillside we went, with the Rhine winding languorously below us. We could observe trains on the eastern side of the river steaming along from our holiday town of Linz-am-Rhein through tunnels and past fairy-tale castles, tiny like an elaborate model railway, some passenger – with four and six-wheelers, as well as bogie-coaches for more remote destinations – but mostly freight, long, fast, air-braked, headed by large 2-10-0s, some with Franco-Crosti boilers. We could see ferries and many freight barges, some self-propelled and some pushed by what one might inaccurately call 'tugs'. One, at least, was a steamer, with big, thrashing paddle wheels and two long funnels, the smoke from them curling away lazily through the heavily-scented, insect swarmed, fruit-laden vineyards that climbed dizzyingly up the steep sides of the gorge. It was all entrancing and wonderful; like taking part in a cinematic travelogue. We were engrossed. We were charmed. We were flying.

I couldn't blame my brother.

He was, as I have said, only eleven. But at a particularly substantial pylon, he assumed we were at our destination and opened the restraint in preparation to disembark – if that is the right word to use where chairlifts are concerned. We jiggled over the pulley wheels as my slow brain gradually appreciated the situation unfolding before us.

We were not at the end of the line.

Not by a long chalk.

I should add that the restraint bar that loosely crossed our tummies was also attached to the one and only footrest. So, bar pushed forwards, the footrest dropped away below our feet. We were, thus, restraintless and footrestless. I did mention the lack of seat belts, didn't I?

We jiggled over a string of pulley wheels and changed direction while I wrestled with the bar and our feet swung freely below us, any ability to force ourselves back into the seat effectively removed by the loss of the footrest. My brother only slowly realised our true predicament. He turned helplessly for comfort towards our parents who quickly disappeared from view as we turned from an up-gradient of perhaps one-in-ten to a similar down grade as soon as we left the pylon behind – cables always being relatively slack on chairlifts. Furthermore, that pylon was situated on a high bluff where the countryside ahead of us dropped away alarmingly. Having followed the gradient of the hillside for perhaps half a mile from where our journey started close by the river, we were now looping dangerously across a deep valley. Pleasant views of the river were no longer high on our list of priorities, even though unsuspecting parents were frustrated by our seeming lack of interest in the view.

We were too busy trying to stay alive for wide-eyed contemplation.

By this time, of course, my brother was totally co-operative and we both managed to close the bar which, as I have indicated, raised the footrests to their proper travelling position. From then on our hands gripped the bar as if our lives depended on it … which they did, especially so as the drop below became one of two or three hundred feet as the cable swayed across a deep valley in one gigantic, sagging loop, the fabled German pines waving a sinister welcome to us from far below.

For his pains, my brother was included in a general admonition for not getting the visual most we could from the journey, while I, as usual, was accused of exaggeration when I tried to explain the opening of the restraint-bar and my heroic rescue of the next generation of Lows.

I can understand my parent's disappointment at our behaviour. All we did was grip the bar as tightly as blood-flow would allow and concentrate on the blessed sight of the upper station. Nothing else mattered.

Mum, having overcome her fear of heights, at least temporarily, we returned to the riverside after a while in a more satisfactory parent / child formation.

♦

Returning from a holiday in Germany in 1960, it was clear, as we approached Ostend, that it was blowing a gale. Washing flapped on lines in back-gardens in a demented attempt to escape their pegged restraints; elderly women struggled across roads, their loose clothing billowing in the wind, turning them around and rendering them as unsteady as an early-morning alcoholic; and, at the frequent level-crossings, men and women held on to hats and scarves, their eyes squeezed shut against the billowing dust, added to by the passage of our electric locomotive-hauled international express.

This did not augur well. Four hours in the tender caring arms of the Belgian Marine faced us. Two weeks before, we had made the journey from Folkestone, and I had been surprised at how sick I felt on what was, to all intents and purposes, a calm sea. Far from being fitted with stabilisers, my father was convinced it had a flat bottom, which would be fine if we had been travelling on the Grand Union Canal.

As suspected, when we arrived at the port and detrained, struggling with belongings and coats in a veritable hurricane, the sea resembled a scene from 'Above us the Waves'. It boiled, it roared, it crashed over the dockside and the ship, while we walked at about forty-five degrees from vertical clutching luggage and each other.

'We'll be fine when we get on board', our parents announced.

As I found out for myself much later where my own two children were concerned, parents are frequently pathological liars.

The ship groaned against the berth, one second trying to tear itself away, the next threatening to mount the harbour wall.

'We'll go and get something to eat,' the adults suggested.

I must say I was surprised at the strange metal hoops, about two inches deep and the size of a plate, clipped to the table-tops with industrial-quality butterfly nuts, but I took no real notice. We had been travelling for much of the night in a couchette, and had been constantly awakened by engine changes, the vigorous pounding of a banker up from Aachen, and the demands of passport control as we both left Germany and arrived in Belgium. In short, we were exhausted. A tasty, if greasy, omelette was consumed before attempting to go up to the deck.

The ship had already set sail and I, for one, was feeling distinctly odd. It resembled the dizzy unreality of coming-to after an extraction at the dentist. On getting to my feet, I quickly sat down again as some loose china crashed to the floor somewhere along the restaurant. The waiters more-or-less ran with lightly-laden trays but, even so, clutching at plate-sides with curled thumbs, gravity doomed their best intentions. I took to my feet again and, with the rest of my family, lurched from table to table, grasping at each other and the furnishings on that old, battered ship. Not so much 'touch' – more a case of grasp.

One view out to the deck, closed as a matter of necessity to the public, revealed a scene that could hardly be imagined. The ship slipped in and out of huge, green troughs, so deep that the bow went down at forty-five degrees with the sea all around us. I looked up once and saw the sky as if I was looking at it though the bottom of an outsized green drinking glass. Then, with an ear-shattering groan, the ship twisted upwards and climbed out into the improbable sunshine, only to return immediately to its nose-dive into the depths of the ocean.

I am sure this extraordinary spectacle continued for the following six hours – it should have been only four, but it travelled so much further than mere nautical miles that day. However, I have to admit I was not a witness to this phenomenon for very long. Deciding that it was every man for himself, I struggled, hand-over-hand, into the stinking lavatory and locked myself in for the rest of the journey. Yes, and I did see that tasty, greasy omelette again, plus probably the majority of what I had eaten for a couple of days before.

On the journey back from Folkestone Harbour, I asked my parents what we would do next. They said we would sleep – which seemed odd at that time of the day, it still being only mid-afternoon.

But before the electric multiple unit had ground its way to the top of the bank, I was dead to the world.

CHAPTER EIGHT

CONCLUSION

Driver Bill Hoole in contemplative mood, Tan-y-Bwlch,
Ffestiniog Railway, 7th August 1961.

The things of which I write are, for the most part, history.
And for those of you who read these words and mutter,
'yes, I remember that', or spot evidence of an imperfect
memory, we, too, are heading for the history books.
Bygone ages are not measured by lost transport but by
passing generations.

Everything can be recreated, although not always
accurately, but we can again see 'everything'. Recreations
of Civil War battles, horse-drawn carriages, false gas
lamps in restored town squares, mediaeval dinners, lost
architecture, rickety bi-planes, yes, and a growing fleet of
railway rolling stock – both new and resuscitated. Even
old trains, other than those incarcerated in museums
forever, are not, in all senses, old. A machine deteriorates,
and every time parts wear out, the choice is clear. Put it

into a museum as it is, to retain its authenticity, or replace the worn out component. So, if I see a light Pacific on some preserved Southern branch-line, and a quick scan of my records tells me I saw it last in Waterloo in 1964 … well, I didn't. Oh, it looks the same, and they have done a wonderful job in bringing the old locomotive back to life, but everything I now see simply fills the space formerly occupied by the engine I once saw.

Surreal, I know, but what we are doing is making manifest the ghosts of the past.

Who would have thought we'd ever see another LNER A1? It looks and sounds like an A1 and brings back a nostalgia that is hard to ignore, but it is not a genuine A1. And what about some of the even more ambitious projects, where they have to recreate the very drawings, since there are few alive that even remember seeing them; the North Eastern G5, the London and North Western 4-4-0, and objects lost from the memory like a 'Bloomer', an Eaton Hall miniature 'Katy', or the curious 'Elephant' at Beamish. Every project is utterly worthwhile but, while they represent what has gone before, that is what they are – representations, pastiches, clones resurrected from whispers of the past. And those of us who 'were there' – who saw the traditional railway, tramway or whatever – will also soon be gone, but, and here is the rub, *we* are genuinely irreplaceable. Our memories will no longer be shared and, just as the last person to fight in the First World War has passed away, so future generations will have to rely solely on the written word, and, of course, the artefacts.

Our memories of the 'real thing' matter less and less, however. The country is criss-crossed by railways lovingly recreated by armies of young people – men and women – who are doing all those things we witnessed. In fact, they are building their own folklore, creating their own memories. To them, it is the 'now' that fills them with pride – the girl shovelling tons of coal into a big WD goods engine as it battles with the gradient out of

Keighley, the quite senior gentleman at 'Flying Scotsman's' regulator who was still in his pram when 60103 signed off at King's Cross, the young man expertly nudging ten tons of tramcar over the crossover and winding on the brake as another load of tourists, who are too young for genuine recall but who love to ride on an old tram, clamber aboard.

I recently went to a delightful open day on the Ffestiniog Railway, where we were encouraged to wander about; visiting Boston Lodge, taking photographs from every possible angle, and even getting cab rides at the works and in the old exchange sidings at Minffordd. I walked there from Porthmadog, across a Cob bathed in unexpected sunshine, waving to acknowledge the warning whistles of passing trains anxious about the uncertain, head-down, stumbling of an old guy in an all-weather coat weaving along the path that parallels the track, down the steps to the retired toll-house and then up the road, getting slightly lost – forgetting access to Minffordd yard is before the main line and not after, and gazing at all the changes. Where once there was charming decrepitude – a narrow-gauge bone yard – new buildings and an impression of lively industrial activity greeted my eyes, not to mention the odour of horse-droppings from the animals temporarily stabled there to provide motive power for the carriages plying their trade back and forth across the Cob for those who wanted to visit in style.

There, at the encouragement of a kindly yard foreman eating his sandwich from a large plastic box and cracking open a can of Coca-Cola, I climbed aboard 'Marchlyn', a one-time Penrhyn engine I had last seen in my boyhood.

A pleasant young man welcomed me aboard and we pottered about the yard, collecting some wagons and doing a spot of genuine shunting. It was great fun.

'I've been here before,' I volunteered, by way of conversation. 'Many years ago.'

'Oh yeah?' came his reply. 'When was that, then?'

'Oh, it must have been about 1964.'

He chuckled. 'Blimey,' he said. 'Long before I was born. Long before.'

'Yes,' I said, my chest visibly swelling with pride, adding, with a little exaggeration, 'I fired to Bill Hoole, down here in these sidings. On 'Prince'' I said, in faltering justification.

'Oh yeah?' he replied. 'Who's he, then? Don't know him.'

I felt an urge to explain, make reference to my hero's credentials, describe how I was told he is buried not a quarter of a mile from where we wobbled down the hill with our string of bogie wagons, enthuse him with descriptions of that exhilarating ride back to Boston Lodge so many years before, whirling along at breakneck speed with a string of slate wagons clattering and swaying behind.

But I didn't.

Bill Hoole has become just one of the thousands of personalities associated with the railway, from 18th Century William Madocks, through the likes of Spooner, Fairlie, Stephens, and Garraway, to the present day. Bill certainly should be remembered, but most of us are not venerated pioneers, nor the respected elder-statesmen of the discipline, and certainly not the 'vital sparks' – dead or alive. We are only a bunch of old people with sweet, irrelevant memories.

There is still a thriving 'now', and long may it continue. I am so grateful to those who work so hard to fill my old age with interest and who keep the magic alive and well.

But the days of which I speak are, indeed, another story.

◆

I was pondering on the subject of change as my wife and I cruised out of Manchester Piccadilly the other day. In my early experience, when it was proudly called London

Road, there were always electrics there – either split-new ones going out to Glossop or, over the wall, the Manchester, South Junction and Altrincham stock – but it was essentially a steam station in my youth. And it was divided as profoundly as Berlin had been – as though Nationalisation had passed it by.

On one side, the vestiges of the LMS, with 'Scots' and noisy 2-6-4 tanks, Class Fives and 'Jubilees', and the beginnings of modernisation with swaying and odoriferous diesel multiple units wandering out to Stockport and Macclesfield. On the other side, the new electrics, and Great Central 4-6-2 and 4-4-2 tanks shunting empty coaches in and out, or taking the back road to Macclesfield, our preferred route for the return to relatives in Upton. But, in those days, as soon as you breasted the end of the station platform, you were mixing it with an entire transport system wedded to rail. And that meant freight – masses of it. Freight meant unbraked wagons and a thousand sources and destinations. It meant lots of shunting and a track-bed alive with shabbily-dressed, acute-eyed, nimble-footed, railwaymen. It meant a daunting level of logistical management before the term was invented, and all without the benefit of computers.

For, in those days, freight was not about block trains of quarry stone, and containers scrawled with Chinese characters going out and back, off on a world tour, and then doing it all over again. It meant millions of combinations of wagons, cargoes, starting points and ending points – a veritable Rubik's Cube of possibilities. It was also a balanced economy, with traffic generated in vast quantities all over the country, and going hither and yon from locations that no longer exist on the railway map. Road haulage has placed that traffic firmly on the roads from which it will never stray, but the balance has gone.

So, whereas we were quite used to new farming equipment emerging from private sidings in Lincoln or Ipswich, and travelling to every country station in the kingdom, we now know that will never go by rail again –

nor will it usually emerge from British engineers. And we saw flocks of sheep going by train from hillsides in Wales to be fattened up in farms in the West Country, or Irish cattle landed at Holyhead or Heysham, and dispersed all over the north of England to put on weight. That traffic, also, is lost forever from rail. Flowers and vegetables rarely travel by rail now and the images of lobsters being loaded into an HST in Cornwall for transport to London in a recent newspaper article is, frankly, laughable. The authorities are probably secretly hoping that piece of initiative will never catch on as they have no way of handling that sort of traffic in any volume. Soon there won't even be a proper guard's van.

It is now a railway largely devoted to moving millions of people in and out of cities so congested that the joys of the open road are as old-fashioned as the little branch-line that is no longer available to the village-dwelling executive. He now has to resort to an overly-quick drive to the railway station that once served as a junction to the very place he now lives in.

I expect the irony is lost on him.

Our run back from Manchester Piccadilly to North Wales passed a dozen or more former stations at former junctions where former goods and marshalling yards used to assemble large numbers of trucks to be moved skilfully and as quickly as possible between the passenger trains of the past. Instead, we bounced efficiently along with nothing in our way, although the dirt and decay of the past was still with us on that shabby, unloved, Arriva Trains Wales multiple unit.

When we mourn the loss of the old railway, we need to think in terms of the character and purpose, rather than just the rolling stock. And the signalling – always a basket of mysteries to me – but as evocative of the past as it is possible to be, is changed forever. Now, simplification of the layout and the loss of sidings and branches has resulted in the felling of semaphores and their replacement by a handful of colour-lights. And these, too, will be on the way out as further progress removes the need for external signalling. From a practical point of view, it is already redundant.

There is, therefore, another generation of *old 'uns* coming up who go all damp-eyed over the passing of the first-generation diesels and colour lights operated from ugly brick and concrete monstrosities shabbily littering station throats – always standing back and at odd angles with the track, unlike their predecessors that invariably seemed proud of their intimacy with the rails.

Nostalgia, therefore, is dynamic. It moves on, generation by generation, in a sort of measurable renewal, almost like a geological period – Cambrian, Silurian, Jurassic, and so on. And just as in the study of geology, new generations are added as the years go by. Geology does not stand still. We are always learning more about the past but, equally, we are aware of the constant addition of material – both sedimentary and volcanic – to the surface of our planet. Parallels can be found in the railway world.

The preservationists talk about the 'classic' or 'traditional' railway, and we know what they mean. The terms conjure up an image of manual signal-boxes, old-fashioned stations with flowerbeds and luggage trolleys, loose-coupled wagons with heavy chain couplings and, above all, steam. But some preservation sites have, cleverly, deliberately tried to recreate the railway in transition, where we can see a whistling English Electric Type Four on a string of maroon Mark 1s on one platform, while an LMS Class Five in BR livery, sporting the second emblem on its tender, sits alongside on a similar train.

In truth, those are my mid-interest memories. I cannot entirely expunge the 'modern' from my mind. Indeed, it was there almost from the beginning of my enthusiasm. For every proud Great Western express leaving Paddington behind a 'Castle' or a 'King', there was a quaint, banana-shaped diesel van shuffling off to some West London destination to collect letters and parcels, or the indescribable din emanating from the Swiss gas-turbine. For every 'Coronation' roaring through Watford Junction with an Anglo-Scottish express, there was a ludicrous string of four-wheeled railcars taking me to that steam heaven from St. Albans Abbey station. For every marshalling yard peppered with enigmatic, frustratingly-unidentifiable locomotive chimneys peeping over wagons and vans across countless sidings, there were diesel shunters invading our happy world. And for every proud tramcar joining a queue on Princes Street, Edinburgh and sliding off to right and left, like a slow but precise military routine, there was a wide, straight road, perhaps still with granite setts, and black-painted iron rosettes, with neatly-cast hooks, bolted to the walls of road-side buildings long-since shorn of their span-wires.

One of the most rewarding things about the preservation era has been the recreation of the distant past – where no memory remains and even photographs are a curiosity. But we can get equally nostalgic about those. Beamish gives us what the Americans call 'grasshopper' engines – a network of cranks driving out of vertical cylinders to the wheels via the tops of boilers. So, when, as a boy, I marvelled at these stuffed, delicate, priceless objects in the museums of Edinburgh and London, I can now actually travel behind one and hear the soft voice of Georgian locomotion. And while trams were modernised and then swept away in my childhood, we can now travel on an open-topped car that started out life when Queen Victoria was still on the throne and whose character could only be imagined in my youth from a grainy black-and-white photograph.

So, I shouldn't be surprised or even critical of plans to preserve an HST – probably the best post-war train – or of people who want to restore a first-generation diesel multiple unit of the type that, basically, broke my heart.

♦

It was blowing fit to sweep the unwary into the sea.

The date in the calendar said we were at the beginning of August, 1961 and, if careless and overly-romantic, it might well be remembered over fifty years later as sunny and warm, with a blue sky overhead, gulls crying, and Monet clouds passing gently by – too ephemeral even to cast a shadow on this idyllic memory. The houses of Barmouth would shine under their improbable coats of lovingly-applied paint – mostly white, with occasional contrasting primary colours adding to the jollity of the view. The faint sounds of a band playing on the promenade and drifting over the estuary might make a perfect scene even more perfect. Cheerful children, laughing and skipping this way and that, brandishing ice-creams dangerously and largely ignoring warnings from their parents that if they carelessly drop them, they will be ignominiously consigned to the throats of those wheeling, crying gulls without replacement, might fill our memories with an animation that could well have been painted by a French Impressionist.

But, the authentic memory is too strong and too clear.

Instead, it was blowing a gale. It was cold. The clouds were grey and threatening. And the houses in Barmouth yonder were largely colourless under an unhappy sky.

A pair of grubby steam engines – what we used to call a '2251' and a Standard 2-6-2 tank – coupled together, shuffled towards us. They had just brought a train into Barmouth and were going to avail themselves of a turn-around on the triangle at what used to be called Barmouth Junction but which now enjoyed a spread of unpronounceable Welsh consonants. Photographs were taken but without appreciating the adverse effects of vibration on the viaduct that added to the shortcomings of being a bad photographer with poor equipment that took an age to open and close the shutter.

The smoke flattened from the chimneys and waved about angrily as it jetted inland on the invisible wind. The fireman of the first engine was sweeping down the footplate and I was momentarily incapacitated by sweet-smelling coal dust that defied the normal advantages of wearing glasses, finding its way into my eyes. Hot oil and clanking valve-gear rolled past, voices exchanged over the roar of the wind, a gasp of warm air and then another – each engine sharing the consequence of its labours with us – a welcome moment of heat in the cold, the summer special train, engineless and waiting, just visible at the platform.

We turned back, knowing the pictures would be failures, to find shelter and move off inland to our next port of call. We paused briefly to see the pair, still inseparable, as they moved slowly back and forth to end up facing north again with the prospect of more work taking their train back.

The senses satisfied.

The five senses nourished again.

The five senses consigned to precious memory.

Lightning Source UK Ltd.
Milton Keynes UK
UKHW01f2144060918
328454UK00002B/309/P